"In this extraordinary feat of high-powered scholarship, Christian Fierens tackles some of the most challenging aspects of Lacan's critical engagement with the ethical systems of Kant and the Sadean libertines. Broadly conceived yet tightly constructed, this book will appeal to philosophers and psychoanalysts alike, and will effectively provide access to texts and arguments that have hitherto remained hermetically sealed for many an ordinary soul. Had Lacan still been alive, he would undoubtedly have said that he had rarely been read with such acumen, scrupulousness and care."

Dany Nobus, professor of psychoanalytic psychology, Brunel University London; author of The Law of Desire: On Lacan's 'Kant with Sade'

"This work will challenge readers from a diversity of backgrounds who wish to understand the foundational work of Kant and Sade, which inspired Lacan to give an absorbing and unique perspective into the frequently misunderstood Principle of Jouissance. Fierens offers a special insight into the interface between three authors who have contributed to our thought on the central topic. This is a truly remarkable work reflecting the seriousness and artistry of its creator. A superb text."

Tony Hughes is a psychoanalyst of the Irish School for Lacanian Psychoanalysis. He practises in Dublin and lectures in the School of Psychotherapy at University College Dublin.

"Whether one agrees or disagrees with the proposal of a principle of *jouissance* as grounding the unconscious as *éthique* (ethical), reading and interrogating this new book by Christian Fierens will be worthwhile and productive. Fierens' rigorous questioning of the fundamental terms of psychoanalysis is required 'to relaunch them' and 'put them to work' (to use his apt phrases.) Thereby clinical and theoretical practice can remain alive, alert and able to respond to the ever-new forms produced by the work of the unconscious, a fundamental concept for any serious approach to mental life. This is a crucial *instrument de travail* for the psychoanalytic field and beyond."

Barry O'Donnell, PhD, practises psychoanalysis and is a member of the Irish School for Lacanian Psychoanalysis (ISLP). He is director of Psychotherapy Programmes in the School of Medicine, University College Dublin, and director of the School of Psychotherapy at St. Vincent's University Hospital, Dublin.

"Christian Fierens' *The Jouissance Principle* is unlike any other book on the topic. Fierens breaks new ground in his inventive analysis of Lacan's 'Kant with Sade'.

Setting out from psychoanalysis, he gives a novel reading of Kant's *Critique of Practical Reason*, before interrogating Lacan's own reading of both Kant and Sade. Freud established the pleasure principle as the principle of the functioning of the *Ich*, or ego. Fierens produces its counterpart from this brilliant and meticulous working of Kant and Sade, literally the jouissance principle: the very principle of the functioning of the unconscious."

Michael Gerard Plastow, psychoanalyst
(Analyst of the School, The Freudian School of Melbourne;
Analyst Member, Association Lacanienne Internationale)
and child psychiatrist (Alfred Child
and Youth Mental Health Service)

"*The Jouissance Principle* cross-examines Lacan's appraisal of Kant's *Critique of Practical Reason* which he confronts critically, using Sade's most incisive manifestos. In an illuminating way, Christian Fierens, a leading authority in Lacanian studies, sets the record straight and shows that Lacan's most profound views on jouissance actually reconcile Kantian major operators – virtuousness and happiness – while fitting exactly the very subtle theorization of the categorical imperative. Undoubtedly, this work is bound to become a classic, as it renews our approach to both Kant and Lacan by making the most consistent use of their respective methodology, i.e. architectonics and topology. This very brilliant and sound contribution to psychoanalysis and philosophy will benefit both practitioners and scholars eager to get back to the original texts . . ."

Frank Pierobon, the author of Kant et les mathématiques
is a philosopher established in Belgium (I.H.E.C.S.)

The Jouissance Principle

This book examines the concept of jouissance, a Lacanian term that refers to enjoyment experienced in different ways, from the enjoyment taken in an action that is ethically disapproved to the hidden pleasure taken by the patient in and from his symptom.

Christian Fierens offers a new and rigorous explanation of jouissance as a third principle in the functioning of the unconscious, in addition to the technical and pleasure principles. *The Jouissance Principle* presents a detailed cross-reading of two key works: Kant's *Critique of Pure Reason* and Lacan's paper 'Kant with Sade', explaining how the functioning of the unconscious is a genuinely ethical process. The book also focuses on the role of psychoanalysis in relaunching the functioning of the unconscious, outlining the fourth form of Lacan's *object a* and its stakes in the psychoanalytic process.

An intriguing discussion of the relationship between pleasure, ethics and rationality, *The Jouissance Principle* will interest scholars of psychoanalysis and European philosophy, as well as helping clinicians to find a practical and ethical pathway through their practice.

Christian Fierens is a psychoanalyst and psychiatrist based in Belgium. He holds a PhD on the question of psychosis in Freud's work and has published several books on Freudian and Lacanian psychoanalysis, including *The Soul of Narcissism* (Routledge, 2019).

The Jouissance Principle

Kant, Sade and Lacan on the Ethical Functioning of the Unconscious

Christian Fierens

Translated by Kieran O'Meara

LONDON AND NEW YORK

First published 2022
by Routledge
2 Park Square, Milton Park, Abingdon, Oxon OX14 4RN

and by Routledge
605 Third Avenue, New York, NY 10158

Routledge is an imprint of the Taylor & Francis Group, an informa business

© 2022 Christian Fierens

The right of Christian Fierens to be identified as author of this work has been asserted by him in accordance with sections 77 and 78 of the Copyright, Designs and Patents Act 1988.

All rights reserved. No part of this book may be reprinted or reproduced or utilised in any form or by any electronic, mechanical, or other means, now known or hereafter invented, including photocopying and recording, or in any information storage or retrieval system, without permission in writing from the publishers.

Trademark notice: Product or corporate names may be trademarks or registered trademarks, and are used only for identification and explanation without intent to infringe.

British Library Cataloguing-in-Publication Data
A catalogue record for this book is available from the British Library

Library of Congress Cataloging-in-Publication Data
Names: Fierens, Christian, author.
Title: The jouissance principle : Kant, Sade and Lacan on the ethical functioning of the unconscious / Christian Fierens ; translated by Kieran O'Meara.
Other titles: Principe de jouissance. English
Description: Abingdon, Oxon ; New York, NY : Routledge, 2022. | Includes bibliographical references and index.
Identifiers: LCCN 2021025657 (print) | LCCN 2021025658 (ebook) | ISBN 9780367519025 (hbk) | ISBN 9780367519018 (pbk) | ISBN 9781003055662 (ebk)
Subjects: LCSH: Pleasure principle (Psychology) | Kant, Immanuel, 1724–1804. Kritik der praktischen Vernunft. | Lacan, Jacques, 1901–1981. Kant avec Sade. | Psychoanalysis and philosophy.
Classification: LCC BF175.5.P54 F5414 2022 (print) | LCC BF175.5.P54 (ebook) | DDC 150.19/5—dc23
LC record available at https://lccn.loc.gov/2021025657
LC ebook record available at https://lccn.loc.gov/2021025658

ISBN: 978-0-367-51902-5 (hbk)
ISBN: 978-0-367-51901-8 (pbk)
ISBN: 978-1-003-05566-2 (ebk)

DOI: 10.4324/9781003055662

Typeset in Times New Roman
by Apex CoVantage, LLC

Contents

Introduction: jouissance and the unconscious — 1

SECTION I
Reading Kant — 15

PART I
Groundwork of the Metaphysics of Morals (1785):
the moral law — 17

Introduction: the principle as principle — 19

1 Good will, duty, and the moral law: on the basis
of popular moral philosophy — 23

2 Analysis of the moral law: unearthing the metaphysics
of morals based on popular moral philosophy — 29

PART II
Critique of Practical Reason (1788): the principle
of practical reason — 41

Introduction: the place and structure of practical reason
(and of the unconscious) — 43

The analytic in the first and second critiques 43
The dialectic in the first and second critiques 44

3 The principle of the autonomy of the moral law
(... and of jouissance) — 46

4	The concept of good/evil	61
5	Respect (*Achtung*)	67
6	The necessary articulation of the principle of morality with the pleasure principle	70
7	How to promote the principle of the moral law (and of jouissance)	82
	Conclusion of the doctrine of method	84

SECTION II
A reading of Lacan   87

PART I
***The Ethics of Psychoanalysis* (1959–1960): the real**   91

8	Critique of "ethics" centred on happiness and perfection	93
9	The hole in reality, the real and the thing	96
10	The universality of the moral law	99
11	The human being's essential relationship to the Thing	102

PART II
"Kant with Sade" (1962–1963): the object *a*   107

12	Introduction to Kant and to Sade	109
13	Sade's contribution to psychoanalysis	130
14	Lacan's struggle against Kant	152
15	The practice of psychoanalysis	171

SECTION III
Practice of the unconscious — 187

16 From one reading the other on Kant and on Lacan — 189

17 The unconscious and the jouissance principle — 192

18 How can the jouissance peculiar to the unconscious be presented? — 196

19 It must be made: The practice of the unconscious — 203

Conclusion: The jouissance principle and the object *a* — 209

Bibliography — 213
Index — 216

Introduction

Jouissance and the unconscious

Jouissance: a (theoretical) concept or a (practical) principle

The *concept* of jouissance seems from the beginning not just to be ambiguous but also contradictory in the field of psychoanalysis. Being sometimes equated with the concept of pleasure, and sometimes opposed to the pleasure principle, it remains unquestioned despite being used as if everybody knew what was involved when we speak of "jouissance".

We can in no way define jouissance once and for all. As a *concept* it remains forever problematic. "What is jouissance?" remains a question without a definitive answer. We can do no more than relaunch the question, not just at the most general level of the concept of jouissance both for observers and theoreticians, but most of all at the level of a singular jouissance: What brings me to say that there is jouissance at such a moment and in such a situation? Where does this lead me? What process is at work in this singular jouissance? What is its operating *principle* [*principe de fonctionnement*], that alone can respond to the question of jouissance while endlessly relaunching it?

The concept of jouissance equated with pleasure

"*Jouir*" (to enjoy) in French is defined in Littré's *Dictionnaire de la langue française* as "*tirer plaisir, agrément, profit de quelque chose* – to derive pleasure, enjoyment, advantage from something", and "*agrément est la qualité de ce qui plait* – *agrément* (enjoyment, pleasure) is the quality of that which pleases". Everything seems to unfailingly revolve around pleasure. Everybody is in search of their pleasure and their jouissance.

Whatever the twists and turns of this infinite quest might be, the im-patient patient always comes to analysis asking for an increase of his or her pleasure and jouissance. Freud patiently responded to this ordinary quest for jouissance. Jouissance, *Genuss* in German, understood as satisfaction, *Befriedigung*, and wish-fulfilment, *Wunscherfüllung*.[1] This is the pleasure principle: one must avoid unpleasure and obtain pleasure. Reality, too, which imposes many obstacles in the way of this search for pleasure and avoidance of unpleasure, must be taken into account – the pleasure principle involves the reality principle.

Let us then rejoice at the favourable response that can be given to the common demand for pleasure or jouissance. In French, "*réjouir* – rejoice", can be used transitively, meaning "to delight, to give joy". Joy, therefore, would only be the faithful repetition of pleasure. Pleasure, pleasure, and more pleasure. We are never finished with it.

But why does this demand for jouissance and pleasure return so insatiably? The basic dissatisfaction inherent in repetition assures us that psychical activity does not respond to concepts, but to principles, and not solely to the pleasure principle. It also responds to a principle which does not seek pleasure and for which we can henceforth reserve the name of "jouissance".

The split between the pleasure principle and the jouissance principle

We first understand the *concept* of jouissance as an equivalent of pleasure. Freud does not elude this equivalence. It was not until 1920 (*Beyond the Pleasure Principle*) that he managed to drive a little wedge into the monolithic *conception* which seemed to manage all psychical reality in accordance with pleasure. Now this split between pleasure and that which is not pleasure ("jouissance") is not settled once and for all. Pleasure and jouissance are not the concepts of twin realities or twin tectonic plates of the psychical world, which would have separated by a huge crack, each drifting away to opposite sides of the ocean of the psyche.

Pleasure and jouissance can only be approached because they determine how we act *without themselves being concepts* (which would offer us a theoretical grasp on what they are). They are always already working in tandem even before we are aware of it and, even more so, before we can theorise it. They can only be approached as *principles* (and not as concepts), as operating principles. We might ask, "How is the thing that is agitating me determined by the pleasure principle?" But also, "How is what is agitating me determined by a completely different principle, the jouissance principle?" Everybody must constantly repeat the articulation and the splitting of these two principles for themselves.

Why does this splitting exist? In the second part of this introduction, we will examine how it unavoidably derives from the *work of the unconscious*. This is what inspires the topic of this book, as well as the work it demands of the reader. It is also what enables the bringing of new life to psychoanalytic practice, as much as to its theory.

Before taking on the task of separating out the pleasure principle and the "jouissance principle" once more, it is worthwhile specifying the different, often contradictory, meanings of the concept of jouissance in Lacanian psychoanalysis and how they derive from the unconscious.

The ambiguity of jouissance

Because of language – as we will see, by the very fact that "the unconscious is structured like a language" – we can distinguish between *pleasure* as the satisfaction of a need by an appropriately fulfilling object and *jouissance*, connected to language and the lack of an object which it entails. Jouissance is therefore "*forbidden*, not in the facile sense of being crossed out by censors, but *inter-said*,[2] meaning that it is formed from the very fabric from which desire takes its impact and in which it finds its rules".[3]

There is an essential ambiguity [*équivoque*] involved in jouissance: what we might call a "*homophonic*" ambiguity, in French, in the play on the words *interdit*, meaning "forbidden" and the neologism *inter-dit* or "inter-said". We will see how it also involves a "*grammatical*" ambiguity between the signifier of the big Other [S(A)] and the signifier of the *barred* big Other [S(A̶)] and also a *logical* ambiguity between the *concept* of jouissance and the *jouissance principle*.[4]

The *homophonic* ambiguity between the forbidden and the inter-said seems initially to present an explanation of jouissance wholly in the opposition of these two *significations*. Firstly, the simple one of an interdiction: jouissance is what must be forbidden, cut, suppressed, devalued, castrated. Secondly, the more subtle one of something unsaid: jouissance being located in the blank spaces between what is said: "That one might be saying remains forgotten behind what is said in what is heard",[5] more precisely: *that one might be enjoying* [*qu'on jouisse*] remains forgotten behind what is said in what is heard. The two significations coexist in the field of Lacanian psychoanalysis: each can be approached either as a (theoretical) concept or a (practical) principle. It is easy to conceptualise the forbidden and to stick to it "on principle". The blank space of jouissance, however, eludes the grasp of the concept, and its principle is never plotted out in advance.

The simple opposition of the two preceding significations cannot, however, suffice. It is "empty speech". A position must be taken up and meaning, or a number of meanings [*sens*], must be accorded to them. We could envisage a solution to the *homophonic* ambiguity in a *grammatical* ambiguity. Here, "grammatical" refers to the *gramma*, the letter, in this case the dash which separates or does not separate *inter* and *dit* in the French terms *interdit* (forbidden) and *inter-dit* ("inter-said"). However, the dash must be put to work, bringing into play the movement inherent in *meaning* [*sens*] rather than the statics of a signification, in other words a principle rather than a concept. It is the function of grammar to put concepts to work in the syntax in which "full speech" unfolds. Now, this use of the dash and its absence remains ambiguous itself. The grammatical ambiguity echoes the homophonic one rather than resolves it.

ON THE SIDE OF THE FORBIDDEN

What direction does this superego go in? Does it come from the outside, from society, or does it come from the inside, from structure? To keep this ambiguity alive, it must be understood at one and the same time as being determined by the social and family structure, as well as arising from the most intimate nature of the unconscious. The big Other, it will be said. Where, however, is the big Other to be found: in the exteriority which startles and frightens us? Or in the intimacy of my speech?

ON THE SIDE OF THE INTER-SAID

What direction does the blank space between things said go in? Is it to be said? Or not said? Who will say it? Again: the big Other?

Lacan's conception of the big Other is essentially ambiguous. It is written both as a capital A[6] and as a barred capital A (Ⱥ). In the forbidden as well as in the inter-said, the big Other must be both barred and unbarred.

If the big Other is written as unbarred, if it exists, all I need to do to satisfy it is to follow its commands and its prohibitions (*interdits*). In this way, I can devote myself to providing it with "jouissance" (a degenerated concept in which the operating principle is to obey) like a good neurotic. And I just have to trust in the big Other, as far as the inter-said which eludes me is concerned, which was Descartes's position in relation to God.

If the big Other is written as barred, if I cannot ground myself on its hypothetical existence, all I can do is raise the question of what can be done without it, without any reference point to tell me what it is I must do. Without a concept to guide me, all that is left to me is to question the principle of what is being played out within me, which always stems from that which eludes me – the "unconscious".

The homophonic ambiguity *forbidden/inter-said* only finds its sense in the grammatical ambiguity barred *big Other/unbarred big Other*. In the latter ambiguity, the *concept* of jouissance will therefore be divided between an overwhelming belief in a limitless pleasure-jouissance guaranteed by the big Other (as a pusher of the opium of the people or of drugs to the subject), on the one hand. On the other hand, a jouissance as the place deserted by the big Other itself:

> I am in the place from which "the universe is a flaw in the purity of Non-Being" is vociferated. And not without reason for, by protecting itself, this place makes Being itself languish. This place is called jouissance, and it is jouissance whose absence would render the universe vain.[7]

Concretely, in clinical practice, this place deserted by Being itself seems unworkable. What is more, within practice and within the theory which results from it, jouissance is unfortunately understood as a pleasure which wants to be limitless, as a search for pleasure detached from its rational conditioning, as a pleasure principle which would no longer be curbed by the reality principle. It would seem obvious that such a jouissance must be devalued, cut, castrated, reduced, or forbidden. From this point of view, jouissance is introduced as a primal concept (a supposedly realistic and obvious datum of the clinic), to then be mastered by a principle which curbs it (a therapeutic or psychoanalytic correction) finally and secondarily in order to approach the place of Non-Being, to see the subject's *désêtre* and the second sense of jouissance.

This trajectory is certainly possible, but it is still dependent on its starting point, namely the realist conception of the big Other providing a foundation for the neurotic.

Yes, we can distinguish different aspects of jouissance: jouissance as *j'ouis sens* (another homophonic ambiguity), phallic jouissance (a grammatical ambiguity of the letter phi), and the Other jouissance (which does not exist). This threefold, seemingly geometrical division leads us to believe that there was at the beginning a big pie of jouissance which is now cut into three slices. But the triad presented by Lacan in "La troisième" is both more complex and simpler because it completely depends not only on the logic of the Borromean knot but also on its flattening for the purposes of imaginary exposition, simpler because there is *only one* jouissance that the symbolic real and imaginary dimensions of the Borromean knot are trying to measure. There is no cut between the different aspects of jouissance, other than in the exposition which flattens the Borromean knot.

In order to approach jouissance, we must first enter into the logical ambiguity underlying the difficulties inherent to an examination of jouissance (which are both practical and theoretical). The logical ambiguity appears in the Borromean knot between, on the one hand, the statics which highlights the different figures in diagrams, and on the other hand, the movement which both generates and transforms these figures (errors of construction, repairs, and different acts of "surgery" on the knot).[8] We cannot make the least progress in understanding the jouissance presented in the Borromean knot if we do not grapple with the logical ambiguity between the diagram intended to conceptualise jouissance, and the movement, principle of formation and transformation, which precedes both the image and the concept. It is this logical ambiguity which justifies and provides a foundation for the homophonic ambiguity of jouissance. The approach through the concept (drawing, image) corresponds to a search for knowledge (What can I know?), whereas the approach through the principle (the movement of formation) corresponds to a search for action or operation [*du faire ou du fonctionnement*] (what must I do?) The first (which goes hand in hand with Kant's *Critique of Pure Reason*) starts out from *concepts* rooted in sensory experience to tease out principles (in the transcendental analytic, the analysis of concepts precedes the analysis of principles). This is the common way of approaching jouissance in psychoanalysis – the theoretical path. The second (which is in line with the *Critique of Practical Reason*) starts out from *principles* and then sees concepts rooted in ethical experience begin to emerge (in the analytic of practical reason, the analysis of principles precedes the analysis of concepts). This is a practical path that must be brought to light in order to find one's way in jouissance.

The unconscious has an ethical status; it is a practical path. It alone can enlighten us as far as jouissance is concerned.

The unconscious and its principle

In psychoanalysis, we begin with the practical path of the unconscious: How does it operate?

The unconscious does not operate according to a technical principle

Technique is the art of achieving what one wants. It focuses action on a goal; it is stretched between a current state of the question and the sought-after modification of this state. All techniques can be modelled as a mathematical function, in which a starting point is mapped on to a goal, a point to be reached, by means of an arrow. The starting point is given in perception; the problem can be pinpointed or diagnosed. The destination point is not yet given in reality; it presents itself as an answer which can be perfectly determinable in the technique. It *thinks* of a goal, *calculates* the means of attaining it, and *judges* the decisions to be taken. Technique concerns both the physical or material work of the worker, artisan or machine, and the abstract or intellectual work of the thinker or the computer. It also concerns a kind of psychical work of the affects: starting out from a painful or unpleasant psychical state, how can we *think* of a happy point of arrival, how can we calculate the way to get there, and how can we *judge* the decisions we need to take?[9] In this way, human life would respond to a series of technical principles.

This in no way applies where the unconscious is concerned

We know neither its point of departure nor its point of arrival. Our ignorance in this regard is so great that one could ask if there had ever been a determinate point of departure or a point of arrival to hope for. The unconscious does not think of a goal to be reached, it does not calculate the means of getting there, and it does not judge any outcomes. The unconscious does not at all operate as a mathematisable technique. It operates as a relaunched movement which fundamentally eludes us. It was the study of dreams (*The Interpretation of Dreams*) which led Freud to the recognition of the radical absence of the technical processes of thinking, calculation, and judgement in the dream work. The work of the unconscious "does not think, calculate or judge in any way at all; it restricts itself to giving things a new form".[10] The work of the unconscious dispenses with every technical principle – it does not think, calculate, or judge – it proceeds in a completely different way: "giving things a new form". This operating principle of the unconscious is a foundational one for psychoanalysis. From its beginnings, Freud understood that he could do no better than borrow his method of interpretation from the modus operandi of the unconscious (Chapter 2 of *The Interpretation of Dreams*), and in turn psychoanalysis borrows his method for interpretation. Each time, it is a case of "giving things a new form".

The work of giving things a new form is carried out by means of the four major mechanisms of condensation, metaphor, the consideration of representability, and secondary revision. (Chapter 6 of *The Interpretation of Dreams*).[11]

There is, however, a great temptation to squeeze the method of the unconscious, interpretation, and psychoanalysis back into the framework of technical principles. In this case, one might imagine a given material which would simultaneously comprise representations, ideas, perceptions, intuitions, trends, and unspecified psychical content, including thoughts, calculations, and conscious or preconscious judgements.[12] Using an appropriate technique – one would have to think of and calculate its effects, then judge the right moment to apply it – the anticipated results could be attained – healing, raised awareness, personal development, etc. Dream material would be primary, and it would be only secondarily, through the application of technique, that it would take on a thousand and one new forms in the dream-work, but also in the end result of psychoanalysis.

However, not only is the dream material [*matière*] never given in advance, independently of the transformations peculiar to the unconscious,[13] but even more so, it stages the creation of a new form which goes against all technique (the unconscious "does not think, calculate or judge in any way at all"). The material itself seems not to exist other than according to the unconscious, according to a non-technical principle. If we pay some attention to the four sources or types of dream material (Chapter 5 of The *Interpretation of Dreams*): 1) recent and indifferent material, 2) infantile material as a source of dreams, 3) the somatic sources of dreams, and 4) typical dreams – we notice that what is *consistent* in these types of material is the ability *to be given a new form*. Indifferent memories from the previous day are chosen as material because they are highly tractable to such a transformation. Infantile material leads us into the dynamics of sexual life, the "Oedipus", in which everything can be transformed. The somatic sources of the dream immerse us in the erratic work of the drives. Typical dreams tirelessly return to the unconscious's work of relaunching, ungrounded in technique.[14] In short, the material is systematically predetermined by the work of the unconscious, which consists in giving things a new form. Here it is not matter [*matière*] which precedes form, it is form which precedes matter. It is transformation and transformation alone which lends consistency to different matters.[15]

The "new form" created by the work of the unconscious can no longer be thought of as a form added to pre-existing material. The new form can no longer be thought of as one of the thousand and one shapes that a ball of modelling clay could take on through the technique of the sculptor. The new form is not one of a number of technical translations of signifiers already present before condensation, displacement, the application of considerations of representability, and secondary elaboration is brought into play. The new form creates and determines the signifying material in its movement of "formation" and "transformation".

If the machine for giving things a new form does not "think, calculate or judge in any way at all", if it does not conform to *any* technical principle, must we conclude that it operates purely by chance, blindly and without any principle? The transformations peculiar to the unconscious would then lead to the systematic degradation of all meaning. Psychoanalysis, in as much as it draws its method from the unconscious, would itself be senseless.

However, there are principles other than the technical principle.

The unconscious operates according to the pleasure principle, among others

The dream has no technique for producing a story. Interpretation does not have a technique for discovering the truth of the unconscious. Psychoanalysis has no technique for triggering dreams, finding interpretations, or curing patients. This does not prevent dreams, as well as all of the other formations of the unconscious and their interpretations, from having a meaning. Even though the dream does not possess a technical meaning, it does seem to have a unique meaning and seems to obey an absolutely general principle: "dreams are the fulfilment of a wish" (Chapter 3 of the *Traumdeutung*). In the "new form", the work of the unconscious would always be seeking an interest, an advantage, a source of satisfaction, a short- or long-term pleasure. The work of the unconscious (both at the level of the formations of the unconscious and of the formations of psychoanalysis) would solely be trying to obey a generalised pleasure principle. All transformations in psychoanalysis would be aiming at pleasure. They would thereby fit in perfectly with all the other ethical systems (apart from Kant's), commanded by the quest for happiness under one modality or another and under one morality or another. Of course, what is pleasant on one side may not be pleasant on the other. Due to the divergence of systems and agencies, the search for happiness or for pleasure leads to inevitable conflicts: pleasure gained on one side sets off unpleasure on the other. It is to respect one side's pleasure that the other's pleasure must be disguised or repressed. The general principle, therefore, needs to be clarified: "a dream is a *disguised* fulfilment of a *repressed* wish" (Chapter 4 of *The Interpretation of Dreams*).

This meaning is not complete or settled in a fixed interpretation. It is eluded and eludes us in a continuously relaunching interpretation [*dans une interprétation de relance continuelle*]. There is always another meaning, another form which is not determined by a goal, a precise purpose, or a technical principle (in the wider sense). The general aim, however, is still in keeping with the pleasure principle. Each of the psychical agencies – conscious, preconscious, and unconscious – would really operate according to their own minor pleasure principle while attempting to avoid offending that of the other agencies.

All of our actions would be commanded according to the pleasure principle in one form or another, and psychoanalytic practice would consist of confronting the different types of pleasure sought for (on the conscious, preconscious, or unconscious levels) in the field of consciousness, which would judge them according to a generalised pleasure principle unifying all pleasure. The principle would extend its empire to all thought – everyday, critical, or philosophical. We would think under the aegis of the search for pleasure. The utility of psychoanalysis and of all its developments would itself be dependent on the search for pleasure or happiness, for both the patient and the practitioner, for the individual and for society. From a practical point of view, the goal would be always, and without exception, to reduce unpleasure.

However, the pleasure principle is not a characteristic specific to the unconscious. It is an absolutely general principle.

The unconscious specifically operates according to the "jouissance principle": that which we call "unconscious" in psychoanalysis is the "jouissance principle"

The disguising of desire ("the disguised fulfilment of a repressed wish") can be understood in two different and opposing ways: Is it pleasure which disguises itself as unpleasure? Or is it unpleasure which disguises itself as pleasure? On the one hand, in *accordance* with the pleasure principle, it might be thought that it is ever present pleasure that is disguised, that the dream always represents pleasure, whatever grimace might disfigure it. On the other hand, in *opposition* to the pleasure principle, it might also be thought that the dream is always only a disguise (in the shape of pleasure) of something completely different, of a completely new form. Under the disguise of the fulfilment of a wish, a "Real", irreducible to desire, would be hiding. Every dream would only be a nightmare disguised as a wish fulfilment. In this way, the dream would reveal a way of working radically different from the pleasure principle, and with it, the creation of a new irreducible to the goal of pleasure. The new form given to things by the unconscious would be fundamentally *other than pleasure*, not in keeping with and not formatted by pleasure. *Beyond the pleasure principle* (1920), the death drive would rule. The aforementioned death, which would justify the "new form" cannot, however, be reduced to the inexorable decay of all living things, which end up returning to a formless state in one way or another. As a real drive giving things a new form, the "death drive" indicates a living force, which would be unique in seeking anything but pleasure, anything other than wish fulfilment or the attainment of happiness. The death drive would not seek the death of the individual, but *the death of the monopoly or hegemony of the pleasure principle*, to the advantage of a new form, to the advantage of another working principle for the psyche, to the advantage of what we would call *jouissance*.

However, naming "jouissance" does not suffice, because it is too easily understood as the intensification of pleasure, as the fulfilment of pleasure stripped of all its rational regulatory mechanisms. Normally, according to the norms of pleasure, pleasure regulates itself: too much pleasure kills pleasure, and I must rein in the pleasure I take in eating so as not to experience the unpleasure of indigestion. (The reality principle is a corollary of the pleasure principle.) "Jouissance" would be nothing other than an aspiration to pleasure disconnected from its control mechanisms. Disconnected from the reality principle, jouissance would be nothing but an unbridled pleasure. From this point of view, "jouissance" appears to be a pathological variety of pleasure. To bring it back to a well-tempered pleasure, it would be enough to "castrate" "jouissance", to limit it, to curb it, to bring it into line with the reasonable part of the pleasure principle known as the reality principle. This way of understanding "jouissance" changes absolutely nothing about a method which is fundamentally focused on the pleasure principle. We must introduce a completely different meaning of jouissance.

Every technical principle is supposed to lead to a concrete realisation. The pleasure principle never manages to be completely realised. A third possible principle seems even more problematic: perhaps it never reaches *any realisation at all*. This possibility does not cancel out the relevance of the principle. A principle is not based on what exists or on what has already been realised, but on what *should* be, without any guarantee of having been realised before, or being realised in the present or in the future. The technical principle's "*devoir être*", its "ought to be", or necessity, is determined by the aim of an action: its concrete realisation is thought of as possible, concretely calculated, and objectively judged as appropriate. The "*devoir être*" of the pleasure principle is determined by the subjective well-being of the people or agencies involved and is only partially realised. The "*devoir être*" of the third principle might never be realised, without it ceasing to be to be a principle and to operate as a principle.

We regularly come across the shadow of such a principle in *guilt*. It emerges in the wake of a "*devoir être*", which has not been realised and may never be. We generally try to explain guilt by referring to a technical error – "I didn't do what I needed to do to reach my goal" – or a conflict between two opposing pleasures. Contrary to this naive, mechanistic, and realist explanation, in the clinic we come across guilt feelings which do not arise from any technical errors and which cannot be explained by a conflict between pleasure and unpleasure either. We regularly come across guilt feelings which go so far as to carry out transgressions in order to justify their very existence.[16] Guilt is also generally completely out of proportion to the sin which has been committed. However, guilt is not a fulfilment of our third principle. On the contrary, it is indeed evidence of the *non-realisation* of this principle, at the same time as it insists *on the principle as a principle*. If we lend our attention to it, we come up against a gaping chasm between the "*devoir être*" and "concrete being", between the principle and its realisation, in all the formations of the unconscious. This is an integral part of all the work of the unconscious, but also of the psychoanalytic method.

For example, let us look at the original example of the psychoanalytic method, taken from Freud's own life (Chapter 2 of *The Interpretation of Dreams*), the dream of Irma's injection. This is used to present the method of free association, which involves first recounting the dream and then freely associating to each of its elements. This method can be verified with any part of a dream or even with any other mental event. The method would necessarily imply to a general thesis, namely "a dream is the fulfilment of a wish" or "every mental event takes place under the primacy of the pleasure principle".

However, this first dream leads to something else entirely. While the dream does appear to be a plea of innocence (pleasure),[17] Freud can do no other than recognise in it something completely different from innocence. This plea

> reminded one vividly of the defence put forward by the man who was charged by one of his neighbours with having given him back a borrowed kettle in a damaged condition. The defendant asserted first, that he had given it back undamaged; secondly, that the kettle had a hole in it when he borrowed it; and thirdly, that he had never borrowed a kettle from his neighbour at all.[18]

In the very act of proving himself innocent, in accordance with the pleasure principle, the plea of innocence well and truly makes the case for a new form, Freud's fragmented guilt, which corresponds *de facto* to a principle opposed to the pleasure principle, even if Freud did not recognise this until much later, with the publication of *Beyond the Pleasure Principle* in 1920. Every dream could be and should be developed according to a method which unveils the underlying guilt. Guilt, or the gap between the third principle and its concrete realisation, is always already at work behind the appearance of a quest for wish fulfilment. This is true for every dream and every formation of the unconscious. Every dream disguises a basic guilt under the guise of a wish fulfilment.

Freud very quickly understood that the unconscious did not operate according to a technical principle, but instead according to the pleasure principle. He needed another twenty years to glimpse that the work of the unconscious widely eluded the pleasure principle. What is more, a few more decades were needed for Lacan to teach us that the *specificity* of the unconscious was none other than what we call here "the jouissance principle".

An examination of the operating principle of the unconscious must therefore involve a consideration of this third principle.

Kant first of all managed to clearly distinguish the three types of principles which governed all human action: the "technical" principles, the "pragmatic" pleasure principle, and a third type of "practical" principle, "duty", which serves as a kind of foundation to guilt. This third principle is touched on in *Groundwork of the Metaphysics of Morals* (1785), and it is the topic of Kant's second critique, devoted to morality or ethics, *The Critique of Practical Reason* (1788). While the question of the third principle is fundamental to an approach to the workings of the unconscious, it goes without saying, however, that Kant was not able to take either the unconscious or repression into account.

The study of the Freudian unconscious shows, however, that the status of the unconscious is fundamentally an ethical one. To demonstrate the distinctiveness of the unconscious, Lacan, therefore, read Kant's second critique very seriously in *The Ethics of Psychoanalysis* (1959–1960) and *Kant with Sade* (1963). As we shall see, calling on Sade as a tool for tackling Kant will serve to reveal the truth of the latter thinker, that is, the importance of the third principle for psychoanalysis, the unconscious and repression. In other words, the third principle, that of morality or ethics in Kant, finds its truth in the jouissance principle governing the operation of the unconscious. The jouissance principle (Lacan) both answers and corresponds exactly to Kant's morality principle.

In the first section of this book, we will read Kant's *The Groundwork of the Metaphysics of Morals* (1785) and *The Critique of Pure Reason* (1788) (the latter work reprising the former after a three-year gap, providing it with a structure).

In the second section, we will read Lacan's *The Ethics of Psychoanalysis* (1959–1960) and *Kant with Sade* (1963). (As with the works of Kant mentioned earlier, there was a gap of three years between the two works, with the latter work providing a more structured treatment of themes of its predecessor.) These *also* essentially offer a reading of Kant (obviously predating our own), so much so that the first two sections of this book are devoted to our reading of Kant and to our reading of Lacan's reading of Kant, respectively.

In the first section, we will attempt to reproduce as faithfully as possible the structure of *The Critique of Practical Reason*. This endeavour is all the more important because what Lacan attributes to Kant differs at a number of points from what Kant himself had written and may even contradict it. These divergences and contradictions must be taken note of, which entails reading *The Critique of Pure Reason* as carefully as we read *Kant with Sade*.

We distance ourselves from the position of a fanatical Lacanian who is happy to trust Lacan alone and spares himself the task of reading Kant: it is vital to carefully read Kant's text. We also distance ourselves from a position which would involve denouncing Lacan's errors in order to simply return to Kant's text. This is because Lacan's relationship with Kant's text is not a simple one: he had in fact studied Kant's text in great depth. His correction of a passage on happiness in the French translation is an example of this. A careful reading of Lacan's text is essential, taking note of its divergences and corrections, so we can ask ourselves how and why they were made. This with a view to highlighting the unique way that the unconscious and psychoanalysis operate, according to the jouissance principle.

Well before Lacan, Kant's practical reason was very commonly the object of a fundamentally distorted reading. According to this reading the problem of practical reason would have thus been reduced to that of an individual subject confronted with a choice between two objective courses of action: What must this individual do in order to do good? And this was to have been answered in a purely formal manner: act in accordance with the law and its universality. In this incorrect understanding of Kant, morality is still understood as a set of technical rules to be observed in order to achieve the goals of a society (or of a humanity) organised around a search for happiness.

Such a reading, of course, has nothing to do with the unconscious, which does not involve the individual, or a pair of objective courses of action, or doing good, or universality. It has nothing to do either with Kant's morality, where neither a determinate individual (such a subject was radically criticised in the paralogisms of pure reason), nor with two objective (or technical) courses of action, nor with a quest for correspondence with a predetermined good, nor with corresponding to a universal law introduced from the outside. However, as we shall see, Lacan did take Kant's morality as if it basically concerned an individual who had to determine themselves in their choice of action according to a good to be attained and according to a universality. One could quite simply dismiss Lacan's reading as inadequate both to how the unconscious works and to Kant's text.

However, this distorted reading is none other than that of *every reader* of Kant, inevitably compelled to adopt the perspective of an individual subject seeking the Good by means of a purely formal universal law. We will not analyse the reasons for this quite common bad reading of Kant right now, even though we can already suspect that repression plays a part in it.

Let us content ourselves with taking note that these three blunders, which Lacan does not evade in his reading of Kant, are just as quickly counteracted by Lacan himself by bringing in *de Sade*, designed to correct these blunders by 1) destroying the individual-subject 2) putting Evil in the place of Good, and 3) creating something different from a lifeless universality. Sade would also make the re-establishment of Kant's truth possible.

Armed with Sade's support, Lacan can then, also in "Kant with Sade", confront Kant in a fight to the death and, in doing so, unleash the operation of the death drive, as we shall see. The goal of this struggle, of which we will follow the ins and outs in detail, is not to declare a winner, even though Lacan pretends to think it is. The goal, rather, is to bring into play a more fundamental struggle, stopping short of individuals, Good and Evil, and of a universality of the law. This is the struggle inherent to the *unconscious* more particularly structured by *repression* as a conflict.

Kant knew both radical desire ("the higher faculty of desire") and the law well. The struggle with Kant lead by Lacan aims to show how the law is none other than repressed desire; in other words, it shows *repression and the unconscious within Kant's problematic itself*, even though Kant, of course, could not have known of them.

Where the unconscious and repression are concerned, today's reader is often hardly more advanced than Kant was, sometimes even behind him. Even if he has heard of the Freudian unconscious, he has no idea how it operates. In order to highlight this, we must not start out from the descriptive unconscious, but from the very *principle* of the unconscious, which develops from a *practical principle* (in Kant) to a new form as the *jouissance principle* (in Lacan).

In his reading of Kant, Lacan neglected the primordial place of the principle as a principle (even though the word appears in the first line of the first chapter of *The Critique of Practical Reason*). This is what allows him to promote, in its place, his *object a*. This, however, does not behave like an ordinary object, but rather as that which articulates the jouissance principle, provided the object *a* is understood not only as an oral object of frustration, but also simultaneously as an anal object of conflict and opposition, a scopic object in which the fantasy is organised, and most of all as a vocal object which energises the unconscious in jouissance. The reading of the object *a* (in Lacan) can only be correct starting from its working *principle* (in Kant). Conversely, Kant's principle can only find its true value by means of the *object a*.

Finally, in the third section, we will briefly show how the jouissance principle clarifies the practice of the unconscious.

Notes

1 [TN – The original reads "un accomplissement de souhaits (*Wunsch*)"].
2 [Translator's note – On the "inter-dit" or "the inter-said", see Lacan, "Subversion of the Subject and the Dialectic of Desire", in *Écrit: The First Complete Edition in English*, translated by Bruce Fink, New York, W.W. Norton & Company, 2006, p. 677].
3 Christiane Lacôte, "Jouissance", in *Dictionnaire de la psychanalyse*, edited by Roland Chemama, Paris, Larousse, 1993 [Translated for this edition].
4 This triple equivocation potentially at play in all interpretations is introduced by Lacan in "L'Étourdit", in *Autres Écrits*, Paris, Seuil, 2000, pp. 491–492.
5 Ibid., p. 449. English translation by Cormac Gallagher in *The Letter* 41, Summer 2009, p. 32.
6 Or in French: Capital A.
7 Lacan, "Subversion of the Subject and the Dialectic of Desire", op. cit.
8 See Lacan, *The Sinthome: The Seminar of Jacques Lacan Book XXIII*, Cambridge, Polity Press, 2016. Also, Fierens, *Lecture du sinthome*, Toulouse, Érès, 2018.
9 Such questions could be considered characteristic of behaviourism.
10 Freud, S.E. V, p. 507.
11 This work of transformation takes place very concretely in language and, as the unconscious is known to us only through the filter of its work of transformation, it necessarily appears to be "structured like a language".
12 [TN – *Matière* can also be translated as "matter" or "subject" (in the sense of a subject studied at school)].
13 Cf. Fierens and Pierobon, *Les pièges du réalisme*, Louvain-la-Neuve, EME, 2017.
14 Cf. Fierens, *La relance du phallus*, Toulouse, Érès, 2005.
15 "[A]s regards the Real, people want to identify it to matter (*la matière*)- I would rather propose to write it like this, 'l'âme à tiers' [. . .] for this there would need to be a ternary logic [. . .] this is indeed what authorises me to speak about 'l'âme à tiers' as something which necessitates a certain type of logical relationships." Jacques Lacan, *L'insu que sait de l'une-bévue s'aile à mourre*, Lesson The "third" precisely implies giving things a new form.
16 "It was a surprise to find that an increase in this *Ucs* sense of guilt can turn people into criminals. But it is undoubtedly a fact. In many criminals, especially youthful ones, it is possible to detect a very powerful sense of guilt which existed before the crime and is therefore not its result but its motive. It is as if it was a relief to be able to fasten this unconscious sense of guilt on to something real and immediate." Freud, S.E. XIX, p. 52.
17 Let us recall that Freud had sent his patient, Irma, to have her nose sliced up by his colleague and friend Fliess and that he obviously wanted to be seen as innocent in this tiresome affair.
18 Freud, S.E. IV, pp. 119–120.

Section I

Reading Kant

Thanks to a reading of Kant, we must rigorously continue examining the jouissance principle, which is simultaneously opposed to technical principles, to the pleasure principle, and to the obedience of outside authority. Or else, to question "jouissance" (which is beyond the pleasure principle, or rather *short of* it) in as much as it is the principle at the core of how the unconscious works.

The new form given by the work of the unconscious must also come to terms with the pleasure principle to some extent, but it fundamentally answers to the jouissance principle. The two principles are mixed together. No pleasure without jouissance, and no jouissance without pleasure. How can we specify the stakes of jouissance when pleasure is essential as an ever-present partial and possible accomplishment, whereas jouissance seems only ever to be accomplished as a degraded pleasure?

The consequences of this third principle make themselves known in the form of guilt, the superego, and anxiety or inhibition, in all of the pathologies and in the so-called normal human being, despite every kind of denial. It is not enough, however, to take note of these phenomenal formations. It must be taken into account that this principle is related to a "new form", differing from things which exist and can be observed. The fable of the damaged kettle[1] demonstrates this new form, not as a set of things (that the kettle is undamaged, that it had already had a hole in it, that it had not been borrowed), but as what *had to be*, what *must be*, and *should be*. The clinic does not first of all consist of observing that which is. It consists, rather, of taking account of that which imposes itself as *coming into being* (*werden, devenir*) and what *ought to* be (*sollen, devoir*), an ought to be which leans on a lack in being, well represented in guilt.

We cannot therefore start out from what is done, from what is, or from what we notice in a clinic of observation, but instead what *ought to* be done, what *ought to* be, what *ought to* come to be in a clinic undertaken from the starting point of a lack in being. In order to grasp jouissance, one cannot start out from an anthropology of morals or from a human ethology which observes certain cultures, or pathologies, etc., but from what ought to be, from what is not yet completely done but which, however, *ought to* be done. In other words, the method which will take jouissance

DOI: 10.4324/9781003055662-2

(and the unconscious) into account cannot start out on the basis of a given fact (that which is), but instead on the basis of *principles* (that which *ought to* be). The object *a* will bear witness to this.

Note

1 Freud, S.E. IV, pp. 119–120.

Part I

Groundwork of the Metaphysics of Morals (1785)

The moral law

Introduction
The principle as principle

The "moral law" (as Kant is concerned with it), which is to enlighten us as to "the new form" inherent to the unconscious, can seemingly be approached by being differentiated from the pleasure principle ("beyond the pleasure principle") along two separate paths. The first would deduce the moral law from a transcendent principle – "beyond". The second would infer it from empirical, clinical observations – "on the near side". Now, both of these precise paths constitute the two wrong tracks which fail to determine the "moral law" and what is at stake in it, by which we mean its value in itself as a first "principle", therefore independent of any beyond or near side.

The first wrong track (the "beyond") postulates that the "moral law" would logically ensue from knowledge. It would suffice to simply deduce it from a higher principle. This principle might be found in[1] the existence of a Supreme Being, in a certain way of organising the world, or else in a pre-constituted subject. If the "moral law" or basic guilt are truly primary, if they really count as *the principle* which orders things rather than being a consequence of them, they can only gain their existence from a hole in knowledge, from a lack of knowledge (an *Aufhebung* or abolition of knowledge). This hole in knowledge simultaneously means that the "moral law" and guilt can be based neither on a Supreme Being as an ideal of pure reason, nor on a pre-determined organisation of the world into which one would have to insert oneself, nor on a subject or a pre-existing and subsistent individual soul which would have to ask itself ethical questions secondarily.[2] In other words: *firstly*, there is no big Other to tell me what I should do, *secondly*, there is no law of the world to determine the "moral law", *thirdly*, there is no prior subject in search of a moral law to guide him or her in their actions. The "moral law" is the "moral law" of the unconscious, before any knowledge of a God, world or subject.

The second wrong track ("on the near side") postulates that the "moral law" and guilt are dependent on pre-existing customs – ethics would thus be reduced to an ethology. Certainly, one can examine the mores, laws and customs of a given society and this can lead to a practical anthropology or a human ethology (the done thing). However, observation of the done thing cannot lead to determining what it is that ought to be done. If ethology serves as a foundation for ethics, what should be done, or what should be the case, would be reduced to the duplication of what is already done, or of what is.[3] So-called "morals", drawn from a practical anthropology, are only an attempt at empirical adaptation to a purely empirical and contingent human ethology, without absolute necessity. We must loosen ourselves from all contingent conceptions of the moral Law and the superego, to take into account the absolute necessity with which the Law and the superego impose themselves.[4]

The interest in reading the *Groundwork* is precisely the consideration of the absolutely principled primary imperative of the "ought to be", the "ought to do", of the "moral law", and, for us, the superego. The radicality of the principle of "duty" implies that it is impossible to reduce the "moral law" to an empirical fact and to a purely clinical observation. To uphold a true ethics, it must be purged of all that, in one way or another, belongs to practical anthropology, which is always grounded in a series of empirical facts. Ethics cannot be grounded on an ethology of the human being, or on a form of humanism. "The ground of the obligation [. . .] must not be sought in the nature of the human being, or in the circumstances of the world in which he is placed, but a priori solely in concepts of pure reason".[5] So-called "ethics" (those of Mendelssohn, for example, a contemporary of Kant, and also the majority of present-day "ethics"), turn towards ethology to the extent that the empirical is mixed up with the rational in determining the "moral law". Ethics must rest entirely on the pure reason of all rational beings (human or non-human). "All moral philosophy rests entirely on its pure part and, applied to the human being, it does not borrow the least thing from our acquaintance with him (anthropology), but gives him, as a rational being, laws a priori."

However, in fact, our morality is exposed to all kinds of "corruption" – it is "human", they say – and selfish motivations in determining what we should do never fail to corrupt the purity of the moral law. Where can this purity be found? "[I]n the case of what is to be morally good it is not enough that it *conforms* with the moral law, but it must also be done *for its sake*".[6] It is the *intention* which counts. Wishing to be faithful to the *letter* of the law on principle is already a corruption of the moral law, because a literal prescription only ever gives us a blueprint to copy while letting the intention slip down to secondary importance. From the outset, Kant sets out the primacy of a *principle* which does not depend on what has already been given. But what then is the principle of the moral law which will be able to give rise to a "new form", rather than something which conforms?

Psychology, as well as a certain tendency in psychoanalysis, do not fail to analyse the motivations, determinations and over-determinations which would explain the human will and the actions which consciously or unconsciously ensue from it. All of these explanations, however – including those which appeal to a particular letter encrypted in the unconscious, or elsewhere – do not weigh up the importance of the principle which gives things a new form (rather than making them conform) and which transmits a new law. The Freudian superego itself, seen as a sediment of social or familial rules, does not fall under the purity of the "moral law", but has to do with its corruption by a whole series of secondary motivations arising from one's family or societal, more generally speaking, upbringing. Lacan defined the superego as the radically refined imperative: "*Jouis,* – enjoy!"[7] (However, as we have seen, mentioning the concept of "jouissance" cannot suffice so long as we have not shed further light on our third principle.)

Readings of Kantian morals almost systematically drift towards an individual ethics or yet again an ethics applied to the individual. Now, the hole in knowledge (*Aufhebung*) implies, as we have seen, not solely the absence of a God or World which would determine the moral law, but also the absence of any pre-existing subject who would apply the law. An emptying-out, therefore, of the spiritual subject or the soul, but also an emptying-out of the empirical subject. The "moral law", therefore, is imposed, we might say, as a *law of the unconscious*, and it is stemming from this law as principle, the third principle or jouissance principle, that the Big Other (and its non-existence), the World (and its phallic way of operating) and the subject (its division and its *désêtre*) can appear.

The *Groundwork* has no other goal than the "identification and corroboration *of the supreme principle of morality*"[8] In our reading of the *Groundwork*, our goal is to shed light on the unconscious through this supreme principle, distinct from the pleasure principle.

The *Groundwork of the Metaphysics of Morals* is comprised of three subdivisions. In the first, Kant starts out from the traditional rational common consciousness of morality, that is to say, good will. In analysing it, he discovers the pure principle of the moral law. (It is not deduced from any higher principle, nor is it inferred from particular experiences; it is observed in each person's singularity.) In the second subdivision, Kant *analyses* this principle of the moral law so as to draw its consequences for every moral being. In the third subdivision, Kant sketches the mechanism of *synthesis* or construction, always at play in morality. This topic will be taken up again and fully developed in the *Critique of Practical Reason*. We will not discuss the third subdivision of the *Groundwork*. After reading the first two subdivisions, we will pass directly to an examination of Kant's second critique.

Kant's starting point in good will indicates that Kantian morals involve a popular philosophy. They are really addressed to everybody. However, despite this popular starting point, they make no compromises in methodical rigour. An amalgam of positions leading to a guide to action is not involved (as in the "popular philosophy" of Mendelssohn, a contemporary of Kant). Rather, Kant starts out from what is "popular" or from the common rational consciousness of morality in order to reveal its *principle*, the purity of the categorical imperative, of the moral law as it concerns each and every person.

Notes

1 Kant, had to "abolish (*aufheben*) *knowledge* to make room for *faith*", without which there is no morality. (Kant, *Critique of Pure Reason*, Preface to the Second Edition, edited by Vasilis Politis, London, J.M. Dent, 1993, p. 21).
2 The hole in knowledge therefore entails the whole Transcendental Dialectic of pure reason: a deconstruction of the Cartesian subject in the paralogisms of pure reason, a radical

critique of the world in the antinomies of pure reason, and a radical absence of the proof of the existence of God in the ideal of pure reason.

3 This question, among others, resonates in the drama of Antigone, confronted with pre-existing customs and rules, Creon's laws – "human" laws, as they say – which establish themselves in the perspective of a practical anthropology as that which everyone should do, meaning to copy the laws. However, the law which is forced on Antigone is completely different. It is not at all founded on pre-existing law making. It appears as a "categorical imperative", in other words not predetermined by that law making.

4 Thinking that we need to relax this radicality, to undo the stranglehold of the superego, to free the subject of their guilt, etc., belongs to a technique in which the question of the third principle has completely disappeared. On the pretext of a pleasure principle which should be in command of everything, the psychotherapist's strategy is then exclusively guided by technical principles, and the question of the "new form" of the unconscious is kept completely silent.

5 Kant, *Groundwork of the Metaphysics of Morals*, translated by Mary Gregor, Cambridge, Cambridge University Press, 2012, p. 5 Reason, in its practical usage, is first discussed by means of *concepts*. The *Critique of Practical Reason* will more precisely emphasize that it is the *principle as principle* which counts for practical reason.

6 Kant, *Groundwork of the Metaphysics of Morals*, op. cit., pp. 5–6.

7 Lacan, *On Feminine Sexuality: The Limits of Love and Knowledge*, translated with notes by Bruce Fink, New York, W.W. Norton & Company, 1999, p. 3.

8 According to Kant, this problem had not been dealt with in a satisfying manner before him (Kant, *Groundwork of the Metaphysics of Morals*, op. cit., p. 7).

Chapter 1

Good will, duty, and the moral law

On the basis of popular moral philosophy

The first subdivision of the *Groundwork* shows how the simple analysis of *good will* as an ethics of common reason leads to the discovery in turn of *duty* and the *moral law*.

Good will[1]

Kant sets out from a universal principle, acknowledged by all rational beings (both human and non-human): the good (*gut*). What is there that is absolutely good?

The Good [*le Bien*] is only one of the three great universals which are thought to transcend all categories: the Good, the True, and the Beautiful. In what way might it permit the discovery of the moral law in all human beings? How might it provide access to our third principle, to the "new form" proper to the unconscious, to "jouissance"? Because despite the popular consensus where the Good [*Bien*] is concerned, good will appears foreign to our actual lives, naive and illusory. On the one hand, the Good as Good seems disconnected from the empirical conditions of experience and seems to be a "transcendence", which is imaginary and unrooted in any tangible, concrete reality. On the other hand, particularly since the advent of psychoanalysis and the discovery of the unconscious, it has been revealed as the disguise of something completely different from the good, up to and including, a murderous ferocity opposed to every good. Kant already asked the question: does good will not boil down to a "high-flown fantastication"?[2] Should we not go further and say that the Good is solely a form of resistance in the face of the complexity of the psychical agencies (conscious, preconscious, unconscious) which all operate according to the pleasure principle? Does good will not in the end boil down to the will to feel good, to a quest for what is pleasant [*bon*] as the sole aim imposed on human beings by their nature?

If there is a "good" [*bien*], it must already be said that it is always a good that is missing, in as much as it does not exist. It is the same for "jouissance": "a certain jouissance might have been to blame": failing, deficiency, something that isn't working out. Something skids off track in what is manifestly aimed at, and then it immediately starts up with the good and happiness. The good, the bad and the

DOI: 10.4324/9781003055662-5

oafish! (*Du bi, du bien, du benêt!*)"[3] Moreover, the oafish is only Well-being or the Pleasant [*Bon*] skidding off track towards an illusion of the good.

As the good is always caught in this naive skidding off track, it is never given or acquired. "Good" is always uttered according to a *will* rather than according to a state of reality – the will to carry out a technical action (in the wider sense), the will to attain pleasure (for oneself or for other people), or moral will. The will stands for the faculty of ends and it always entails "an activity, a power (*efficace*) of the intellect, it is *practical reason* itself".[4] However, in will in general, the Good [*Bien*] is always already contaminated by the Pleasant [*Bon*], unless it is pure (good) will: "It is impossible to think of anything at all in the world, or indeed even beyond it, that could be taken to be good (*gut*)[5] without limitation, except a good will (*ein guter Wille*)."[6] Nothing is good apart from good will. So, the different talents of the mind – "[u]understanding, wit, judgement [. . .] confidence, resolve, and persistency of intent" are only "good" according to the will that puts them to use. They can be "extremely evil and harmful if the will that is to make use of these gifts of nature [. . .] is not good".[7] It is the same for "[p]ower, riches, honor, even health", which can either be used for good or for evil. Moderation itself, which Aristotle regarded as the height of the practical intellect, is not the good: "the cold blood of a scoundrel makes him not only far more dangerous, but also immediately more loathsome in our eyes than he would have been taken to be without it".[8] We will not find what is good in an action, in its results, nor in the ability to attain a result, but solely in its willing. The will alone, the deep intention alone counts in evaluating the good. And, as it *always* fails in purifying itself (cf. Overdetermination), should we not conclude that human nature is solely dependent on the pleasure principle and that our third principle is only a pipe dream?

As Kant remarks, if human nature solely sought happiness and what pleasant in accordance with the pleasure principle, it could have been constructed entirely from the starting point of the instincts (the drives would in this case be identical to instincts). Rational beings would be completely directed by these instincts and the "reason" which is allotted to them would be purely speculative or would contemplate the operation of the instincts. Reason would have no place in practice. Now, reason does in fact have a place in practice: good will and the unconscious present themselves as irreducible to instinct and the quest for the pleasant. The good is opposed to the pleasant, but it is a good in negative, an unattainable good, a failing jouissance (*une jouissance en défaut*). It always seems to go together with a *basic guilt* for not having done the right thing.

Reason, as used in practice, gets in the way of the operation of the pleasure principle. From the point of view of the search for the pleasant which corresponds to the pleasure principle, the practical reason which seeks the good without being able to attain it would appear hateful. And, in accordance with the pleasure principle, a certain degree of "misology", or hatred of reason, is found in everyone.

The true aim of reason in its practical usage is "to produce a *will that is good*, not for other purposes *as a means*, but good *in itself*"[9] This will is the highest good (*höchste Gut*) as it is "the condition of everything else, even of all longing for happiness." It is always coming up short of the good and of jouissance, the jouissance which should be there but is not. It is always already mired in the basic guilt, prior to any transgression, which is its unsurpassable underside.

The conflict between principles and duty (*Pflicht*)

Good will always appears along with its underside, guilt, and it is always contaminated by the quest for happiness or the pleasure principle. However, it is always opposed to the principle of happiness, not without implicating some conflicts of interest which must be taken into account. *Duty* is identical to the concept of good will, taking these conflicts into account.

It is *conflict* as conflict which interests us here. It is because "good will" is always involved in a conflict of principles that it must be developed as *duty*. Duty is therefore the position of good will in relation to the conflict which always opposes it to other principles, the technical principle and the pleasure principle. This position can be explained in three propositions. The first two are negative: *firstly*, the driving force of moral action cannot be the inclination (*Neigung*) towards happiness (the pleasure principle); *secondly*, the driving force of moral action is not explained by the goal to be attained (the technical principle). The third proposition spells out the positive motivation of moral action: "*duty is the necessity of an action from respect for the law*".[10] Outside of the influence of pleasure and technique, "nothing remains for the will that could determine it except, objectively, the *law* and, subjectively, *pure respect* for this practical law, and hence the maxim of complying with such a law, even if it infringes on all my inclinations."[11] Respect – *Achtung*, attention! Danger! – is a subjective, positive principled focus on the objective law. As this law cannot be drawn from inclination nor the sensible[12] goal to be accomplished, it does not fall under the heading of sensibility, it "*can take place only in a rational being*",[13] and the "rational being" is reduced to being the point of operation of our third principle (which must spell out the working principle of what we call "the unconscious"). We have acquired the principle of duty: this is a respect for the law *on principle*. Respect appears to be a feeling, but it is a unique type of feeling in that it is not taken in by sensibility, but directly arises from a consideration of the third principle, as produced by reason.

The moral law

To determine the principle of the law, all particular determinations which would come from sensibility must be excluded, notably the idea of the possible results of compliance with the law. "Nothing remains but as such the universal conformity of actions with law, which alone is to serve the will as its principle, i.e. I ought never to proceed except in such a way *that I also will that my maxim should become a universal law*".[14] Good will should correspond to a *law*.

Is it the same for the unconscious? As the unconscious does not submit to specific characteristics (*particularités données*), does this mean that it should operate according to a universal law?

Let us note that a "universal law" is not given in advance – neither in Kantian morality, nor, of course, for how the unconscious works. It must *come into being* from a maxim. In common understanding, subjective assent submits to what is objectively given in the senses. In respect *for the law*, consent submits to the law because the law derives from reason, in other words because it takes its objectivity from the exercise of reason, independent of sensibility. The objectivity of the law arises, therefore, from willing (*wollen*) itself: "can you also will that your maxim become a universal law?"[15]

For the Kantian moral law, this act of willing is quite simply not possible when the maxim cancels itself out in a logical contradiction when it is raised to the level of a universal law, for example, in case of a promise made with the intention of not keeping it, or in the case of "the lie". This criterion of universality, which judges a maxim according to the supreme principle of all analytical judgements,[16] is never a criterion of *exclusion*: in analysing the maxim in order to perhaps detect in it a logical contradiction, it enables the exclusion of all maxims which cannot become laws. This criterion, however, does not suffice to make a law.

The Kantian moral law is not fundamentally dependent on analytical universality. This is because the moral value of the law is based only on the *exercise* of reason and appears from the *questioning* of the universal scope of a maxim: "can you also will that your maxim become a universal law?" Universal law is not given in advance, it depends on the willing which determines its coming into being. It must be synthesized, manufactured by reason. We will return to this exercise of reason in what follows of our reading of Kant, and to this questioning of universality, in our reading of "Kant with Sade" (Lacan).

While common reason is immediately in step with the moral law, it is also in step with our various inclinations.

> [F]rom this there arises a *natural dialectic*, i.e. a propensity to rationalize against those strict laws of duty, and to cast doubt on their validity, or at least their purity and strictness and, where possible, to make them better suited to our wishes and inclinations, i.e. fundamentally to corrupt them and deprive them of their entire dignity.[17]

It is because of this natural dialectic (which appears spontaneously and as if independent of any philosophy) that common reason must develop a complete critique of practical reason.

***

Good will, duty, moral law. Important objections are raised against each of these three ideas. Good will is supposed to have been given to everyone, and it is only on the basis of this hypothesis that duty and the moral law can be deduced, but is this not a pure prejudice depending precisely on the common way of seeing things, of no revolutionary significance, a habit of common reason which uses disavowal to protect itself against the death drive, against fundamentally destructive tendencies towards other people and towards oneself? Is not the idea of resolving conflict or of doing something "out of duty" merely a decoy and, what is more, a decoy in contradiction with the principle of narcissism, according to which all the libidinal force which drives any of our actions is narcissistic? No action can be performed "out of duty" because, at a fundamental level it is instead performed out of narcissistic egoism. Finally, the *moral law* postulates that we can determine the maxim of our action to the exclusion of all others. Now, do we not learn with the unconscious that every action is overdetermined, that is to say brought about by a multitude of determinations which render any search for the definitive cause of the action in question impossible? In the interpretation of a dream, we necessarily come up against its "navel", i.e., a tight ball of meanings which become more complex the more we try to unravel them. Is it not the same for the interpretation of the various maxims of each of our actions?

Yes, good will conceals the death drive and we must, in our critique, tease out this will from all of the ego's tendencies to appear in a flattering light. Yes, doing something "out of duty" always involves narcissism, in as much as the latter is always torn between the ideal ego of its past and the ego-ideal of an unreachable future, and we must, in our critique, differentiate what is performed "out of duty" from all the pragmatic rules imposed on the basis of ordinary rules and regulations, and raise narcissism to the level of a structural "duty" – *Wo Es war soll Ich werden*. Yes, the moral law stands as the exclusive focus point of all other motivations: as such it represents an empty place which makes the movement of overdetermination possible and we must, in our critique, tease out the moral law not as a new maxim, opposed to the plethora of pragmatic maxims already in existence, but as the third principle inherent to the unconscious – the jouissance principle which never ceases to act and which consists in "giving things a new form".

Notes

1 We translate *gut* as "*bien*" (a moral good to compare with our third principle) and not as "*bon*" (a pleasant good to compare with the pleasure principle) which translates the German word "*wohl*". Translating "*guter wille*" as "*bonne volonté*" [literally "*good will*"] causes problems, as it associates the will with "*bon*", whereas the German language opposes *guter Wille* and *wohl*. In French, due to the lack of an adjective corresponding to the adverb *bien* ["well" in English], this could be translated as "*volonté de bien*". But this translation, which brings in the *noun* "*bien*" is not suitable either, as it lets it be understood that the will is determined by a "good" [*bien*] (as a primary *concept*), which is precisely not the case in the Kantian moral law. The will, however, always *first of all* implies doing/making [*faire*] as a *verb* (the principle) and the "good/well" ["*bien*"] only comes into it as an *adverb*. We shall translate *guter Wille* as "*volonté de bien faire*" ["the will to do well"]. It could certainly also be understood as a will guided

by technical principles (which is not the case). Ambiguity or equivocation is inevitable. Our translation, however, has the merits of clearly retaining the distinction between *gut* (*bien*)/*wohl* (*bon*) and of founding it on the aspect of *faire* ["making" or "doing"]. [Translator's note: In Mary Gregor's English translation of the *Critique*, from which all of the quotations in this text are drawn, *das Gute*, the substantive form of the adjective *gut* is translated as "the good" and *das Böse* is translated as "evil". The cognate concepts, related to the morality principle rather than the pleasure principle, are *das Wohl*, which is translated as "well-being" and *das Übel* (or *Weh*), which are translated as "woe" or "ill-being". I have retained Gregor's translation of *guter Wille* as "good will" for ease of reading and have translated *le Bon* as "the Pleasant", to stress its affinity with the pleasure principle.]

2 Kant, *Groundwork of the Metaphysics of Morals*, op. cit., p. 10.
3 Lacan, *On Feminine Sexuality: The Limits of Love and Knowledge*, op. cit., pp. 54–55.
4 Eisler, *Kant-Lexikon*, Paris, Gallimard, NRF, 1994, p. 1078.
5 [Translator's note: Text in brackets does not appear in Gregor's English translation.]
6 Kant (1785), p. 9.
7 Ibid.
8 Ibid., p. 10.
9 Ibid., p. 12.
10 Ibid., p. 16.
11 Ibid.
12 [Translator's note: "Sensible" and "sensibility" here, and throughout this text, refer to the empirical world of sense experiences.]
13 Ibid.
14 Ibid., p. 17.
15 Ibid., p. 18.
16 "Now the proposition: 'Nothing can have a predicate that contradicts it', is called the principle of contradiction, and is a universal but purely negative criterion of all truth. But it belongs to logic alone, because it is valid of knowledge, merely as knowledge, and without respect to their content, and declares that the contradiction entirely destroys and nullifies them." (*Critique of Pure Reason*, p. 149; A149/B189).
17 Kant, *Groundwork of the Metaphysics of Morals*, op. cit., p. 20.

Chapter 2

Analysis of the moral law
Unearthing the metaphysics of morals based on popular moral philosophy

Good will, duty, and the moral law can be found right within common morality. We should in no way conclude from this that these are empirical concepts concerning a factual reality. In them, we stumble upon contradictions and other forms of impossibility, amplified by the discoveries of psychoanalysis, with the result that these concepts can in no way be reduced to the clinical observation of a given reality.

There are *no* examples of morality

Because of these impossibilities inherent to good will, duty and the moral law, there are no concrete existing examples of moral action. Actions more or less in keeping with the letter of a certain particular "duty" could probably be found, but no concrete moral action can serve as a model or as an example. It is not possible that an action could have been carried out solely "from duty" precisely because of the overdetermination which rules over all our actions. Kant did not wait for Freud to spell this out. There is always a risk of self-love being the motive behind our most apparently noble actions. "In fact, it is absolutely impossible by means of experience to make out with complete certainty a single case in which the maxim of an action that otherwise conforms with duty did rest solely on moral grounds and on the representation of one's duty."[1] Moreover, Kant adds, "we can never, even by the most strenuous examination, get entirely behind our covert incentives". "One need [only be] a cold-blooded observer who does not at once take the liveliest wish for the good as its actuality, to become doubtful at certain moments [. . .] whether any true virtue is actually to be found in the world at all."[2]

The very act of basing ourselves on examples, on sensible experience or the observation of facts involves us in an empirical anthropology or a human ethology, and definitively puts us at a distance from the groundwork of the metaphysics of morals.

Even the Christ of the Gospel is not an example to be imitated: "Why do you call me (whom you see) good, there is none good (the archetype of the good) but one, that is, God (whom you do not see)."[3] Citing Mark 10:18 and Luke 18:19,

DOI :10.4324/9781003055662-6

and through his own commentary in brackets, Kant points out clearly that the concept of the moral good can in no way be presented as something visible, namely an example or an empirical model (belonging to sensibility). In the quote, the reference to the invisible "God" (rather than to Christ) refers back to the operation of reason as reason. We will see that the appeal to an invisible Good is not, however, a sufficient basis for morality, because it is not a case of presenting the idea of morality on the basis of the idea of God (an idea which could be symbolized in religion, for example), but solely on the basis of a *principle* (good will and its accompanying guilt are a direct basis for this principle without the support of any God). It is in this sense that the metaphysics of morals must be founded on the pure operation of reason.

The examples which may appear can only be useful in one way, to lead us back, in a pedagogical manner, to the foundations, to the principle of morality, which is dependent on practical reason and not on what one might observe of human nature. A mixture of determinations is falsely taken to be the goal of moral action, "now perfection, now happiness, here moral feeling, there fear of God, a bit of this and a bit of that".[4] In contrast to this diversity observable in human nature, in contrast to this humanism, a metaphysics of mores must be found, "mixed with no anthropology, no theology, no physics or hyperphysics, still less with occult qualities (which one might call hypophysics)" and this, non-humanist, but purely rational metaphysics has "an influence on the human heart so much more powerful than all other incentives".[5]

***

The psychoanalytic method itself is not founded on any examples. This is because all examples are already caught in the framework of the one who thinks they are presenting it objectively. It inevitably confirms the pleasure of the person presenting it. In other words, it has already excluded the question of the third principle, the question of the new form given to things by the unconscious or rather, it has already brought it back to the familiar nature of the all-powerful pleasure principle. The only possible use of examples lies, on the other hand, in putting things in question.

The question of morality must, therefore, be taken up again above any example: on the basis of the principles of action.

Morality is a question of *principle*

Moral laws (which are never embodied in examples) are completely different from the laws at work in nature, empirical anthropology included. The former are only ever represented as what *must or ought to* be, as a *duty*, and take effect through their *representation*, whereas the latter primarily take effect in nature such as it is effectively realised.

We should carefully distinguish what *ought to* be (and which action in general) and what *is* (and can be contingently observed), even before we can distinguish moral laws from the laws of nature. We should also grasp the different possible principles of action according to this necessity (*devoir être*).

The verb "ought" (*devoir, sollen*) expresses an imperative. All imperatives postulate a *relationship* between duty and the non-accomplishment of this duty: I ought to do what has not yet been done. Where no gap exists between the representation of a goal and its accomplishment, where the goal is not associated with an at least temporary absence of accomplishment, there is no imperative. For example, divine will knows no duty or imperative, because an act of divine willing is at the same time its achievement. Lack (to be precise, the lack of accomplishment in the present) is therefore fundamental to the question of the imperative or of "duty".

We must now distinguish different types of imperative or duty along with different types of *principle* which command action in general.

Three types of imperative, three types of principle

1 *If* I want to attain a certain goal, if I want to arrive at a concrete end, I must use the correct means. This duty is dependent on my initial hypothesis, it is a *hypothetical* imperative. The hypothesis in question is that the right means are needed to solve the *technical problem* in the wider sense – technique also includes the domain of thought and the problems which arise within it. Here the hypothetical imperative is *problematic*, that is, related to a *problem* which must be solved. "The prescriptions for the physician thoroughly to cure his man, and for a poisoner reliably to kill him, are of equal worth, in so far as each serve to effect his purpose perfectly."[6] These are questions of skill (*Geschicktlichkeit*), and they are the aims of education and training in general. They are technical imperatives. The obligations imposed by this type of imperative are the *rules* (*Regeln*) of skill.

2 The second imperative is also *hypothetical*. However, the hypothesis on which it depends is not connected to any particular problem to be solved. It is, on the contrary, completely general. It is the search for happiness, which is much wider in scope than particular problems: "if I want to move towards well-being or happiness, I must also will the means of getting there". The pleasure principle is *pragmatically* part of the essence of the human being. The second imperative is a *pragmatic* imperative (in the sense of pragmatism aiming at well-being). However, I do not know the rules which assure happiness: the obligations of this imperative come down to mere counsels (*Ratschläge*) of prudence (*Klugheit*), advice with regards to "the choice of the means to one's own greatest well-being."[7]

3 The third imperative is not hypothetical because it is not determined by the goal to be attained (the possible result of an action or the attainment of happiness). "This imperative is **categorical**. It concerns not the manner of the action or what is to result from it, but the form and the principle from which it does itself follow; and the essential in it consists in the disposition, let the result

what it may. This imperative may be called that of **morality**."[8] It is the moral imperative. The obligations are here commands (*Gebote*) or laws (*Gesetze*).

The two hypothetical imperatives basically appear as *analytic*: it is enough to analyse the hypothesis to discover the imperative. This goes without saying for the problematic imperative. Its principle is *technical*. Where happiness or the pleasure principle is concerned, analysis immediately comes up against an unsurpassable limit, because "[no human being] can never say determinately and in agreement with himself what he actually wishes and wants."[9] Where is happiness? "*Che vuoi?*" This question remains without a definitive answer. In both cases, "whoever wills the ends also wills the means", as the saying goes. "The imperative that commands willing the means for someone who wills the end is in both cases analytic."[10] These analytic positions do not cause any theoretical difficulties, except that the analysis of the imperative of happiness (the pleasure principle) does not lead to any concrete solution, for want of knowing what is really desired.

The technical imperative is *possible* (it is dependent on its hypothesis). The pragmatic imperative appears as *real* – the pleasure principle is a fact (*donnée de fait*), even if the means of attaining this pleasure elude us. The third imperative, the categorical imperative, is both *synthetic* (it must be made) and *necessary* – it corresponds to Kant's principle of morality and our "jouissance principle" (which "does not stop being written", even when we are unaware of it).

The three imperatives are thus divided up according to the three categories of modality and of its principles, "the postulates of empirical thought in general".

1   That which agrees with the formal conditions (intuitions and concept) of experience, is *possible*.
2   That which is connected with the material conditions of experience (sensation) is *real*.
3   That whose connection with the real is determined according to universal conditions of experience is necessary (exists necessarily).[11] The principle of the technical imperative is problematic because it is subject to the contingent nature of the goal to be reached and analysis easily determines the means of arriving at that end. The principle of the pragmatic imperative (of happiness) is real and assertoric. It is found in everyone, but analysis fails to determine what must be done in order attain happiness. The principle of the moral imperative (including the jouissance principle) is categorical and apodictic (necessary), but there is *no analysis* that could determine it because it has no concrete material, no pre-existing condition that we might analyse. It must therefore be constructed, "synthesized", it must be made. It is found through "*synthesis*".

Determination of the moral imperative

The formula of universality

How can we pinpoint the third principle, of morality (and jouissance), which comes under the heading of necessity, when we have no assumptions at the outset, as it is an imperative without pre-existing hypotheses? Kant insists on the fact that we cannot start out from any example or with any goal for our action in mind. The difficulty with grasping the how and the why of the formation of this imperative is considerable. It results from the fact that "[i]t is an a priori synthetic practical proposition".[12] It had already been difficult to understand the synthetic theoretical principle of judgement (a synthetic proposition like a mathematical theorem is dependent on the action which proves it: "it must be made"). For a practical synthetic judgement, "the difficulty will be no smaller."

Kant, however, starts out from the pure general, necessary (but not sufficient) "formula" for there to be a categorical imperative. As such an imperative does not contain any conditions (it is not hypothetical), that force it to conform completely to the law, no matter, no particularity can be of use, "nothing is left but the universality of a law as such, with which the maxim of the action ought to conform, and it is this conformity alone that the imperative actually represents as necessary." There is no way of avoiding this necessary (*but not sufficient*) condition for there to be a categorical imperative corresponding to good will. The categorical imperative reads, therefore, as follows: "act only according to that maxim through which you can at the same time will that it become a universal law".[13] All imperatives of duty should answer to this universal criterion.

This universal law raises a question, however. There are no example, no moral actions, no concrete realizations of this principle. Is the concept of duty not completely empty, even if it purports to be universal?

Let us take up the question of universality again from scratch. We have universal laws in nature. The existence of objects "is determined according to universal laws". We do not at all have (supposedly universal) laws of morality. What do we do? All that is left for us to do is to put ourselves in the position of the creator of those laws: "*act as if the maxim of your action were to become by your will a* **universal law of nature**". This position of the moral "subject"[14] is possible according to the solution of the third antinomy, namely, while the world is indeed determined according to the principles of phenomenal causality, there is still a place for an extra phenomenal causality (which would be the starting point for a new phenomenal causal series), a noumenal causality which creates a new world, a divine freedom. But again, this is not a case of imitating God or of modelling oneself on the universal laws of nature. The sense of "ought" (*sollen, devoir*) would be lost in the simple duplication of what already is. Therefore, there is no example that would serve to develop moral duty.

Short of this creation of the law by the moral "subject", this criterion only serves to rule out a certain number of subjective wills which can *in no way* count as duties. Kant therefore examines four well-organized counterexamples "according to their usual division, into duties to ourselves and to other human beings, into perfect and imperfect duties".

Four counterexamples or four maxims that cannot be duties (how the criterion of analytic universality enables us to discard false duties).

1   *Euthanasia* cannot be considered a "perfect" duty towards oneself. The maxim (or the subjective will) for euthanasia would be as follows: "from

self-love I make it my principle to shorten my life if, when protracted any longer, it threatens more ill than it promises agreeableness. The only further question is whether this principle of self-love could become a law of universal nature".[15] No, this law would mean the destruction of life in general. A nature behaving according to this principle *is in contradiction with itself*. Death is destructive of life. Euthanasia can in no way constitute a moral duty. (*This does not mean than there is a moral law which forbids euthanasia.*)

2 *Breach of trust* cannot be considered as a "perfect" duty towards others. The maxim of a breach of trust would be as follows: "when I believe myself to be in need of money I shall borrow money, and promise to repay it, even though I know that it will never happen". Such a maxim would mean the destruction of lending and borrowing, and of the pact which connects human beings. A human nature based on the principle of false promises is *in contradiction with itself* and destroys itself. (*This does not mean that there is a moral law which forbids the breach of trust.*)

3 *Idleness and the gratification of pleasures (Genuss)* cannot be considered an "imperfect" duty towards oneself. It is absolutely impossible to "**will** that this become a universal law of nature, or as such be placed in us by natural instinct. For as a rational being [one] necessarily wills that all capacities in him be developed, because they serve him and are given to him for all sorts of possible purposes."[16] This maxim is most probably not contrary to human life. However, *it is in contradiction with what is willed by reason*, which articulates *all* of the capacities. (*This does not mean that there is a moral law which forbids idleness.*)

4 *A retreat into oneself* cannot be considered an "imperfect" duty towards others. "May everyone be as happy as heaven wills, or as he can make himself, I shall take nothing away from him, not even envy him; I just do not feel like contributing anything to his well-being, or his assistance in need!" This maxim is, of course, not contrary to the life of human society. It is, however, *in contradiction with what reason itself wills*: "it is still impossible to **will** that such a principle holds everywhere as a law of nature".[17] Here again it is the will which would contradict itself in excluding solidarity between human beings. (*This does not mean that there is a moral law which forbids one from retreating into oneself.*)

The first two maxims cannot be "conceived" as universal law because of a *conceptual* contradiction (the supreme principle of all analytic judgements forbids the universalization of these maxims.) The latter two maxims cannot become universal laws, cannot be "*willed*" as universal laws because of what reason *does*. "The first conflicts with strict or narrower (unrelenting) duty, the second only with wider (meritorious) duty."

Of course, in the eyes of Kant the man, the opposing maxims (respect for life, respect for one's word, respect for all one's capacities and for solidarity) are real duties, "or at least what we take to be such". For if Kant had determined "the content of the categorical imperative, which would have to contain the principle of all duty",[18] he adds just as subtly, *"if there were such a thing at all"*, if there are concretely determined duties. Tempting as it might be to subjectively admit four maxims, opposing the four counterexamples as *duties*, he has not at all proven them as such, he has not shown them arising from any deductions (*Abteilung*). In contrast, their four-part division (*Ableitung*) "can clearly be seen" according to the twofold dichotomy of, on the one hand, duties towards oneself or towards others, on the other hand, duties relating to conceptual possibility or impossibility ("perfect" or "unrelenting" duty) or of the possibility or impossibility of the *will* (*vouloir*) ("imperfect" or "meritorious" duty).

Let us already note that if jouissance is an imperative ("*Jouis!* – Enjoy!"), we have not managed either to determine the slightest *duty* of jouissance, the slightest concrete application of the third principle to reality.

From the impossibility of the determination of duty to the second formula of the categorical imperative: respect for the end in itself

How can we manage to determine what duty is? We cannot in any way start out from the particular constitution of human nature, because duty only exists as a conflict in which the human will is always divided between inclination and complete conformity to reason. We can, however, determine the *principle* of the moral law which holds for all human will. To determine the moral law we should find "a [...] standpoint, which is to be firm even though there is nothing either in heaven, or on earth, from which she is suspended, or on which she relies".[19] Without this standpoint in a higher principle (heaven) or in phenomenal reality (earth), we can only count on reason or on will itself: "The will is thought as a capacity to determine itself to action *in conformity with the representation of certain laws*. And such a capacity can be found only in rational beings."[20]

The "representation of laws" comes into play in representing the ends of action. "End", however, can have two different meanings, according to whether the end is external to action or internal to it. *Firstly*, to reach a particular end or to attain my well-being, I must use a certain means (technical or pragmatic imperatives). This "will" or this "desire" is dependent on my *subjective* situation in relation to a particular end and the "incentive" of my action will be spoken of: "The subjective ground of desiring is the *incentive (Triebfeder)*". The German term, *Triebfeder*, can literally be translated as the "spring"(*Feder*) of the drive (*Trieb*). Here the drive is oriented towards pleasure and outside the action performed. *Secondly*, if I set aside any particular end, the *inherent* end of will, *independently of the rest, objectively* remains. Such an end is an "end in itself" (*Zweck an sich selbst*). Objectivity is determined here by reason itself: "the objective ground of willing [is] the *motivating ground (Bewegungsgrund)*",[21] the basis of the movement at the heart of action.

The human being is precisely characterised by an act, the basis of whose movement is included within itself [*L'homme se caractérise précisément par un fondement de son mouvement à l'intérieur de son acte*]: "a human being and generally every rational being *exists* as an end in itself, *not merely as a means* for the discretionary use of this or that will, but must in all its actions, whether directed towards itself or also to other rational beings, always be considered *at the same time as an end*". In the quest for the application of the categorical imperative to particular duties and therefore to the determination of the ends of action, we do not manage to determine concrete duties, but rather a new formulation of the imperative: "*So act that you use humanity, in your own person as well as in the person of any other, always at the same time as an end, never merely as a means.*"[22] We can see how the four counter-examples, mentioned in the framework of universality, do not respond either to the second formula of the categorical imperative: they never treat the person as an end in themselves.

From this new formulation of the imperative, it will be understood that jouissance should necessarily have to do with the treatment of humanity as an end in itself. The four counter-examples also cannot serve of examples of "jouissance" in the strongest sense of the term.

The third formula of the categorical imperative: the autonomy of the moral law

The third formula is not stated by Kant in the manner "So act that . . . ." Such a formulation would be equivalent to saying, "So act that you do not obey a command" or "So act in a way that you are spontaneous". If the end ought to be "in itself", it must be established by the will itself alone. The first formulation of the categorical imperative states the necessary (but not sufficient) condition for a maxim to become a moral law (analytic universality, without any contradiction in the way it is formula). The second formulation stated that moral action should correspond to the essence of a human being or other rational being (the end in itself and respect for the person). The third practical formulation of the will does not enunciate a logical formula or a formula in accord with human dignity. It says what the moral will *makes* or *manufactures*. It is "the idea *of the will of every rational being as a universally legislating will.* [. . .] [T]he will is not just subject to the law, but subject in such a way that it must also be viewed *as self-legislating*, and just on account of this as subject to the law (of which it can consider itself the author) in the first place".[23]

The autonomy of the law making will is complete not only in relation to all the inclinations but also in relation to any other will (God, for example) and in relation to all interests.

All the attempts at discovering the principle of morality prior to Kant had failed because they had overlooked this autonomy to the benefit of another principle or interest, outside the moral law. "For one never got duty, but the necessity of an action from a certain interest, be it one's own interest or that of another. But then the imperative always had to be conditional and could not be fit to be a moral command at all."[24] It was the *third* formulation of the categorical imperative that had been missing from all the pre-Kantian "morals", even more than the first or second.

The kingdom of ends

Autonomy leads to the concept of a systematic connection of all ends (ends in themselves and objective ends, but also subjective or particular ends): the kingdom of ends (*Reich der Zwecke*). Every rational individual belongs to the kingdom of ends, as a member subject to "universal laws", but also as its *head* who makes the laws without submitting to the will of another.[25]

"In the kingdom of ends everything has either a **price**, or a **dignity**." Something with a price can be replaced with an equivalent thing (and is thus capable of being brought back into a market economy), whereas something with dignity has no equivalent and cannot be replaced (remains unmarketable). "Skill and diligence in work have a market price; wit, lively imagination, and humor have a fancy price; by contrast, fidelity in promising and benevolence from principles (not from instinct) have a inner worth."[26] They have no price, because they cannot be exchanged for something of an equal value. Such is their *dignity*: non-exchangeable. That which determines all moral value presupposes dignity, meaning "unconditional, incomparable worth, for which the word respect alone makes a fitting expression of the estimation a rational being is to give of it".[27]

***

Articulation of the three formulations of the categorical imperative.

Each of the three ways of determining the principle of morality imply the others: the first consists of the universal form, the second presents the end in itself as the matter of morality, and the third finds the reason for its determination in the autonomy of the will. These correspond to the three sub-categories of quantity: the first corresponds to the unity of the form of the will, the second deals with the plurality of the matter of the will, and the third deals with the totality of the will, stemming from the singularity of autonomous reason. We could probably also relate these three ways to the other triads of the sub-categories. Therefore, there would be form as reality (quality), substance (relation), and as possibility (modality). There would be the end in itself as negation (quality), causality (relation), and as existence (modality). Finally, there would be autonomous determination as limitation (quality), as reciprocal causality (relation), and as necessity (modality).

If we wished to pass a judgement (*Beurteilung*) on the *possible* moral quality of such and such a maxim,[28] it would be the universality of form which is most suited to this (this is the sole criterion retained by Sade and, in some way, by Lacan in his reading of Kant, as we shall see).

> If, however, one wants at the same time to obtain *access* for the moral law, it is very useful to lead one and the same action through the said three concepts (universality, respect for the end in itself and autonomy) and thereby, as far as can be done, bring it closer to intuition.[29]

In other words, we must proceed through all of the three formulations together – and therefore, through all of the twelve categories.

In the first manner (the universal form), we would give a *symbolic* consistency to the maxim. In the second manner (the matter of ends and in particular the end in itself, respect), we would give an *imaginary* consistency to the maxim. In the third manner (autonomy), we would provide access to the real mechanism of determination of the moral law, because it is the autonomy of the will which is "the supreme principle of morality".[30]

The heteronomy of the will, source of all false principles of morality

The heteronomy of will – that is, a will determined by something other than itself – "is the source of all spurious principles of morality".[31] All heteronomous principles of the will are either empirical or rational. In the first case, the will is determined by empirical experience, according to the search for happiness and through the use of the right technical means. In the second case, the will is determined by the rational idea of perfection, perfection as the possible effect of an action or perfection as existing in God's will.

One can, of course, identify these heteronomous principles in Sade, both as empirical (in the staging of the scenes in his novels) and as rational (the perfection implied in "Yet Another Effort, Frenchmen, If You Would Be Republicans"). As we shall see, Lacan recognized in Sade the merit of having had the maxim "com[e] out of the Other's mouth".[32]

Now, it is heteronomy and the Other which are at the heart of the misunderstanding of Kant's morality (and perhaps that of jouissance?). Should we simply dismiss the autonomy of the moral law to make way for the big Other of psychoanalysis? In Kant's examination of the heteronomy of the will, we find a catalogue of the false understandings of the big Other of psychoanalysis. In the first misunderstanding, the Other is taken for an empirical character (father, mother, psychoanalyst, etc.). In the second, it takes the place of a pure idea of perfection.[33] How can these two misunderstandings be avoided other than by situating the question of the big Other *within autonomy*, movement, and the unfolding of the subject (*Wo Es war soll Ich werden*)?

How, though, can autonomy be understood?

It can only be done by leaving the analytic approach behind (the analysis of "good will" as it was developed in the first two subdivisions of the *Groundwork of the Metaphysics of Morals*) and passing to a *synthetic* approach: we must walk alongside reason and immerse ourselves in what it *makes*. This question is better developed in the *Critique of Pure Reason*. Also, without lingering on the third subdivision of the *Groundwork*, we will address Kant's second great *critique* straightaway.

Notes

1. Kant, *Groundwork of the Metaphysics of Morals*, op. cit., pp. 21–22.
2. Ibid., p. 22.
3. Ibid., p. 23.
4. Ibid., p. 24.
5. Ibid., p. 25.
6. Ibid., p. 29.
7. Ibid.
8. Ibid., p. 30.
9. Ibid., p. 31.
10. Ibid., p. 32.
11. Kant, *Critique of Pure Reason*, p. 190; A218/B265.
12. Kant, 1785, p. 33.
13. Ibid., p. 34.
14. Let us remember that this "subject" is not an individual at all, but instead the emergence point of the moral law and this point is unconscious, strictly speaking. It is called up not by the paralogisms (which have to do with the soul or the Cartesian subject), but by the antinomies (which have to do with the idea of the world).
15. Ibid., p. 34.
16. Ibid., p. 35.
17. Ibid., p. 36.
18. Ibid., p. 37.
19. Ibid., p. 38.
20. Ibid., p. 39.
21. Ibid., p. 40.
22. Ibid., p. 41.
23. Ibid., p. 43.
24. Ibid., p. 45.
25. However, a rational being can only assume the role of head "only if it is a completely independent being, without need or limitation of its capacities adequate to the will". (Ibid., p. 46).
26. Ibid., p. 47.
27. Ibid., pp. 47–48.
28. Ibid., p. 48.
29. My text in brackets.
30. Ibid., p. 51.
31. Ibid., p. 52.
32. Lacan, *Écrits: The First Complete Edition in English*, translated by Bruce Fink, New York, Norton, 2006, p. 650.
33. Let us note that Kant's four counterexamples were divided according to the criteria of perfection and the individual vs. social opposition.

Part II

Critique of Practical Reason (1788)

The principle of practical reason

Introduction
The place and structure of practical reason (and of the unconscious)

In the *Groundwork*, Kant started out pedagogically from the popular conception of morality centred on the good (*gut*) to show that the good as good is always dependent on the *will* (and not the other way round), in other words, that the Good is not primary. We set out from the *concept* (the Good) to arrive (through analysis) at the *principle* (the will) which is its necessary condition. In its practical operation and in the *Critique of Practical Reason*, reason is concerned first of all with the determining *principle* of the will.

The *Critique of Practical Reason*, like the *Critique of Pure Reason*, begins with a presentation of elements (an elementary doctrine) in order to show in what way they operate in tandem (a methodology).

The elementary doctrine of the *Critique of Pure Reason* begins with the question of knowing how we receive or take in that which *is* (transcendental aesthetic) to subsequently explain how we conceive or understand it (transcendental analytic). The *Critique of Practical Reason* does not start out from what *is* (and which it is enough to just take in) – it prescribes what *ought to be*. There is no aesthetic (of what is) in practical reason, and it all begins instead with the analytic of practical reason.

In both critiques, an analytic is followed by a dialectic. "[A]n *Analytic*, as the rule of truth, as the first part, and a Dialectic as the exposition and resolution of illusion."[1]

The analytic in the first and second critiques

In its speculative (theoretical) usage, reason (which must determine what is and not what it wants) is founded on sense experience, on something apart from itself, rooted in sensibility. That is why the *Critique of Pure Reason* begins with "the transcendental aesthetic", the examination of the forms prior to all sensibility (space and time). After that it studies *concepts* (the categories), the function of which is to understand the sensations given in sensibility, and only subsequently deduces the *principles* by which it operates, principles which are therefore dependent on sensibility and concepts. The transcendental aesthetic devoted to sensibility comes first, then comes the analytic of concepts, followed by the analytic of principles, and finally, dialectic.

DOI: 10.4324/9781003055662-8

In the *practical* usage of reason, the aesthetic is absent and the order of the analytic is reversed. Reason (which must determine what it wants, what should be, not what is) is grounded only in itself (the analytic is not preceded by a transcendental aesthetic). As the *Critique of Practical Reason* is in no way founded on what *is*, on sensibility or on an aesthetic, its "concepts" (Good, Evil) are not determined by sensibility – they are completely dependent on principles (moral law, freedom). The equivalent of the aesthetic in Kant's second critique, developing an awareness [*sensibilisation*] of the moral law, can only ensue from principles via concepts. The analytic of practical reason first presents principles, then concepts, and finally sensible motives.

The dialectic in the first and second critiques

Reason is always at risk of going astray. *Dialectic* analyses and deals with these inherent possibilities of reason. In its *speculative* usage, reason must correspond to what *is*, namely to phenomena given in sensibility. Driven by its own momentum, reason risks getting lost beyond these phenomena amidst inaccessible (the soul, God), or even contradictory ideas (the world). Speculative reason must take a stand in relation to these ideas which are radically unknowable, but which necessarily present themselves to speculative reason (*dialectic of pure reason*). In *practical* usage, there is a completely different way to go astray. In its concrete realisations, reason necessarily remains confronted by sensibility, and virtue (the good emerging from the principle of reason) is necessarily opposed to pleasure (the pleasant). Reason must take a stand in relation to this basic opposition (*dialectic of practical reason*). This is the question of the opposition between the pleasure principle and the jouissance principle: How do we deal with their articulation?

Contrary to speculative reason, which must correspond to *what is*, practical reason determines its own will or *what ought to be*. The only remaining question is knowing if what it wishes for or puts forward as what should be corresponds to the principle of the moral law. Is practical reason capable of determining the will on its own? Or is the will also always determined empirically by what is? The way in which our motivations are overdetermined, discovered by psychoanalysis, seems to radically exclude the first branch of this alternative. If this is the case, practical reason will never be pure, in the sense of being autonomous or independent of determinism.

Whatever the impact of overdetermining factors on the will, indeed their utter determinism, it is not ruled out, however, that reason might enjoy [*jouir de*] a completely different form of causality, a new undetermined causality, a causality in freedom, without us being able to pinpoint what that freedom might be, phenomenologically speaking. This question of a type of freedom capable of creating a form completely different from those which are determined reprises, furthermore, the third antinomy of pure reason (contradictions inherent to the idea of World). The *thesis* of this third antinomy is stated like this: "Causality according to the laws of nature, is not the only causality operating to originate the appearances of the world. A causality of freedom is also necessary to account for these appearances."[2] The antithesis reads: "There is no such thing as freedom, but everything in the world happens solely according to the laws of nature."[3]

In the dispute between the followers of the thesis and the followers of the antithesis, each of the opposing sides draws support from the opposing argument. However, as Kant showed in the *Critique of Pure Reason*, the thesis and antithesis of the third antinomy should both be taken to be *true*, according to different modalities – on the one hand, faith in the ability to fundamentally change things, to give things a new form and, on the other hand, the project of building up the knowledge of the laws of nature. We will not follow the development of Kant's argument here. Let us content ourselves with pointing out parallels with the practice of psychoanalytic listening. Antithesis: "there is no freedom, everything happens instead according to the laws of overdetermination"; we must, in fact, ceaselessly enable the infinite knowledge of the overdetermining factors which govern the life of our psyche in its entirety, to come to light. Thesis: "the fact that everything takes place in the psyche along with an infinite number of overdetermining factors, does not make it any less necessary to allow for freedom, which is not solely a point at which the mechanism emerges, but also a point at which a new story or history can emerge." We can and we ought to believe in the possibility of creating a new meaning, a new form, a new history which eludes the overdetermining factors and their history. This point of emergence, moreover, is the unconscious, the essential property of which is to create a new form. Without this *thesis* as a counterweight to the antithesis, psychoanalysis would be reduced to the unending duplication of overdeterminations.

Our reading of the *Critique of Practical Reason* aims to highlight this possibility of creating something new, this freedom, not in order to deny the actual causality of countless overdeterminations, but so as to refuse to stick to those overdeterminations and to reduce everything to them. It follows the exact design of Kant's second critique.[4]

To highlight this *principle* of freedom and the possibility of giving things a new form, which is the specific nature of the unconscious, we cannot overemphasise the importance of the order of the chapters in which the examination of practical reason takes place. It is the *principle* of the autonomy of the moral law which comes first (Chapter 1), and then produces and determines the moral *concept* of good and bad (Chapter 2) and its sensible consequences: the respect for the law and the good (Chapter 3). Further on there are chapters devoted to *dialectic* (Chapter 4) and the *methodology* of practical reason (Chapter 5).

Notes

1 Kant, *Critique of Practical Reason*, translated by Mary Gregor, Cambridge, Cambridge University Press, 2015, p. 12.
2 Kant, *Critique of Pure Reason*, p. 329; A444/B472.
3 Ibid., p. 329; A445/B473.
4 "It is therefore incumbent upon the Critique of Practical Reason as such to prevent empirically conditioned reason from presuming that it, alone and exclusively, furnishes the determining ground of the will." (*Critique of Practical Reason*, op. cit., p. 12).

Chapter 3

The principle of the autonomy of the moral law (... and of jouissance)[1]

The first chapter of the *Critique of Practical Reason* is structured according to a form which seems to have been borrowed from geometry. The presentation essentially contains three types of statement: *definitions*, which say what words mean without saying whether or not they correspond to things which exist; *axioms* or *principles*, which are statements which set out the necessary relations between concepts; and *propositions* or *theorems*, which are deduced from the definitions and axioms (these are secondary constraints or obligations).[2] Let us note that a fourth type of statement – postulates – plausible, but not obligatory, statements[3] – are absent from this chapter; they form the majority of the dialectic of practical reason.

This geometrical mode of presentation had already been present in Descartes, in his responses to the objections to his *Meditations on First Philosophy*, and in Spinoza, *"ordine geometrico demonstrata* – Demonstrated in Geometrical Order". It is adapted to how reason works, because in Descartes, Spinoza, and Kant's time, reason found its paradigm in geometry.

Descartes and Spinoza began by defining concepts (for example, thought, idea, substance, God, etc., in Descartes,[4] and cause of itself, substance, God etc. in Spinoza).[5] Kant, on the other hand, does not define any concepts at first (notably that of the "good"), beginning solely with the definition of "principles". Starting out from principles (and not concepts) is the very principle of morality in Kant.

Definition of "principles"

(§ 1 *Definition of practical principles*)

> Practical *principles* (*Grundsätze*) are propositions that contain a general determination of the will, having under it several practical rules. They are subjective, or *maxims*, when the condition is regarded by the subject as holding only for his will; but they are objective, or practical *laws*, when the condition is cognized as objective, that is, as holding for the will of every rational being.[6]

The definition of practical principles implies from the very beginning a dichotomy between subjective principles (commanded by the pleasure principle) and objective principles (commanded by reason). Be careful, however: the "subjective" here

DOI: 10.4324/9781003055662-9

must not be referred back to the ontology of a "subject" understood as an existing individual – such a subject is only a fiction. The "subjective" means only that it has to do with something purely local, not truly objective, dependent on the conditions of a particular sensible experience.

As knowledge essentially aims for objectivity, this distinction between subjective principles (or maxims) and objective principles (or laws) is not found within it. Theoretical principles are *essentially objective*. On the one hand, there are the principles of *physics* (for example, the principle of the equality of action and reaction) and, on the other hand, the *a priori principles of pure* (speculative) *reason*. These theoretical principles are principles inasmuch "they themselves are not grounded in higher and more general knowledge".[7] They are proven in the fact that without them there would be no possibility of an object (no possibility of the object of physics, no possibility of the object of knowledge in general). For the object to *be*, it must necessarily be according to these principles. They are thus eminently objective – they are laws. First among the *a priori* principles of *pure reason* must be counted the supreme principle of all analytical judgements, in other words, the principle of non-contradiction.[8] Second, the supreme principle of all synthetical judgements,[9] and third, all the synthetical principles of pure understanding: the axioms of intuition,[10] anticipations of perception,[11] analogies of experience,[12] and the postulates of empirical thought in general.[13]

In contrast to theoretical principles, which are all *laws*, practical principles are divided into maxims and laws. Maxims are purely subjective (by which is meant, local, particular rather than related to a clearly defined individuality). They do not impose themselves as (general) imperatives. The imperatives inherent to action in general are most often not laws. So, (pleasure-seeking) technical and pragmatic imperatives are not laws, as they are dependent on a hypothesis. They are hypothetical imperatives – precepts or prescriptions (*Vorschriften*) which aim to achieve a particular technical result or, more generally, to attain happiness.

Are there any practical principles which are not hypothetical? Does at least one categorical imperative, that is, a practical law, exist? We have seen in the *Groundwork* from the experience that everyone has of "good will", that there is a moral law. And for reason to succeed in making that law, "it should need to presuppose only *itself*, because a rule is objectively and universally valid only when it holds without the contingent, subjective conditions that distinguish one rational being from another".[14]

Kant gives an example here: Can "making a lying promise" be valid as a moral law? "Making a lying promise" can certainly operate as a practical principle under certain a circumstances. However, it can never be anything more than a hypothetical imperative attached to the quest for a certain technical result or the goal of happiness. It is also a counterexample of moral duty. It in no way follows, however, that "never make a lying promise" is a moral duty.

***

From this definition (§1) alone, concerning the principle of the moral law and the difference between the moral law and the subjective maxim, Kant will go on to "prove" four "theorems". The first two (§2 and §3) deal with subjective practical principles (maxims), which are dependent on a hypothesis and cannot therefore become moral principles. They fall under the pleasure principle, having to do with the "lower faculty of desire". The other two (§4 and §8) deal with objective practical principles (laws). They have to do with the "higher faculty of desire". These latter theorems concerning the moral law are separated and connected by two symmetrical problems (§5 and §6) and by the enunciation of the moral law (§7).

Practical principles which cannot be moral

(§2 and §3 of Kant's text)

Theorem I devoted to technical practical principles

"All practical principles that presuppose an *object* (matter) of the faculty as the determining ground of the will are, without exception, empirical and can furnish no practical laws."[15] Desire for an object precedes the enunciation of the practical rule. This is determined by the pleasure the subject would feel if the object were technically acquired. "But it cannot be cognized a priori of any representation of an object, whatever it may be, whether it will be connected with *pleasure* or *displeasure* or be *indifferent*". As much from the technical side as from the side of pleasure, we are brought back to empirical experience, which is valid locally, in a certain detail, in a certain "subjective" context. Such principles are only purely local, "subjective" maxims. They are *hypothetical* imperatives. For lack of objectivity, they are not practical laws.

Theorem II devoted to the general pleasure principle

"All material practical principles as such are, without exception, of one and the same kind and come under the general principle of self-love or one's own happiness."[16] Pleasure is always grounded in the "subject's" faculty of feeling. (The "subject" is once more to be understood as a certain localisation, a certain particular point, and not as an individual.) It falls under the heading, therefore, of a certain local sensibility. "It is, then practical only insofar as the feeling of agreeableness that the subject expects from the reality of an object determines the faculty of desire." The sought-after object appears here as the final cause of desire and it is an object to be realised in sensibility.[17]

All the material practical rules mentioned in theorems 1 and 2 "put the determining ground of the will in the *lower faculty of desire*". The faculty of desire is called "lower" because of its very contingency, connected to a certain particular characteristic of an object. Moreover, the origin of the representation of the object which would provide pleasure does not matter (the senses, the understanding, or even reason). The pleasure or agreeableness expected from the object or happiness in general is always of the same type – it is a matter of sensibility and material practical rules are always hypothetical. "For, although the concept of happiness *everywhere* underlies the practical relation of objects to the faculty of desire, it is still only the general name for subjective determining grounds, and it determines nothing specific."[18] Whatever the nature of the desired *object*, the desire for it seems to be completely inscribed within the pleasure principle (it is the "lower faculty of desire"). There would not therefore strictly speaking be any practical laws, but only purely subjective principles commanded by the search for happiness.[19]

There is another remaining possibility, however, namely that the will is not determined *by any matter*, by any particular object, but *by pure form* (that is, independently of all the hypotheses connected to a particular object and to sensibility). It is only thus that we could talk of a "higher faculty of desire". We call it "higher", not because it might depend on a "higher" origin for the object or for its representation (a divine origin for example), but because it is not dependent on the object (therefore not on the Good or on God either). If all practical rules could be determined by the object of desire or by matter, "[if there were] no *merely formal* laws of the will sufficient to determine it, then neither could *any higher faculty of desire* be admitted".[20]

First approach to the moral law

Practical laws are formal

§4 Theorem III. *Practical laws can determine the will only in regard to their form.*

The matter of various types – whether they are viewed as goals to be attained (technical principles) or the subjective or local search for happiness (pleasure principle) – only determines an action in its dependence on a (technical or pragmatic) hypothesis. It cannot determine anything of necessity, it cannot determine anything universally. It cannot, therefore, determine any *laws* strictly speaking and, consequently, no moral laws.

To find the determining principle of a moral law, all matter must be set aside: "all that remains of a law if one separates from it everything material [. . .] is the mere *form* of giving universal law".[21] This proposition is purely analytical:[22] if it is not matter, it is the "other" of matter, namely form. It is form which must determine the necessary, universal "law", in other words, the categorical imperative.

Kant claims that the most common understanding can easily discern "what form in a maxim makes it fit for a giving of universal law and what does not".[23] The simplest man can perform the test which excludes one maxim or another from the field of moral laws. Again, he only gives us counterexamples, namely two examples of maxims which *cannot* count as the moral law. The first operates according to technical principles, the second according to the pragmatic principle of the search for happiness.

The first counterexample resembles the second counterexample in the *Groundwork* (which situated itself as the antithesis of a perfect duty towards others). It also concerns a breach of trust: "Now I have a *deposit* in my hands, the owner of which has died and left no record of it" and "I have [. . .] made it my maxim to increase my wealth by every safe means". This maxim cannot take on the form of a law, because "such a principle, as a law, would annihilate itself since it would bring it about that there would be no deposits at all". We see that the story does indeed a maxim ("to increase my wealth by every safe means"), but this goal wipes out both the deposit and trust. Such a maxim annihilates itself as soon as it takes on the form of a universal law.

The second counterexample is built around the fact that one's person's will to happiness necessarily conflicts with that of another. Certainly, "the desire [for happiness], and so too the *maxim* by which each makes his desire the determining ground of his will, is universal". However, this so-called "universality" remains abstract and is concretely inapplicable because what gives rise to happiness in one place systematically rides roughshod over happiness in another place.

Not alone is one person's pleasure opposed to that of another, but pleasure in one part of the psyche (the unconscious) is opposed to the pleasure of another part of the psyche (the preconscious and the conscious). All that remains then is the compromise "solution" (which is Freud's definition of the symptom) and that is not a law. In Kant's counterexample, it is the contradiction between one person's will and another's which makes universalisation impossible. If we postulated a possible agreement on the level of "subjects", individuals, or different loci in the psyche, it would result in "a harmony like that which a certain satirical poem depicts in the unanimity between a married couple bent on going to ruin: "*O marvellous harmony, what he wants she wants too*" and so forth, or like what is said of the pledge of King Francis I to the Emperor Charles V: "What my brother Charles would have (Milan), that I would also have".[24] The will on both side is to have, but what counts as having for one person is in contradiction with that of the other. "[F]or each person puts at the basis of inclination his subject – another person, another subject."[25] Kant finds it strange "that intelligent men could have thought of passing off the desire for happiness as a universal *practical* law".[26] It is also strange that Freud remained loyal for so long to the monopoly of his pleasure principle, even though he saw that the pleasure of the unconscious was in contradiction with the pleasure of the conscious mind, and even though Sabina Spielrein had understood the importance of the death drive and of a different principle as early as 1912.[27] The quest for pleasure is always a source of conflict as much at the intrasubjective level as at the intersubjective level. Will is certainly present, but there is also an opposing will which destroys the other one. It is at the level of the will that contradiction arises. It is completely impossible to find a law which regulates the inclinations as a whole by bringing in them into agreement.

The (universal) moral law cannot depend either on technical principles or on the principle of happiness. It is in this sense that it is "free".

The relationship between the universal form of the moral law and freedom

This relationship is introduced by an examination of two opposing problems. And it will then be illustrated by a double parable.

§5   *First problem*: what would a will which is determined by a lawgiving form alone be like? As such a law cannot be an object for the senses and cannot take part in appearances (or phenomena), "the representation of this form as the determining ground of the will is distinct from all determining grounds of events in nature in accordance with the law of causality, because in their case the determining grounds must themselves be appearances".[28] The will, therefore, should be thought of as entirely independent of the natural law of appearances. In other words, it should be thought of as *freedom* (according to the thesis of the third antinomy of pure reason).[29] Every will determined by the law-giving form of the moral law is therefore a free will.

§6   *Second problem* (the opposite problem to §5): What would a law determined by a free will be like? As free will is completely independent of empirical conditions, it is independent of the matter of the law. Apart from the matter of the law, there is only lawgiving *form*. Free will is therefore necessarily a will which is determined solely by the form of the law.

These two problems lead to two reciprocal propositions: freedom entails the moral law (§6) and the moral law entails freedom (§6). It is not a case here of knowing whether the moral law and freedom must be "factually" differentiated, namely within appearances as, in the case of the moral law and freedom, we have already left the level of appearances behind and are outside the observable facts. The questions raised from these reciprocal propositions do not belong to the empirical, but to *principles*. It is not a case either of understanding "unconditioned law" as the pure self-consciousness of a practical reason in which "duty" postulates a "power", logically prior to "duty", the freedom to be able to carry out the duty commanded in the moral law. It involves asking oneself "from what our *cognition* of the unconditionally practical *starts*, whether from freedom or from the practical law".[30] The starting point of the *cognition* [*connaissance*][31] of practical reason cannot be freedom, because cognition comes solely from appearances and there is no empirical cognition of freedom (cf. *Critique of Pure Reason*). The starting point comes from the moral law, "of which we become immediately conscious" (cf. *Groundwork of the Metaphysics of Morals*).

It is therefore through the cognition of the moral law that we may have access to a certain "cognition" of freedom. To stress the point and to show that the *moral law* (guilt) always comes before *freedom* in the order of cognition, Kant imagines two situations, two parables (or apologues), the first of which is untouched by any moral law, whereas the second completely revolves around the moral law. The first, therefore, does not enable us to become aware of any freedom. The second undoubtedly introduces the question of freedom, even if it is not concretely put to use.

The first story postulates that everything is determined by inclination, towards pleasure, carried to the highest level of voluptuousness and lust. In other words, it remains *hypothetical* from start to finish and no moral law becomes involved in it: it does not, therefore, lead to any freedom.

> Suppose someone asserts of his lustful inclination that, when the desired object and the opportunity are present, it is quite irresistible to him; ask him whether, if a gallows were erected in front of the house where he finds this opportunity and he would be hanged on it immediately after gratifying his lust, he would not then control his inclination. One need not conjecture very long what he would reply.[32]

This situation only brings the pleasure principle into play (including what might be called a certain "jouissance", but one which only stands for extreme, unbridled *pleasure*). The situation presented in this way does not postulate any moral law and is explained by means of a device comprised of two conditions (lust and the scaffold). In accordance with a radical generalisation of the pleasure principle, one of the conditions (lust) would purport to be absolutely compelling, and the other would contradict this generalisation, by means of a much more radical penalty. Such a device, wholly constructed according to the pleasure principle, does not entail *any* freedom in the Kantian sense of a non-empirical causality (we have here a construction of hypotheses and the imperative here is purely hypothetical, simultaneously technical and pragmatic). The "choice" proposed in this situation is simply subject to a double "constraint": that of lustful pleasure and that of the counter-pleasure of the scaffold.

The second situation puts forward a completely different structure. Besides the inclinations of pleasure and counter-pleasure, they are situated *within the framework of the moral law* (which was radically absent from the first case).

> But ask him whether, if his prince demanded, on pain of the same immediate execution, that he give false testimony against an honorable man whom the prince would like to destroy under a plausible pretext, he would consider it possible to overcome his love of life, however great it may be. He would perhaps not venture to assert whether he would do it or not, but he must admit without hesitation that it would be possible for him. He judges, therefore that he can do something because he is aware that he ought to do it and cognizes freedom within him, which, without the moral law, would have remained unknown to him.

This second story also postulates a series of hypotheses (dependence on the prince, the threat of death, the desire to destroy an adversary, the love of life, etc.), but it fundamentally differs from the first story in so far as the *moral law* is represented in the form of sin, which consists in giving false testimony against an honest man. The question is not one of judging whether this example of duty, consisting of not giving false testimony, is relevant to the moral law, we already know that no example suits the moral law. It is a question of seeing that the recognition of the freedom to carry out this duty appears from the consciousness of a moral law and of a duty: it is "possible". Freedom appears as something possible.

These two stories thus perfectly illustrate the general principle: *without the moral law, we would never know freedom*. Freedom would never, moreover, have been introduced into speculative reason (in the third antinomy), "had not the moral law, and with it practical reason, come in and forced this concept upon us".[33]

As freedom is preceded by the moral law, theorem III, which had shown the principle of the *moral law* as a *formal* principle, itself also precedes theorem IV, which shows how *freedom* is entailed by the principle of the moral law. Before tackling freedom and autonomy (§8), we must state the moral law qua form, the formula of the universal moral law (§7).

The universal formulation of the moral law (... and of jouissance?)

§7 *The fundamental law of pure practical reason qua formal principle.*

"So, act that the maxim of your will could always hold at the same time as a principle in a giving of universal law."[34]

The formulation of the moral law is followed by two remarks.

First remark (p. 28). The *factum* (reason gives the moral law).

Geometry postulates hypotheses (definitions, axioms, postulates), from which results (theorems) ensue. Someone who does geometry, therefore, has an imperative which is conditioned by these hypotheses, it is "hypothetical". The moral law is unconditioned and categorical, independent of all empirical conditions (matter), but also of definitions, axioms, etc., and it only has itself (its form or its principle alone) to determine it. "The thing is strange enough and has nothing like it in all the rest of our practical cognition."[35]

However, the consciousness of this fundamental law is a fact (*Faktum*) of reason. This law cannot be reasoned out through the antecedent data of reason (*herausvernünfteln*). One must act, it must be produced, it must be made. It imposes itself upon us as a "synthetic a priori proposition". The *Groundwork* analysed the common moral conscience to show that it had always already contained this production of the moral law, this "synthetic a priori proposition". If it is said that the moral law is "given", it must well be understood that it is not given by any empirical facts but *by pure reason* alone, in as much as it makes and proclaims the law. It is given in its act of enunciation.

Second remark (p. 29). The *factum* is given as a formal and universal determining principle of reason as reason. This is why it imposes itself upon all rational beings, including "the infinite being as the supreme intelligence".[36] The only difference between the infinite being and finite beings, is that God has a holy will, "such a will as would not be capable of any maxim conflicting with the moral law". For lack of this opposition, for lack of this conflict, God *never* has any *duties*, as he is in no way pathologically affected (by sensibility). On the other hand, finite beings are incapable of holiness (they are always involved in conflict, as they are always affected by sensibility). Holiness is completely inaccessible to us and we must content ourselves with duties. Holiness can only serve as a model (*Urbild*) which we can only approximate without ever being able to reach. Virtue (*Tugend*) can never be completely achieved (*nie vollendet*).

The autonomy of the moral law

Autonomy has nothing to do with the solipsistic acting out of one's caprices. On the contrary, it involves creating, constructing a universal law, capable of transmuting the matter of the world. It is an immense project.

The formula of autonomy

§8   *Theorem IV*. The first formula of the categorical imperative in the *Groundwork*, that of universality, is taken up again by Theorem III of the *Critique of Practical Reason*. The third formula, that of autonomy, is taken up again in Theorem IV. The second formula, that of respect for humanity, which involves the possible matter of the imperative, will be dealt with further on, in Chapter III of the Analytic.

The independence of the moral law from all matter (object and aim) leads to the formal formula of a universal law. This independence is "freedom" in the negative sense of the term, as non-dependence. Freedom, however, above all has a positive sense, namely the *creation* of laws, the purely formal lawgiving of practical reason. "Thus, the moral law expresses nothing other than the *autonomy* of pure practical reason, that is, freedom, and this is itself the formal condition of all maxims, under which alone they can accord with the supreme practical law."[37] In order words, the maxim can only accord with the practical law if it implies in itself freedom, or autonomy, or the creation of the moral law. The moral law must be *constructed*, it is necessarily given as a "synthetic a priori judgement" (and not as an analytic judgement).

Let us note that, in Kant's text, the third formula of the imperative is never given as such. The third formula cannot be formulated. Its statement would in fact contain its own negation – it would contradict the free enunciation which it promotes: "So act according to a maxim that would be taken up in complete autonomy, in complete freedom", in other words, "Be spontaneous".

A remark on the happiness of others

It is undeniable that all willing has an object and a matter and that a general pleasure principle exists. Can *the happiness of others* serve as a determining principle of the moral law? Happiness does not count as a universal principle. Moreover, as we have already seen, one person's happiness is opposed to another person's happiness and can possibly bring him unhappiness. More fundamentally, at the level of the different psychical agencies, what is pleasure to the unconscious may give rise to unpleasure for the conscious mind. If the quest for the happiness of others can be included within the moral law, it is in no way by way of *happiness* (the need for sympathy, empathy, etc.) or charity, but through the simple *universal* lawful form, by which I limit my maxim founded on an inclination (happiness, for example), to open on to the *universality* created by reason. "[O]nly from this limitation [by universality], and not from the addition of an external incentive [happiness], could there arise the concept of *obligation* to extend the maxim of my self-love to the happiness of others as well."[38] Let us note already the difference between the maxim of the search for the happiness of others from the Christian commandment, "You shall love your neighbour as yourself", in which "love" is not necessarily linked to "happiness", and therefore leaves room for our third principle, the principle of jouissance (even if "love" does risk bringing us straight back to the problematic of happiness). The commandment to love your neighbour is dealt with by Kant in the third chapter of the analytic of practical reason (see later).

Remark on the radical opposition between autonomy (the voice of reason) and heteronomy (personal happiness)

"The direct opposite of the principle of morality is the principle of *one's own happiness* made the determining ground of the will." What appears to be in radical opposition to the principle of personal happiness and its empirical conditioning, is the "voice" (*Stimme*), *not of conscience, but of "reason"* (*Vernunft*). It is absolutely "distinct" (*deutlich*) and thunderous, "so irrepressible" (*unüberschreibar*). This heavenly (*himmlich*) voice is "audible" to all human beings without exception. The voice is not characterised by a realisation, nor by the little voice of a conscience or of a guardian who would whisper to us what needs to be done. It does not give out an empirical sound either. It arises within the framework of sensible experience, but it radically arrives from somewhere else. It corresponds to the fourth form of nothing, the *nihil negativum*, the form of nothing which counts as impossible because it contradicts the conditions of possibility of experience. It really is the voice, as the fourth form of Lacan's object *a*. It introduces the absolutely Other, which cannot be pinpointed in any way within the framework of sensible experience. It is from this that the universality of the moral law ensues.

In contrast to the voice of reason, which appears as absolutely universal, the principle of happiness can only give "general" rules, which would correspond to the average of what people want. Those rules are not really "universal".

Henceforth, "the maxim of self-love (prudence) merely *advises*; the law of morality" alone "*commands*".[39] In the maxim of happiness, all sorts of forces are considered, and it is only rarely possible "to satisfy the empirically conditioned precept of happiness". On the other hand, "to satisfy the categorical command of morality is within everyone's power at all times". This sentence may seem to contradict the assertion that "there is no example of a moral action". It is not a case, however, of satisfying or being good enough for the *accomplishment* of a perfectly moral action; rather, it has to do with satisfying or being enough to situate itself within the framework of the principle of morality, and this is always possible despite the constant presence of the principle of happiness and despite the impossibility of a perfectly moral action.

Transgression of the moral law goes hand in hand with "*deserving punishment*", its punishability (*Strafwürdigkeit*).[40] But punishment should not be thought of either as an evil that the guilty party must incur or as a means of deterrence. All such means cause us to forget autonomy and the freedom of the moral law. "In every punishment as such there must first be justice (*Gerechtigkeit*), and this constitutes what is essential in this concept." In other words, it is because of justice understood as *conformity to duty* that a punishment can possibly be imposed. It is in this exact sense that Kant was a supporter of the death penalty for what one might call crimes against humanity (see later).

The voice of reason cannot be reduced to a particular moral *sense*. The awareness of virtue is not connected to pleasure and the awareness of vice is not connected to mental unease or pain. It does not have to do with personal happiness (or unhappiness). Certainly, we may "feel that satisfaction in consciousness of one's conformity with [the moral law] and bitter remorse if one can reproach oneself with having transgressed it".[41] It is right to cultivate this "moral feeling" in order to support morality. But "the concept of duty cannot be derived from it". Duty comes solely from autonomy, from the freedom of reason.

Heteronomous principles which have been the (false) basis of moral systems prior to Kant

Before Kant, all moral systems were based on heteronomous principles. The principles were taken either from experience (and are thus subjective principles) or from reason (and are thus objective principles).

Empirical and subjective principles can be drawn either from experience external to the moral subject themselves (education and the civil constitution) or from experience internal to the moral subject (physical and moral feelings). These empirical principles presuppose "an *object* (matter) of the faculty of desire as the determining ground of the will (. . .) and can furnish no practical laws".[42]

Rational and objective principles refer to *perfection*, which can again be understood as a *characteristic* (of the human being), but also as (an eternal) *substance*. The characteristic of perfection is still hypothetical and so is supreme perfection, external to the human being. Agreement with the will of God as an *object* of our will can only serve as a determining cause by means of the happiness we expect from it, and it also implies a *matter*.[43]

All of the heteronomous principles, without exception (empirical-subjective and rational-objective, internal and external) are *material* principles which cannot serve as a supreme moral law. "[T]he *formal practical principle* of pure reason [. . .] is the *sole* principle that can *possibly* be fit for categorical imperatives, that is, practical laws."[44]

Supplementary explanation of freedom and autonomy

On the deduction of the principles of pure practical reason

In practical reason, we start out from the *factum*, namely the determination of a world by the moral law. "This law is to furnish the sensible world, as a *sensible nature* [. . .], with the form of a world of the understanding, that is, of a *supersensible* nature."[45] *Nature must, therefore, be subject to the autonomy of reason.* Reason itself gives the law of the supersensible world, the law of an *archetypal world* or nature (*natura archetypa*), the law of an ideal nature which give rise to effects in the sensible world, in the *ectypal world* or nature, in sensible nature.

> The moral law in fact, transfers us, in idea, into a nature in which pure reason, if it were accompanied with suitable physical power, would produce the highest good, and it determines our will to confer on the sensible world the form of a whole of rational beings.[46]

It behaves "as if a natural order must at the same time arise from our will."[47]

On the one hand, there are laws of nature (*natura ectypa*) to which our will is subject. This problem has to do with the critique of pure speculative reason and begins with intuitions. On the other hand, there are laws of the will to which nature *must* submit. This principle has to do with the critique of pure practical reason and begins with the principle of the moral law and freedom. But the critique of practical reason is not focused on the concrete accomplishment of this new world, it is a *volition of principle* [*vouloir de principe*] (concrete realisation, moreover, is dependent on technical principles, external to the critique of practical reason strictly speaking).

> For, provided that the will conforms to the law of pure reason, then its power in execution may be as it may, and a nature may or may not actually arise in accordance with these maxims of giving law for a possible nature; the *Critique* [. . .] does not trouble itself with this.[48]

How are the moral law and freedom possible? And how do they have sensible effects? It cannot be explained, "its admissibility can, however, be defended in the theoretical *Critique*". It cannot be explained because a real *deduction* of moral principles must necessarily begin from experience. Now, the categorical imperative pertaining to pure reason precisely cannot begin from experience. The only thing we can do is to begin from the moral law and deduce freedom from it.

> This kind of credential of the moral law – that is itself laid down as a principle of the deduction of freedom as a causality of pure reason – is fully sufficient in place of any a priori justification, since theoretical reason was forced to *assume* at least the possibility of freedom in order to fill a need of its own.[49]

The solution of the third antinomy of pure reason does indeed hold that, at one and the same time, our actions are completely conditioned by a deterministic causality, while allowing for the possibility of freedom.

On the causality in question

Kant first recalls Hume's critique of the concept of cause. Cause would be a false and deceptive concept because it would be impossible to cognise an a priori and necessary connection between one thing (the cause) and another (the effect). Instead of a cause thought of as purely objective, the whole process of the "cause" would be reduced to a subjective necessity, to a *habit* which would connect the supposed cause with the expected effect. Hume's error is due to the fact that he "took objects of experiences as things in themselves [. . .]; he was quite correct in declaring the concept of cause to be deceptive and a false illusion".[50] Everything changes with the Kantian revolution, however, because "the objects with which we have to do in experience are by no means things in themselves but only appearances", and Kant had shown that causality is a pure category of the *understanding*; in other words, it necessarily appears among the conditions of sensible experience, and it is essential for thinking about any object whatsoever even before any reference to given empirical sources.

"But how is it with the application of this category of causality [. . .] to things that are not objects of possible experience but lie beyond its boundaries?" As causality and the other categories are not deducted from a given experience, but from the a priori conditions of experience, they have their place in pure understanding, even outside all given experience. The objective reality of the concept of causality "nevertheless remains and can be used even of noumena",[51] provided it is kept in mind that this does not lead us to *any* cognition, to any objective object.

Understanding is not limited to cognition alone. Understanding maintains a necessary relation with objects in theoretical cognition, notably by means of causality (*causa phenomenon*). The same concept of causality is taken up again by reason for a relation to the higher faculty of desire and the moral law. The concept of a being endowed with a pure will, that is, a free will "is the concept of a *causa noumenon*".[52] An intuition which would determine its objective value cannot be found; "it has nonetheless a real application which is exhibited *in concreto* in

The principle of the autonomy 59

dispositions or maxims, that is, it has practical reality which can be specified; and this is sufficient to justify it even with regard to noumena".[53]

Notes

1 "Chapter 1 of the analytic of pure practical reason: On the principles of pure practical reason."
2 See, for example, Badiou, *Le Séminaire, L'Un, Descartes, Platon, Kant 1983–1984*, Fayard, 2016, p. 58.
3 Including Euclid's postulate: If a straight line falls on two straight lines in such a manner that the interior angles on the same side are together less than two right angles, then the straight lines, if produced indefinitely, meet on that side on which the angles are less than the two right angles.
4 René Descartes, *Meditations on First Philosophy*, 3rd Edition, translated by Donald A. Cress, Indianapolis and Cambridge, Hackett Publishing Company, 1993.
5 Spinoza, *Ethics*, translated by Andrew Boyle, edited by G.H.R. Parkinson, London, J.M. Dent, 1993, p. 3.
6 Kant, *Critique of Practical Reason*, p. 17.
7 Kant, *Critique of Pure Reason*, p. 148; A147/B187.
8 "Nothing can have a predicate that contradicts it", (Ibid., p. 149; A149/B189).
9 This principle replaces Leibniz's principle of sufficient reason and states, "Every object is subject to the necessary conditions of the synthetical unity of the manifold of intuition in a possible experience." (Ibid., p. 153; A157/B196).
10 "*All Intuitions are Extensive Quantities.*" (Ibid., p. 156; A162/B202).
11 "*In All Appearances the Real, That Which Is an Object of Sensation, Has Intensive Quality, That Is, Has a Degree.*" (Ibid., p. 159; A166/B207).
12 "*Experience Is Possible Only through the Representation of a Necessary Connection of Perceptions.*" (Ibid., p. 165; A176/B218).
13 "1. That which agrees with the formal conditions (intuition and concept) of experience, is *possible*. 2. That which is connected with the material conditions of experience (sensation) is *real*. 3. That whose connection with the real is determined according to universal conditions of experience is necessary (exists necessarily)." (Ibid., p. 190; A218/B265.) This fourth principle entails the position of postulates, by which is meant non-obligatory demands or positions: we do not *have to* situate ourselves in the real, the possible, or the necessary. But we *can* choose one of those non-binding positions. We *can* postulate ourselves on one side or the other.
14 Kant, *Critique of Practical Reason*, p. 18.
15 Ibid., op. cit., p. 19.
16 Ibid.
17 Let us note that Lacan's "object *a*, cause of desire" is completely different because the object *a* is precisely characterized by its absence, impossibility, and un-representability.
18 Ibid., p. 23.
19 "It would be better to maintain that there are no practical laws at all but only *counsels* on behalf of our desires than to raise merely subjective principles to the rank of practical laws." (Ibid., p. 24).
20 Ibid., p. 20.
21 Ibid., p. 24.
22 Let us note that it is not (universal) form that is analytical, but the proposition which states that for lack of matter all that we have left is form as a possible determinant of the moral law.
23 Ibid., p. 25.

24 Ibid.
25 Ibid.
26 Ibid.
27 See Plastow, "L'émergence de la pulsion de mort chez Sabina Spielrein", in *Essaim*, Toulouse, Érès, 2019/2, no. 14. [See also Michael Gerard Plastow, *Sabina Spielrein and the Poetry of Psychoanalysis*, Oxon, Routledge, 2018].
28 Ibid., p. 26.
29 Thesis: "Causality according to the laws of nature, is not the only causality operating to originate the appearances of the world. A causality of freedom is also necessary to account for these appearances." Antithesis: "There is no such thing as freedom, but everything in the world happens solely according to the laws of nature." (Kant, *Critique of Pure Reason*, op. cit., p. 329, A444/B472).
30 Kant, *Critique of Practical Reason*, op. cit., p. 27.
31 [Translator's note – "Cognition" is used by Mary Gregor to translate the German term *Erkenntnis*. Both *Erkenntnis* and *connaissance* can also be translated in English by the word "knowledge"].
32 Ibid.
33 Ibid.
34 Ibid., p. 28.
35 Ibid.
36 Ibid., p. 29.
37 Ibid., p. 30.
38 Ibid., p. 31.
39 Ibid., p. 33.
40 Ibid., p. 34.
41 Ibid., p. 35.
42 Ibid., p. 19.
43 Ibid., p. 36.
44 Ibid., p. 37.
45 Ibid., p. 38.
46 Ibid.
47 Ibid., p. 39.
48 Ibid., p. 40.
49 Ibid., p. 41.
50 Ibid., p. 45.
51 Ibid., p. 46.
52 Ibid., p. 47
53 Ibid., p. 48.

Chapter 4

The concept of good/evil[1]

Derivation of the concept of the good/the evil on the basis of the moral principle

"By a concept of an object of practical reason I understand the representation of an object as an effect possible through freedom."[2] The object which will be the good/evil has not yet been brought into being. It must be brought into being through moral action and can in no way be the final cause of our moral volition or of our higher faculty of desire. It is the moral principle which determines the object.

As a result of the precedence of the moral principle over the concept of the object, there are only two objects of practical reason, one which follows the principle and the one which opposes it: "The only objects of a practical reason are therefore those of the *good* (*Gut*) and *evil* (*Böse*)."[3] The former is determined by the positive will, by the faculty of desiring (*Begehrungsvermögen*), the latter by the negative will (*Verabscheuungsvermögen*). We do not morally desire anything unless it is because of the good (*bonum*). We do not morally reject anything unless it is because of the bad (*malum*).[4] The Latin expressions *bonum/malum* are fundamentally ambiguous because of a deficiency or a certain poverty in the language; *bonum* refers to both the pleasant good [*bon plaisant*] and the moral good [*bien moral*], and *malum* refers to both the painfully unpleasant (in French, there is "*ça fait mal*" – "that hurts") and the morally bad [*le mauvais moral*] or morally evil [*le mal moral*]. The same ambiguity is found in the French language, whereas "the German language has the good fortune to possess expressions which do not allow this difference to be overlooked. For that which the Latins denominate with a single word, *bonum*, it has two very different concepts and equally different expressions as well: for *bonum* it has *das Gute* and *das Wohl*, for *malum* it has *das Böse* and *das Übel* (or *Weh*)".[5] *Gute* and *Böse* refer to objective morality derived from universal reason, while *Wohl* and *Übel* (or *Weh*) refer to subjective sensibility, to what is subjectively (meaning locally) agreeable or disagreeable.

***

This equivocation is of considerable importance: it is at play within all of the equivocations encountered in psychoanalytic experience, if we are willing to pay it attention. It is not the equivocation between good and evil (that of ambivalence)

DOI: 10.4324/9781003055662-10

which is most important, but that between the good and the pleasant (*le bien et le bon*) (vs. that between the bad and the unpleasant [*le mal et le mauvais*]). The equivocation around the good and the pleasant is not, moreover, primarily a question related to one language or another: it *also* exists in the German language, despite its richness. Thus, we can say that a surgical operation is good (*gut*) because it has been successful, because it has attained its sensible goal, namely a cure, which has to do with technique rather than morality. The equivocation of the good and the pleasant is dependent on the amphiboly proper to the concept itself,[6] to the concept of the good and the pleasant certainly; but it can be found within every concept which always appears simultaneously within the perspective of pleasure and the perspective of the moral law (or of jouissance). In "L'Étourdit",[7] Lacan presented a *ternary* articulation of every equivocation we could present as follows. Every equivocation appears to be a linguistic one (*équivoque de la langue*), a homophonic equivocation in which the same sequence of sounds refers to two different significations (*bonum* meaning pleasant and morally good). This first aspect of equivocation is dependent on another type of equivocation, the logical equivocation in which the level of the understanding (and of reason) and the intuitive level of the sensible are intermingled; the logical equivocation is particularly obvious in the case of *bonum* (vs. *malum*), which fluctuates between the good understood on the side of reason and the pleasant on the side of sensibility. Thirdly and finally, every equivocation asks to be inscribed literally (in "grammar"); it calls for a subjective stance in which the ambiguity will persist as a grammatical equivocation, but not without relaunching the logical equivocation. This grammatical equivocation is again particularly obvious in the case of morality having to take a stand, to be inscribed within the ever-present equivocation between the good and the pleasant (this is what will be dealt with in the *dialectic of practical reason*).

The omnipresent equivocation between language, logic and grammar is dependent on the equivocation in reason itself, divided between what is (pure reason) and what should be (practical reason). In the order of knowledge or cognition, every concept must be determined before its principles. In the order of morality, the principle must determine the concept and not the other way round. We are always caught between one order and the other. That is why the method of the critique of practical reason seems fundamentally paradoxical: "the concept of good and evil must not be determined before the moral law (for which, as it would seem, this concept would have to be made the basis), but only (as was done here) after it and by means of it".[8] In the use of any concept at all, we are forever confronted with the question "pleasant or good?" – do we understand the concept as applied in sensibility (pleasure principle) or as already structured in reason (moral law or jouissance)?

Despite the absolute primacy of the principle of the moral law over the good, we are always tempted to first give ourselves the representation, the concept of the goal to be attained (the good) to guide our will towards that good. But this strategy which seeks agreement with the good is dependent on the pleasure principle, because it is determined by an external goal and, with this strategy, we have already taken away the possibility of really thinking through a pure practical law (and jouissance). Dismissing a priori every equivocation between the pleasant and the good, all of the moral philosophies prior to Kant had sought an object of the will, the concept of the good = pleasant, in order to make it the matter and the basis of the moral law. In this, "their principle was in every case heteronomy",[9] and they could only miss the true mainspring of morality, namely, autonomy.

The *concept* of good and evil (the sole object of practical reason) is the *consequence* of the pure practical principle, of the causality of pure reason. It is not originally related to objects thought of as given within the framework of cognition or of knowledge. If moral actions are radically dependent on the *principle* of the moral law and of freedom, they should also, however, concretely fall in with the world of appearances with sensible objects. The different sensible objects to which the concept of the good and the evil are related only count as modalities of the moral law. They "are rather, without exception, *modi* of a single category, namely that of causality", of the causality of *freedom*.[10] This *freedom causality* must be capable of being determinant within appearances, and in order to do this, it is permitted to use the categories of the understanding, not in order to "bring a priori the manifold of (sensible) *intuition* under one consciousness, but only in order to subject a priori the manifold of *desires* to the unity of consciousness of a practical reason commanding in the moral law".

The "categories of freedom" are founded on "the *form of a pure will* as given within reason and therefore within the thinking faculty itself".[11] By means of the categorial framework involved in speculative reason,

> the practical a priori concepts in relation to the supreme principle of freedom at once become cognition, and do not have to wait for intuitions in order to receive meaning; and this happens for the noteworthy reason that they themselves produce the reality of that to which they refer (the disposition of the will).

The four great classes of category (quantity, quality, relation, modality) comprise three categories, of which the third "always arises from the combination of the second with the first", but this does not mean in any way that it is a derived concept. On the contrary, the third category is also "a primitive concept of the pure understanding".[12] The *articulation* of the elements, of the categories, is always already there prior to each isolated element, *prior to each isolated category*. This remark is most significant where the "categories of freedom" are concerned. In each class of categories, the first one presents that which still appears to be morally indeterminate and sensibly conditioned, the second that which appears sensibly unconditioned, and the third that which is solely determined by the moral law. We shall understand that it is the *third* one that is decisive for the moral law, even if it is only understood relative to the two others. From the perspective of quantity, the so-called "universality" of the moral law should be understood not from universal judgements and from the category of unity (first category) but from *singular judgement* and the category of *totality* (third category). It will not have to do with practical rules of commission (affirmation), nor with practical rules of omission (negation), but with practical rules of *exception* (limitation). Freedom thus appears not as the affirmation or the negation of a reality, but as posing a radical *limit* in the sequence of appearances as a new opening, a new creation, that is, always as an exception. At the level of the relation, freedom does not first concern the personality, which would count as the substance of the moral law, nor as the result of a causality, but as a *reciprocal relation* between dynamics each of which is articulated with the others. Finally, at the level of modality, freedom does not boil down to the couple permitted/forbidden (that which is possible), nor the couple duty/contrary to duty (which appears as existing). It is the question of *commitment* to the action made necessary by duty which is crucial, the *necessity* of duty in as much as it is not primarily dependent on the thing ("imperfect duty"), but on will alone, on freedom itself ("perfect duty").[13]

The moral law should always be thought through in its concrete, empirical applications. In its application, it is always the third categories of each class which impose themselves, precisely in the fact that they create, construct something new, something previously unseen.

But how can the concept of good or evil or of these categories, the "categories of freedom", be judged concretely? What is the algorithm for this? What is the test which allows them to be concretely *presented*? It is the "typic" which responds to this.

Presentation of the concept of good/evil through the typic of the faculty of pure practical judgement

The faculty of judgement (*Urteilskraft*), among other things, bears the responsibility for presenting (*darstellen*) concepts in a concrete manner, of schematising them. There are four fundamentally different types of concept.

1 To schematise or present an *empirical concept*, it is sufficient to present an *example*. As we have seen, the moral law, which has nothing to do with an empirical concept, can in no way be presented or schematised by an example. There are no examples of a moral action.
2 To schematise or present the *concepts of the pure understanding* (the categories), the faculty of judgement has recourse to the pure intuition of *time* (quantity being schematised according to the line of time, quality according to empty or full time, relation according to the order of time, modality according to the conditions of time in general). The moral law is not reduced to and is not deduced from the categories of cognition: it cannot be schematised by time, because we are situated completely outside the conditions of sensible experience and of a pre-given temporality. On the contrary, the moral law can command the construction of a new temporality.
3 To schematise or present the *concepts of pure reason*, which are abstract ideas (God, the soul, the world), the faculty of judgement has recourse to the

symbol. The moral law is not deduced from ideas as hypotheses of reason (it would therefore no longer be categorical, but hypothetical instead).

4   For the concepts of morality, it is not a case of finding "the schema of a case in accordance with laws",[14] but the schema of a law as a law. The schema of the pure concept of the moral law (the good/the evil) "must correspond to a natural law [. . .]. But no intuition can be put under the law of freedom [. . .] and hence under the concept of the unconditioned good as well – and hence no schema on behalf of its application *in concreto*". To present empirical concepts, the concepts of pure reason (categories) and the ideas, the faculty of judgement had the possibility of recourse to the *imagination*. To present the concept of the moral law (good/evil), the imagination is not directly at our disposal, we must rely on the workings of reason – to the symbolic and not the imaginary – to judge if the action in sight can go under the heading of a law as law. "The rule of judgment under laws of pure practical reason is this: ask yourself whether, if the action you propose were to take place by a law of the nature of which you were yourself a part, you could indeed regard it as possible through your will". The schematism of the moral concept thus consists in placing oneself in the position of the creator of the law and to verify, through the understanding and reason if this law could really be a law. Indeed, this is how everyone judges whether or not an action is morally good or bad: "how would it be if everyone permitted themselves to perform this action", in other words, if it were a law? But this comparison with the creation of a universal law of nature is not the determining principle of the will. It is only the concrete means of showing and verifying that the proposed action *may* correspond to the principle of the law.

The presentation of the moral law by the "typic" (comparison with a possible natural law) protects us both from the *empiricism* of practical reason (or from presentation through examples) and from the *mysticism* of the moral law (or of a presentation of the moral law through symbols). In mysticism, the moral law is still dependent on *ideas* rather than the principle. Mysticism, however, "is still compatible with the purity and sublimity of the moral law", *because it does not have its basis in sensibility*. As far as empiricism (and the schematism of examples) is concerned, it should be recognised that it is absolutely incompatible with true morality, because it makes everything depend on sensibility and the pleasure principle. Empiricism "destroys at its roots the morality of dispositions [. . .] and substitutes for it something quite different, namely in place of duty an empirical interest, with which the inclinations generally are secretly leagued".[15]

Jouissance also can never be presented either through examples (like empirical concepts), or through a temporal schematism (like the pure concepts of the understanding), or through symbols (like the pure ideas of reason): it can only be presented as the questioning of the invention of a law, of a new form.

Notes

1 "Chapter II of the analytic of pure practical reason: On the concept of an object of pure practical reason."
2 Ibid., p. 49.
3 Ibid.
4 "*Nihil appetimur, nisi sub rationae boni; nihil aversamur, nisi sub ratione mali*", Ibid., p. 50.
5 Ibid., pp. 50–51.
6 "The amphiboly of the concepts of reflection" (Kant, *Critique of Pure Reason*, op. cit., p. 260ff; A260/B316), concerns the use of any concept at all: do we understand it as the concept applied within sensibility or as structured within the understanding and reason?
7 Lacan, "L'Étourdit", op. cit., p. 491ff.
8 Ibid., p. 53.
9 Ibid., p. 54.
10 Ibid., p. 55.
11 Ibid.
12 Kant, *Critique of Pure Reason*, op. cit., p. 88; B110.
13 Kant, *Critique of Practical Reason*, op. cit., p. 56.
14 Ibid., p. 58. Translation modified.
15 Ibid., pp. 59–60.

Chapter 5

Respect (*Achtung*)[1]

The incentives or driving forces (*Triebfeder*), which belong to sensibility, are not the motive, the motivating ground (*Bewegungsgrund*) of the moral law. The will, in fact, immediately determines the will without the intervention of feelings. If action is determined by sensible incentives, it can certainly have a lawful character, it can be in conformity with the letter (*Buchstabe*) of the law, but it is absolutely not moral, because it is not performed according to the spirit (*Geist*) of morality.

It now remains to carefully determine in what way the moral law can and should become an "incentive", a sensible driving force, namely *how it has an impact on sensible reality*. The moral law produces two types of effects on sensibility: a negative effect, pain, and a positive effect, respect.

The moral law is detrimental to sensible inclinations which might determine the will. It necessarily provokes a certain sorrow, a certain pain. But the provocation of pain has nothing to do with masochism, because pain is not the incentive for, but the *undesired* effect[2] of the moral law. "All the inclinations together [. . .] constitute regard for oneself",[3] and this can appear as "*love for oneself*, a predominant *benevolence* towards oneself" or as a self-satisfaction which is nothing but self-conceit (*Eigendünkel*). Practical reason confronts the self-love (*Selbstliebe*) which corresponds to narcissism, *not in order to suppress it*, but in order to limit it, more precisely in order to bring it into agreement with the moral law. It therefore transforms narcissism into a "rational self-love", whereas it strikes down self-conceit. True self-esteem (*Selbstachtung*), true narcissism rests solely on morality (*Sittlichkeit*). The negative effect of the moral law on feelings (pain) is thus directly counterbalanced by a positive effect, true self-esteem, true self-respect (*Selbstachtung*), or to be brief, respect (*Achtung*). Pain is only the counterpart or the reverse side of respect. The feeling of respect "is produced by an intellectual ground", and it is "the only one that we can cognize completely a priori and the necessity of which we can have insight into". The simple fact of situating oneself in the moral law produces an effect on the feeling which, on the one hand, is purely negative, pain or humiliation (*Demütigung*) accompanied by an "intellectual contempt"[4] (*intellektuelle Verachtung*) and, on the other hand, a positive feeling, respect (*Achtung*). Intellectual contempt, which consists

DOI: 10.4324/9781003055662-11

in not taking pleasure and pain into account, fosters the causality of freedom. This feeling – which is simultaneously both negative and positive – may be called "a feeling of respect for the moral law" or "a moral feeling". The moral feeling or "respect" thus inextricably presupposes *Achtung* and *Verachtung*, respect (for the moral law) and contempt (for the obstacle that is empirical sensibility). Respect, however, is in no way a determining cause of the moral law: "it is morality itself subjectively considered as an incentive".[5] It the driving force, "the sole and also the undoubted moral incentive"[6] of practical reason. It can be found in every human being.[7]

Respect or the moral feeling (*moralisches Gefühl*) is presented as a "consciousness" or an awareness of the moral law in as much as it concretely determines the good and it falls within sensibility. "The consciousness of a *free* submission of the will to the law, yet as combined with an unavoidable constraint put on all inclinations though only by one's reason, is respect for the law."

Should we not be capable of imagining, however, that a moral action may be performed according to the principle of the moral law, but independently of the moral feeling of respect? And should we not also be capable of imagining that feelings, incentives, and driving forces other than respect may intervene in mobilising moral action?

As far as the first question is concerned,

> The concept of duty [. . .] requires of the action *objective* accord with the law but requires of the maxim of the action *subjective* respect for the law, as the sole way of determining the will by the law. And on this rests distinction between consciousness of having acted *in conformity with duty* and *from duty*, that is, respect for the law.[8]

Lawfulness is possible without respect for the law, but morality is not possible without respect for the law. Morality must necessarily be inscribed within the register of the drives *by means of respect*.

With regard to the second question: is it not suitable to inscribe morality within the register of the drives by a sensible means other than respect – love, for example?

Here Kant examines the Christian commandment: "*Love God above all, and your neighbour as yourself*". Kant's position is clear and definitive: the moral law "agrees with this [commandment] very well".[9] As a commandment, it demands *respect* (*Achtung*) for the law. However, the concept of "*love*", which would come to rival respect as an incentive of the moral law, only veils the radical differences which are imposed between virtue and happiness, between the practical and the pathological, between the noumenal and the phenomenal. Because, on the one hand, "love for God as inclination (pathological love) is impossible, for he is not an object of the senses." And, on the other hand, if love for human beings is possible as a sensible inclination, "[it] cannot be commanded, for it is not within the power of any human being to love someone merely on command".[10] When the

Christian commandment is taken as the "kernel of all laws", it may be understood as "practical love" in the sense of practical reason – it would quite simply be equivalent to the moral law and to freedom (with universality, autonomy, etc.). But the connotation of "love" added to the practical law does risk introducing a sensible pathological element (in the place of respect), which covers over what is essential in the moral law and in freedom. "To love God means, in this sense, to do what He commands *gladly*; to love one's neighbour mean to practice all duties towards him *gladly*." But "a command that one should do something gladly is in itself contradictory." The moral law is in fundamental opposition with sensible inclinations, this is why it gives rise to a divided feeling (of pain and respect) and not simply a unitary feeling such as love. The moral law appears as a duty, namely as a conflict between the search for virtue and the search for happiness.

Notes

1 "Chapter III of the analytic of pure practical reason: On the incentives of pure practical reason."
2 Pain in itself is not desired by the higher faculty of desire or by the lower faculty of desire.
3 Ibid., p. 61.
4 Ibid., p. 63.
5 Ibid.
6 Ibid., p. 65.
7 The voice (*Stimme*) of practical reason presenting the moral law "makes even the boldest evildoer tremble and forces him to hide from its sight" (Ibid., p. 66).
8 Ibid., p. 67.
9 Ibid., p. 68.
10 Ibid., pp. 68–69.

Chapter 6

The necessary articulation of the principle of morality with the pleasure principle[1]

We have seen how pure reason (*Wissen*) starts out from (imaginary) sensibility and passes through the (symbolic) concept before opening onto the real with principles. Practical reason (*Gewissen*), on the other hand, starts out from the (real) principle which subsequently determines the concept of good or evil (symbolic), to finally express itself in the feeling of respect (imaginary).

Practical reason does not demand that we give up all claims to happiness (which would quite simply be impossible) in the consideration of duty. "It can even in certain respects be a duty to attend to one's happiness, partly because happiness [. . .] contains means for the fulfilment of one's duty and partly because lack of it [. . .] contains temptations to transgress one's duty."[2]

The supreme principle of practical reason remains autonomy or practical freedom, which we can define as the "independence of the will from anything other than the moral law alone".[3] Even if we cannot ascertain any concrete possibility of freedom, any sensible realisation of it, we can be assured that there is no proof of its impossibility (as the *critique of pure reason* showed with regard to the third antinomy). All those who think that a psychological or phenomenal sense can be given to freedom only block the perspective opened up for the moral law, autonomy, and freedom.

Natural deterministic causality and causality through freedom are radically opposed. If a being is completely determined in time, it is impossible to attribute freedom to it. But the same being can be considered as an *appearance entirely* determined in time while being conscious of themselves as a *thing-in-itself* with an existence which is not subject to the conditions of time, determined by laws which they give themselves. The subject is therefore fundamentally divided into a psychological subject and an absolutely empty noumenal subject.

This "wonderful capacity" of the conscience (*Gewissen*) confirms the timelessness (*hors-temps*) of the subject, their freedom, and their morality. There are obvious sensible traces of this timelessness in the phenomenology of guilt. Bad actions could be explained by a thousand phenomenal or psychological reasons: this is thought to get rid of guilt. But the voice of conscience continues to accuse, guilt remains. One could say, "What's done is done", and that there is no sense to feel guilty in the future. Guilt, on the other hand, shows the timelessness of

DOI :10.4324/9781003055662-12

morality and freedom. Time does not wear guilt away. It is outside of all time that freedom must be exercised.

Generally speaking, space and time are not determinations belonging to the existence of things in themselves, but idealities, forms of sensible intuition which belong to the sensible subject's mode of representation.[4]

In the same sense, the timelessness of the unconscious should be thought of as outside the phenomenal, outside any clinic of pure observation, despite what might be observed in the phenomena of guilt and in the formations of the unconscious in general. The timelessness of the unconscious should be thought through in the dimension of jouissance (basis of morality) and not according to the pleasure principle.

General perspectives on this articulation[5]

Reason always "requires the absolute totality of conditions for a given conditioned".[6] In other words, it always requires that the set of conditions for this given be placed under the heading of a singularity, of a One.[7] "*Y'a d'l'un* – There is something of the One", said Lacan, and Badiou speaks of the "count-as-one". But this required totality is never found in appearances. It can only be found through the activity of reason.

However, all concepts should always be related to intuitions and be represented in intuitions. The required totality is therefore always *imagined within* appearances (*Erscheinung*). It thus appears as an unavoidable illusion (*unvermeidlicher Schein*). One would not realise the deceptive character of these ideas of pure reason, of these totalities, if they did not show at the same time a "*conflict* of reason with itself".[8] It is because there is this conflict that reason is led to seek a key to resolving it.

Therefore, in the *Critique of Pure Reason*, the soul (or the subject), the world and the supreme Being (or God) unavoidably appear as totalities (from the point of view, respectively, of substance, the causal series, and the reciprocal action which unites all beings). But within these totalities immediately arises a conflict: the subject is divided, the world is riddled with contradictions, the big Other lacks proof of its existence. The key to escaping these conflicts depends in each case on the supreme principle of all synthetic judgements, namely the activity of reason which produces these totalities: everything depends on the synthesis of our knowledge, everything depends on our experience of knowledge, everything depends on what we *do*. Also, the "subject", the "world", the "big Other" will not count as realities, but as regulatory principles of what we do in this case.

In the *Critique of Practical Reason*, reason starts out from the formal principle of the moral law and freedom, and in this way determines good/evil. It also seeks, however, "the unconditioned totality of the object of pure practical reason, under the name of the *highest good*",[9] meaning a higher Good than the Good produced by the autonomy of the moral law, a Good which would also be presupposed to contain happiness.

From then on, the determination of the highest Good carries with it a conflict: "though the highest good may be the whole *object* of a pure practical reason",[10] it includes within itself the opposition between the good and the pleasant, that is, the conflict inherent to duty as duty. The key to leaving this conflict behind should be again sought in synthetic judgement, in the making of morality itself. We must therefore reject from the outset the interpretation of the highest good reduced to a reward or a payment for doing good in the field of happiness or pleasure.[11]

The highest good and the postulates of the "immortality of the soul" and "the existence of God"[12]

"Highest" ["*Souverain*"] in the expression "highest good" ["*souverain Bien*"] is equivocal, and this equivocation takes up again the equivocation of the good and the pleasant. "The highest [*Souverain, das Höchste*] can mean either the supreme [*das Oberste*] (*supremum*) or the complete [*das Vollendete*] *(consummatum)*."[13] The first sense, that of the highest or most elevated good, is the good determined by the moral law, the good of virtue. This first sense is pleonastic: the moral Good is the highest moral Good, there is no Good higher than it. The second sense implies, on the contrary, that the Good is complete, and for this "*happiness* is also required". Virtue makes it worth being happy according to this highest Good *as supreme*, but it precisely does not guarantee the *complete* Good. The highest Good as complete supposes that virtue and happiness are brought together in harmony, that the Good is made complete by happiness and that the latter be "distributed in exact proportion to morality".[14]

How can that union, that harmony between virtue and happiness, be established, when everything seems to set them against each other? That unity could be called analytic if the aspiration to virtue and the rational search for happiness were basically identical (the maxim of the moral law and the maxim of happiness would thus coincide). The ancient Greek Stoic and Epicurean schools supposed that virtue and happiness fundamentally matched up. "The Epicurean said: to be conscious of one's maxim leading to happiness is virtue; the Stoic said: to be conscious of one's virtue is happiness."[15] The intelligence possessed by these men was unfortunately used to attempt to establish the identity of these two fundamentally opposing concepts. Each was certain that their basic concept was *the whole highest Good*:

> The Stoic maintained that virtue is the *whole highest good*, and happiness only the consciousness of this possession as belonging to the state of the subject. The Epicurean maintained that happiness is the *whole highest good*, and virtue only the form of the maxim for seeking to obtain it.[16]

If happiness and morality are two completely distinct elements of the highest good (this is the conflict inherent to duty, which remains an underlying part of the highest good), their *union* cannot be cognised analytically (that is, through the analysis of the concept of happiness or of the concept of morality). Their union in the highest good, therefore, presupposes a synthesis (and not an analysis); *it must be made, built, constructed*. This union is absolutely necessary; it must be made real, because reason absolutely *wishes* to reach totality, the One of a composite highest good. "It is a priori (morally) necessary *to produce the highest good through the freedom of the will*."[17] This necessary *synthetic production* of the highest good is clarified as follows.

The antinomy of practical reason

The highest good contains a conflict within itself. From then on, producing virtue with happiness (Epicureanism) is *absolutely* impossible (it is the opposite of virtue) and producing happiness with virtue (Stoicism) is impossible to *concretely* accomplish in the world (one cannot expect to attain happiness in the world from observing moral laws). If the highest good is therefore contradictory (but we shall see the key to escaping this apparent contradiction), a moral law that would command us to carry it out could only be false in itself: the moral law does not command us to carry out the moral law.

Principle of the critical solution to the antinomy

In pure reason, the third antinomy set the thesis of a world entirely subject to deterministic natural causality against the antithesis of a world in which freedom can intervene in the causality of the events of the world. The principle of the critical solution consisted in showing that a real conflict was not involved. In fact, the two positions are situated in completely different fields: the events of the world are produced as *appearances* or *phenomena* (and causality there is entirely deterministic and natural), whereas "the acting person regards himself at the same time as *noumenon* (as pure intelligence, in his existence that cannot be temporally determined)".[18]

In a similar manner, in practical reason and for the antinomy of the highest good, if it is absolutely false that virtue can be deduced from the search for happiness as the Epicureans do, it is not absolutely impossible for the morality of the intention to have a necessary connection (but one of which we are unaware) with happiness. Because if it is impossible that this connection is realised in the world, on the level of appearances, it is not impossible at the level of noumena. We shall see how.

The antinomy of the highest good presupposes two moments, *firstly* the distinction and the opposition between morality and the search for happiness, *secondly* the possibility of resolving the antinomy through unity, totality, and synthesis. We can distinguish four positions in relation to this antinomy. *Firstly*, one could deny the opposition; this is what "philosophers of modern times", *Berkeley* and Utilitarianism do, whose morality boils down to a search for the happiness of all: the unity of pleasure (happiness) and form (for all) is ensured from the outset. *Secondly*, one could completely deny the very possibility of resolving the antinomy in unity or synthesis; if this position was not considered by Kant (for him, reason cannot in any way do without seeking this unity and totality), it is, however, upheld by the advocates of *pure love* who were well and truly aiming for a pure morality (consisting in the love of God), without any expectation of happiness in proportion to that "pure love".[19] *Thirdly*, among Epicureans and Stoics, there is a clear distinction between morality and the quest for happiness, but it is cancelled out by the direct connection which can be made between the two, in one sense or another, at the level of the phenomenal world. *Fourthly*, in *Kant*, the basic gap between morality and the quest for happiness cannot be resolved here below, on the phenomenal level, but practical reason – which simultaneously commands the moral law and the quest for totality (unity) – necessarily postulates their unity in the highest good in a "future life", which is, in fact, *outside time, outside the determinations of time*.

Today we find the same four positions in the question of the articulation of the pleasure principle (corresponding to happiness) and the jouissance principle (corresponding to virtue). *Firstly*, there is no fundamental opposition, and the concept of "jouissance" is after all only a variant of the pleasure principle. *Secondly*, jouissance may be thought of as ecstatic, mystical, without any need to reconcile it with pleasure. *Thirdly*, pleasure would be a preliminary stage leading to jouissance (on the Epicurean side) or jouissance would be the basis of pleasure (on the Stoic side). *Fourthly*, the jouissance principle and the pleasure principle are radically opposed, seemingly irreconcilable, *and* we should do everything to concretely bring them together in practice. It is only here that the antinomy of practical reason appears. The task seems strictly impossible. What does this impossibility imply?

Before coming to his own position, Kant in particular, lingers over that of Epicurus, because he begins from the concrete principle of the quest for pleasure, while already placing it within the immediate perspective of virtue (it is pleasure which leads directly to virtue). "The virtuous Epicurus" (because he aimed for virtue) "fell into the error of presupposing the virtuous *disposition* in the persons for whom he wanted first of all to provide the incentive to virtue."[20] But the question is precisely one of knowing how this disposition was possible; it is none other than the respect which itself *ensues from* the moral law and from freedom. "The moral disposition is necessarily connected with consciousness of the determination of the will *directly by the law*."[21] Respect is really the motive, the driving force (*Triebfeder*) of virtue; it is not determined by any other feeling, but by virtue.

Conversely (on the side of the Stoics), do we not have a kind of happiness, "contentment with oneself" (*Selbstzufriedenheit*) which results from the consciousness of a moral action? The expression "contentment with oneself" indicates in fact that "one is conscious of needing nothing",[22] which refers back to "*independence from the inclinations*".

On the primacy of pure practical reason in its relation to pure speculative reason

Synthesis ("making") is at the heart of the solution of the third antinomy of pure reason, and it is also more clearly so in the antinomy of practical reason.

The treatment of the antinomy of practical reason presupposes that there is a *making of what ought to be* (on the noumenal side), more powerful than the *knowledge of what is* (on the phenomenal side). Why and how are the interests of speculative reason subordinated to the interest of practical reason? If practical reason could not admit more what speculative reason offered it, speculative reason would have to be considered as primary and practical reason would consist in applying the data of speculative reason according to adequate technical rules. But practical reason has an original a priori principle which is not given by speculative reason: the moral law and freedom.

Speculative reason failed in the proof of certain dogmatic principles concerning the subject, the world and God. There is no authentic knowledge about these three ideas (*Aufhebung* of knowledge). These ideas, however, inevitably present themselves to reason, which "is still only one and the same reason which, whether from a theoretical or a practical perspective, judges according to a priori principles".[23]

As we have seen in the first chapter on practical reason: according to the moral law, practical reason must accept – and accept it without knowing, it is a postulate – the idea of a world also operating according to a causality of *freedom*. With this first postulate of practical reason, the practical predominates over the speculative. To situate oneself in morality, one must *believe* in freedom; it is not knowledge, but faith (*Glaube*). In the rest of the dialectic of practical reason, we shall see that practical reason must also believe in the "subject" and in God, to develop *totality*, namely the unity (*Y a d'l'un*) of the general conditions of all moral actions (which must be both formal and material at the same time).

When the union of speculative and practical reason is limited to a certain contingent action (according to technical imperatives) or to the quest for happiness, it is speculative reason which is predominant (practice follows the theoretical schema). On the other hand, when this union is necessary according to the categorical imperative of the moral law (what it concerns is at the very foundation of the human experience), it is practical reason which predominates. *Pure* practical (that is, moral) reason is always, therefore, structurally predominant over pure speculative reason.

The immortality of the soul as a postulate of pure practical reason

"*[T]he complete conformity* of dispositions with the moral law is the supreme condition of the highest good."[24] In this conformity, the highest good is understood as supreme and not complete. This complete conformity of inclinations to the moral law is *demanded* by the moral law, but it is not assured. It can therefore only be found "in an *endless progress* toward that complete conformity". One is never finished with the pursuit of the moral law. This is the source of fundamental guilt, as we have seen. But Kant here draws from it the postulate of the aforesaid "immortality of the soul". More fundamentally, and according to the absence of complete conformity, the demand of the moral law entails that the search for it never ceases to impose itself, and alongside it the supposition of the insistence of this demand, the insistence of this principle of jouissance which does not stop not realising itself, is a soul or a subject outside of time. This "soul" or this "subject" has no certain substance in phenomenal time. This is the very supposition of the timelessness of the unconscious, oblivious to the wearing away of time. We are never finished with the question of the so-called subject, because the unconscious and its ethics postulate the complete realisation, the totality of what should be [*la totalité du devoir être*], without being able to find it. It is the complete and necessary realisation of "the first and principal part of the highest good, **morality**".[25] Not without implying the timelessness of guilt, we will add here. The immortality of the soul has nothing to do, therefore, with a yield of pleasure repaying moral action (it would, rather, be a yield of guilt).

The existence of God as a postulate of pure practical reason

If the moral law should lead to the complete and necessary realisation of the second part of the highest good, "**happiness** proportioned to that morality" (the postulate of a timeless unconscious "subject"), it should also lead to "the supposition of the existence of a cause adequate to this effect". In the moral law itself, there is no connection between the morality principle and happiness. But according to the unifying function of reason, morality, as Kant conceives it, *must* remain engaged with sensibility (thus, with the question of happiness) and the connection between virtue and happiness "is postulated as necessary [. . .] Therefore, the highest good in the world is possible only insofar as a supreme cause of nature having a causality in keeping with the moral disposition is assumed".[26] This would be a primitive causality which brings together deterministic natural causality and causality through freedom. The "*highest derived good*" (in which happiness is proportionate to my action) implies the postulate of the "*highest original good*", namely the postulate of a big Other, the highest cause of the agreement of the pleasure principle and the jouissance principle.

However, this moral necessity is not objective, it is not an object of knowledge. It is, above all, not to be thought of as a payment for moral action. It is the necessary connection between causality through freedom and the deterministic causality which commands the postulates of "the immortality of the soul" and "the existence of God". The big Other, God or the highest principle, which unites the two causalities is not, however, the ground of moral obligation, as this "rests [. . .] solely on the autonomy of reason itself".[27] Considered from the theoretical point of view, this postulate of the existence of God is only a hypothesis, but from the subjective point of view of the practical subject, it is a *"belief* and, indeed, a pure *rational belief* since pure reason alone (in its theoretical as well as its practical use) is the source from which it springs".[28] The big Other, the existence of which is radically called into question at the level of knowledge (there is not and there will never be any proof of the existence of the big Other), must be supposed to exist (the big Other must be made exist) so as the unity of virtue and happiness can be concretely achieved, so that jouissance can lead to pleasure, from which, however, it is different.

The Cynical, Epicurean, Stoic, and Christian moral philosophies each presuppose an *idea* of the highest good as *aim* of morals: this moral idea (practical perfection) serves as a yardstick for the action the morality of which needs to be judged. "The ideas of the *Cynics*, the *Epicureans*, the *Stoics*, and the *Christians* are *natural simplicity, prudence, wisdom,* and *holiness.*"[29] However, through the predominant place of the highest good in the evaluation of morality, the *autonomy* of pure practical reason is completely lost – and true morality with it. Morals do not teach us how to attain the highest good or "how we are to *make* ourselves happy but of how we are to become *worthy* of happiness".[30] This worthiness is to be found in autonomy and not in the highest good. What is presupposed in the moral postulate of the existence of God is not that he created the happiness of rational beings, but that a highest good as guarantor of an adequate correspondence between happiness and virtue should exist – must be made to exist.

On the postulates of pure practical reason in general

These postulates – causality through freedom, the immortality of the soul, and the existence of God – are not in any way theoretical dogmas, but hypotheses inherent to practice and the moral law. The critique of pure reason showed the error inherent to the three corresponding ideas: the world (the antinomies of pure reason), the subject (the paralogisms of pure reason), and God (the ideal of pure reason which does not at all prove existence). These three ideas, which are transcendental for speculative reason, become immanent in the operation of practical reason. We necessarily presuppose freedom (the causality through freedom in effect within the world), the subject (the immortality of the soul), and God (the highest good). We understand that freedom – which, let us stress, is not first of all related to the subject, but to the causality of the *world* – is necessary for there to be a moral law, but we cannot know any free acts (other than to open up a place for the jouissance of the unconscious). We understand that it is necessary to uphold the question of virtue beyond phenomenal temporality, but we cannot know this immortal "subject" (except by persevering in the moral law, in jouissance). We understand that virtue or jouissance must proportionately unite with pleasure, we understand that the big Other must enable this articulation with happiness, and we cannot know anything about it (except by making it exist through the jouissance principle).

An extension of pure reason from the practical point of view alone

The three ideas of pure reason, which correspond to the three postulates of practical reason (world of freedom, immortality of the soul, God) were simply thinkable for speculative reason. With the principle of practical reason, these objects "are now declared assertorically",[31] which had not been possible for speculative reason. These objects are now, therefore, given, but for want of intuition, we can know strictly nothing about them: "[as] nothing is thereby given us by way of intuition of them [. . .], no synthetic proposition is possible by this reality granted them". We must make them, must practise them. Reason can make use of these ideas (world of freedom, immortality of the soul, God) not to extend its knowledge, but negatively, "so as on one side to ward off *anthropomorphism* [. . .] and on the other side *fanaticism*".[32] These pure ideas serve to keep morality at a distance from every sensible source (anthropomorphism) and from every supersensible source external to the workings of practical reason itself (the recourse to this kind of supersensible source is called fanaticism).

Freed as much from the sensible side as from the supersensible side, we must nevertheless *think through* practical reason on the basis of the categories of freedom, which cannot be deduced from the categories of the understanding. The categories of freedom "are not of empirical origin but have their seat and source a priori in the pure understanding".

> They indeed bring about *theoretical cognition* only in application to *empirical* objects, but still, applied to an object given by pure practical reason, also serve for a *determined thought of the supersensible*, yet only to the extent that this is determined merely through such predicates as necessarily belong to the pure *practical purpose* given a priori and to its possibility.[33]

Let us remember that the categories of freedom prioritise the third subcategory within each category: for quantity, the autonomous *singularity* of the law-giving "subject"; for quality, the *limitation* which adjudicates and decides; for relation, the *reciprocal action* of rational things; for modality, the *necessity* of the moral law.[34]

Belief (Glaube) as the holding as true[35](führwahrhalten) arising from a need of pure reason

"A need of pure reason in its speculative use leads only to hypotheses, that of pure practical reason, however, to postulates."[36] In speculative reason, I raise myself as high as I can towards totality, towards a unitary principle, towards the One (*Y a d'l'un*), to explain an objective reality, but it is not possible to be certain of the objective reality of this principle (the subject, the world, or God). "On the other hand, a need *of pure practical* reason is based on a *duty*, that of making something (the highest good) the object of my will so as to promote it with all my powers." This is not only possible, but is, more importantly, necessary. This necessity does not lead *to any objective knowledge* of the subject, of the world, or of God. It comes into play in a form of practice.

As the moral law necessarily imposes itself on me,

> I *will* that there be a God, that my existence in this world be also an existence in a pure world of the understanding beyond all natural connections, and finally that my duration be endless; I stand by this [. . .], and I will not let this belief (*Glaube*) be taken from me.[37]

I hold these three postulates as true due to purely subjective motives (the maxim of my action, "I will"), which are no less absolutely necessary. This belief (*Glaube*) is not knowledge (*Wissen*), which would be founded on objectivity, nor is it an opinion (*Meinen*), which only holds it as true although it lacks sufficient arguments from either an objective or a subjective point of view.

One could make the objection here that "willing" or "desire" in no way guarantees the reality of the thing desired and that a form of delusion precisely consists in taking one's desires for reality.[38] It is therefore completely correct to say that an inclination does not suffice to bring forth the *object* in reality. But in the moral law, inclination is not only involved. The moral law – necessary, unconditioned – inevitably determines my judgement: I believe in a world in which there is a place for freedom, as well as in the immortality of the subject and the existence of God, without this faith or this belief ever amounting to knowledge: I can say precisely nothing about what that freedom, subject, or God might be. I can bring them into existence in practice (freedom of the unconscious, persistence of the question of the subject, existence of the dimension of the big Other).

Faced with the necessity of jouissance, I must have faith in freedom, in the immortality of the question of the moral subject, and in the Other who will bring pleasure into agreement with jouissance in the end.

On the wisely balanced relation of the human being's faculties of cognition to its practical destination

The *Critique of Pure* – speculative – *Reason* showed the radical insufficiency of reason when it came to resolving its own goals, namely finding the unconditioned condition, totality, the One (*Y'a d'l'un*) in the order of substance (the subject), in the order of causality (the world), and in the order of community or reciprocal action (God). Knowledge is fundamentally holed, not contingently, but with regard to the most basic things.

Now, this *hole in knowledge* (*Aufhebung* of knowledge) is not simply a lack – it is fundamentally an asset.

Supposing that we had *knowledge* (*connaissance*) of the immortality of the soul and the rightful order of every moral action in the world due to the highest good, we would certainly obey to the letter of an apparently "moral" law. But the *intention* of our actions would no longer be guided by law-giving autonomy. It would be directly focused on the happiness resulting from our actions. Freedom would disappear. And our lawful, but not moral, behaviour would be "changed into mere mechanism in which, as in a puppet show, everything would *gesticulate* well but there would be *no life* in the figures".[39]

Nothing of the sort is the case, though. We do not directly know or cognise freedom, or the immortality of the soul, or the rightful order of the highest good. We have to *make them*. The moral law and guilt force themselves on us and, alongside them, the jouissance principle which, incapable of being reduced to examples or other sensible realisations, continues to uphold the freedom of the unconscious to give things a new form, to always create anew.

Notes

1 "Second book: The dialectic of pure practical reason."
2 Ibid., p. 76.
3 Ibid.
4 If one does not accept this division between a phenomenal and psychological subject, on the one hand, and a noumenal subject, subject of freedom, reducing itself to an empty point, on the other hand, all that remains to us is to think, along with Spinoza, that time and space are essential determinations of the primary Being in itself, God, Nature, and that other things are solely its accidents.
5 "First chapter: On a Dialectic of Pure Practical Reason in General."
6 Ibid., p. 87.
7 The category of totality (*Totalität*) corresponds to singular judgement and not to universal judgement.
8 Ibid., p. 168.
9 Ibid., p. 88. [This has also been translated as "the Sovereign Good", which is the term which is most common in the English-language translations of Lacan's commentaries on Kant.]
10 Ibid., pp. 88–89.
11 This is what Lacan does not do in his text "Kant with Sade", as we shall see further on. Alenka Zupančič, *Ethics of the Real: Kant, Lacan*, London, Verso Books, 2000, follows this interpretation (which devalues Kant).
12 "Second chapter: On the Dialectic of Pure Reason in Determining the Concept of the Highest Good."
13 Ibid., p. 89.
14 Ibid., p. 90.
15 Ibid.
16 Ibid., p. 91.
17 Ibid., p. 92.
18 Ibid., p. 93.
19 Thus, Fénelon's problematic of pure love posed "the possibility of an ill will within God (of the divine *Grimmigkeit* Jakob Boehme spoke of), which for Kant was absolutely impossible" (Jacques Le Brun, *Le pur amour de Platon à Lacan*, Paris, Seuil, 2002, p. 229). We shall see how this hypothesis (divine *Grimmigkeit*) returns in Lacan in "Kant with Sade", *Écrits*, p. 652.
20 Kant, *Critique of Practical Reason*, op. cit., p. 94.
21 Ibid.

22 Ibid., p. 95.
23 Ibid., p. 98.
24 Ibid., pp. 98–99.
25 Ibid., p. 100.
26 Ibid., p. 101.
27 Ibid.
28 Ibid., p. 102.
29 Ibid., p. 103n.
30 Ibid., p. 104.
31 Ibid., p. 108.
32 Ibid., p. 109.
33 Ibid., pp. 113–114.
34 Ibid., p. 56.
35 [Translator's note: "*tenir pour vrai*". Gregor translates *führwahrhalten* as "assent".]
36 Ibid., p. 114.
37 Ibid., p. 115.
38 Cf. Hallucinatory psychosis, of which the canonical example, in Freud (in "The Neuro-Psychoses of Defence", S.E. III, p. 59ff), is that of a bereaved mother who continues to walk around for years with piece of wood in her arms, which is supposed to represent her lost infant child.
39 Ibid., p. 118.

Chapter 7

How to promote the principle of the moral law[1] (and of jouissance)

The method of pure speculative reason would show how to master all of the diacritical breadth of the work of reason in the field of cognition.[2] The doctrine of the method of pure practical reason must make clear the way in which the moral law becomes *subjectively* practical, how it can and must have an "*influence* on its maxims".[3] As we have already seen, this influence is at stake in the passage from the principle of practical reason (first chapter of the analytic of practical reason) to "respect" as the incentive of pure practical reason (third chapter) by means of the Good (second chapter of the analytic of practical reason. The question of methodology is now to show how the *presentation* of pure virtue can "have *more power* over the human mind [. . .] than all the deceptive allurement of enjoyment and, in general, everything that may be counted as happiness, or even all threats of pain and troubles can produce".[4] How can we tip the balance not on the side of the inclinations, but on the side of the moral law?

Methodology [or "the doctrine of the method"] will first "[make] use of this propensity of reason to enter with pleasure upon even the most subtle examination of [. . .] practical questions".[5] But if reason questions the moral value of such and such an action, this is not to put them forward as examples to be imitated. "It is altogether contrapurposive to set before children, as a model, actions as noble, magnanimous, meritorious, thinking that one can captivate them by inspiring enthusiasm for such actions."[6] It is rather a case of taking advantage of concrete actions as occasions in which to return to the movement of pure practical reason, of its questioning, its reflection, and its autonomy. The quality of the "examples" does not matter – it is a question of using them as a pretext for the exercise of practical reason and its critique.

The method first of all consists in

> making appraisal of actions by moral laws a natural occupation and, as it were, a habit accompanying all our own free actions as well as our observation of those by others, and of sharpening it by asking first whether the action *conforms with the moral law*, and with which law.[7]

After this first exercise, which consists in becoming used to and practising the principle, "the *second* exercise" of the methodology is to "draw attention [. . .] to

DOI: 10.4324/9781003055662-13

the purity of will", firstly as a negative perfection, meaning to become aware in the pain of the opposition to the inclinations, but then as a positive perfection, in becoming conscious of inner freedom (as freed from the world of appearances) and of the respect it deserves. "The law of duty [. . .] finds easier access through the *respect for ourselves* in the consciousness of our freedom."[8]

***

Notes

1 "Second part of the *Critique of Practical Reason*: Doctrine of the method of pure practical reason."
2 Certain pitfalls must first be avoided at the beginning (discipline): it must be shown that reason has a positive aim (canon), and the structure (architectonic) of reason must be teased out and inscribed in a history.
3 Ibid., p. 121.
4 Ibid.
5 Ibid., p. 123.
6 Ibid., p. 125.
7 Ibid., p. 127.
8 Ibid., p. 128.

Conclusion of the doctrine of method

"Two things fill the mind with ever new and increasing admiration and reverence, the more often and steadily one reflects on them; *the starry heavens above me and the moral law within me.*" One of these admirable things lowers the value of the human being; the other raises and magnifies it.

The first admirable and venerable thing goes together with a radical humiliation of humanity; it "annihilates, as it were, my importance as an *animal creature*, which after it has been for a short time provided with vital force [. . .] must give back to the planet [. . .] the matter from which it came". From this viewpoint, I am only a minuscule finite object within the immensity of the things in the universe which are offered to pure speculative reason. This first thing inflicts on the human being in general a radical narcissistic wound, the whole importance of which Freud had gauged.[1]

The second admirable and venerable thing "raises my worth [. . .], the moral law reveals to me a life independent of animality and even of the whole sensible world". From this point of view, I am the subject of pure practical reason, and the end which pure practical reason gives my existence "[is] not restricted to the conditions and boundaries of this life but [reaches] into the infinite".[2]

Admiration for the starry sky and the moral law has been cited a thousand and one times. What is important, however, is not admiration or veneration for those two things, but the fact that they give rise to reflection (*Nachdenken*), to inquiry (*Nachforschung*), and to the exercise of reason in its autonomy. Without reflection, the contemplation of the starry sky would end up in astrology (*Sterndeutung*) and its basic determinism. Without reflection, blind obedience to a moral law would end up in fanaticism (*Schwärmerei*) and superstition (*Aberglauben*).

Taking care not to advance "otherwise than on the track of a previously well-considered method",[3] reason has known an "incomparably happier outcome" to that of astrology, namely Newton's physics. That paragon of reflection, beginning from the first admirable thing, namely the starry sky and the humiliation which arises from it, "can recommend that we take the same path in treating of the moral predispositions of our nature and can give us hope of a similarly good (*gut*) outcome", this time beginning from the second admirable thing, namely the

DOI: 10.4324/9781003055662-14

moral law, arriving at "incomparably happier outcome" to that of fanaticism and superstition.

This may lead us not only to understanding the unconscious and the jouissance principle, which is essential to it, but most of all to undertake a renewal of psychoanalytic practice.

Notes

1 It is at the root of humanity's three narcissistic wounds noted by Freud. The first humiliation suffered by humanity's naïve self-love occurred "when they learnt that our earth was not the centre of the universe" (Copernicus). This is also recognised by Kant (notably in the Preface to the second edition of the Kant, *Critique of Pure Reason*, op. cit., p. 17, Bxix). The two further humiliations of the self-love mentioned by Freud occur after Kant's death (1804). With Darwin's *The Origin of Species* (1859), "biological research destroyed man's supposedly privileged place in creation and proved his descent from the animal kingdom and his ineradicable animal nature". And with the discovery of the unconscious, the human ego must realise "that it is not even master in its own house" (Sigmund Freud, *Introductory Lectures on Psycho-Analysis: The Standard Edition of the Complete Psychological Works of Sigmund Freud, (1916–1917)*, Volumes 15 and 16, London, Hogarth Press, 1963, pp. 283–284). Nonetheless, on the one hand, where the second humiliation is concerned, Kant explicitly refers to man as an "*animal creature*". On the other hand, for the third humiliation, the *Critique of Practical Reason* (more precisely speaking, in the conclusion of the doctrine of method), does point out that I am nothing in comparison to the third principle (of morality), which prefigures the workings of the unconscious.
2 Ibid., p. 129.
3 Ibid., p. 130.

Section II

A reading of Lacan

How can we remain faithful to the way the unconscious works? The unconscious operates according to the pleasure principle *and* according to the jouissance principle ("beyond the pleasure principle", which is more of a "short of"). The first overlaps with, wipes out, and represses the second, whereas the latter contains the specific nature of the operation of the unconscious.

The opposition between these two principles only recapitulates the opposition between the principle of the quest for happiness and the principle of the moral law, between the pragmatic principle and the practical principle, or again between the hedonistic pre-Kantian moral philosophies and Kant's moral philosophy of virtue.

How can the Kantian advance of the moral law be given its full weight in order to allow the emergence of the jouissance principle specific to the unconscious? How can the scales be tipped towards the side of the moral law and the jouissance of the unconscious, while it is rather the search for happiness and pleasure which dominate the landscape?

The method of practical reason begins with the principle of the moral law to then determine what the Good is and finally ends with the mobilisation of sensibility towards the moral law (respect). This pathway is never finished with once and for all. It must be made and re-made, and it is only in repetition that it becomes effective.

The method of psychoanalysis, which is none other than the method of the unconscious, should give its rightful place to the specific principle of the unconscious, the jouissance principle. This pathway is never finished with once and for all; it is only in repetition that it becomes effective.

The method of psychoanalysis is thus a recapitulation, a repetition of the method of pure reason. From this double pathway, two admirable and venerable things will be retained. On the one hand, *that which is*: "the starry sky above me" is none other than the sign of the generalised humiliation of humanity's naïve self-love. In the order of knowledge, knowing, sensibility and pleasure, I am worth next to nothing [*je ne suis que quatre fois rien*]. On the other hand, *that which should be* – "the moral law within me" – points towards an extraordinary power of creation (out of the "ordinary" associated with pleasure). In the order of making proper to the unconscious, which is not, but which *should* be, it should be to give things a new form, a new creation from nothing.

Lacan's seminar, *The Ethics of Psychoanalysis* (1959–1960), takes full measure of man's narcissistic humiliation: I am basically nothing not only in the face of the real of the universe, but more radically in the face of The Thing (*Das Ding*), which is absolutely unknowable to me, in the face of the *Real* which completely eludes me. It is from this emptiness that the Kantian moral question which must shed light on the ethical workings of the unconscious takes its place.

The text "Kant with Sade" (1962–1963) first takes what Kant regards as the second admirable and venerable thing, the moral law, into consideration, to give it its full value in sensibility by the intermediary of a reading of Sade. Sade's *Philosophy in the Bedroom* (1795) "yields the truth of the *Critique*"[1] (the *Critique of Practical Reason*, 1788). It is supposed to reveal it in sensibility.

***

By "*lecture de Lacan*", we understand both the reading made by Lacan of Kant's *Groundwork* and *Critique of Practical Reason* and the reading which we make of Lacan reading Kant's writings, though we have already read the same Kantian texts. In the course of this enlightened reading of Lacan's texts, we will be led to take a certain number of deviations and misunderstandings of the part of Lacan towards precisely these Kantian texts into consideration. Let us note, among other things: the primordial and explicit place of the principle as a principle in Kant is erased in Lacan's presentation (but the function of the principle as a principle is most probably taken up again through the introduction of the Thing and the object *a*). The moral law centred around autonomy in Kant is presented as a purely formal universality in Lacan (which allows him to insist *a contrario* on the synthetic side and on the enunciation of the law in Sade). The place of the secondary good in Kant is primordial in Lacan's reading of it (notably to oppose Sade and evil to it). The place of basic respect in Kant is obscured in favour of pain in Lacan's presentation (pain allows the reconciliation of Kant and Sade). The value of the transcendental dialectic centred first of all on the moral law is presented from the perspective of happiness in Lacan. Examples, in Kant, are little more than occasions for illustrating the main moral reflection, whereas in Lacan they function as a basic element of argumentation.

From all these deviations and misunderstandings, we will remember that Lacan presents quite a loose and subtly out of step version of Kantian moral philosophy. His reading, however, corresponds quite well to the common opinion of Kant (including the opinion that Lacanian psychoanalyst have in general about Kant, most often without having read him closely).

In relation to this obvious gap between Kant's text and Lacan's reading, there are several possible options. First, recognising *Lacan's* immense amount of work compels us to trust him. Lacan would thus have corrected what had needed to be corrected and reading Kant would have become useless or obsolete. Second, recognising *Kant's* philosophy takes precedence, and we should simply reject Lacan's reading, which would fail some kind of university examination on Kant's moral philosophy. Third, we must give an account of *Kant and Lacan* and of the *gap* which exists between Kantian morality and its common and Lacanian reading. What should be done with this gap? Here, two sub-positions are possible. The first one consists of an *observation*: one may remark that Lacan generally subverts the borrowings he makes from linguistics, philosophy, mathematics, or whatever author it may be, and it is always in an innovative and creative direction – armed with this observation, we will simply be able to rely on the Lacanian text alone. The second sub-position consists in a *task*, which involves analysing the gaps, deviations, and misunderstandings to restore Kant's radical positions as well as Lacan's propositions. This not in order to end up separating out one group from the other, but rather in order to put them into tension in their common structure. This is the work we undertake with Lacan's reading of Kant.

The value of this work is completely in line with Kant's doctrine of the method of practical reason: to bring the moral law to light (the jouissance principle), to give a sensible access to the invention and the exercise of freedom. This work, which is irreplaceable because it is the exercise of the structure at play in practical reason as well as in the unconscious, will lead us to the clarification of the fundamental principle of psychoanalysis: the jouissance principle specific to the unconscious.

Note

1 Lacan, "Kant with Sade", in *Écrits: The First Complete Edition in English*, New York, Norton, 2006.

Part I

The Ethics of Psychoanalysis (1959–1960)

The real

Chapter 8

Critique of "ethics" centred on happiness and perfection

"Ethics" centred on happiness

Following on from Seminar VI, which was devoted to desire, Seminar VII had to clarify ethics as an ethics of *desire*. But how is desire to be understood? The central thesis of *The Interpretation of Dreams*, "a dream is the (disguised) fulfilment of a (repressed or suppressed) wish", could mean that the work of the unconscious quite simply operates in the direction of the pleasure principle. This quest for pleasure in any case presupposes *prudence*, because one person's pleasure is not another's and pleasure in one part of the psyche (the unconscious) is not pleasure in another part (the preconscious and conscious). This conception of ethics polarised towards pleasure and moderated by prudence on the level of individuals is that of Aristotle's *Nicomachean Ethics*. This same conception of ethics (pleasure and prudence), transposed *to the level of psychic loci*, may also seem to be that of Freud's *Interpretation of Dreams* (we shall see that this is not at all the case). In this sense, psychoanalytic ethics would aim to liberate desire from what is repressing or suppressing it.[1] The ethics of psychoanalysis would thus come within the framework of a general quest for pleasure or happiness.

The Aristotelian conception of ethics is still prevalent today: it would suffice to follow the path of one's desires with prudence (Aristotle's *phronesis*, Kant's *Klugheit*), that is, to take into account their consequences, the ins and outs they involve. It presents itself as natural and therefore has nothing to teach people (the prudent are already immersed in ethics and the imprudent do not, in any case, listen to the advice they might be given). *The Nicomachean Ethics*, just like current, contemporary ethics, is not, therefore, addressed to individuals, but to lawmakers who, through the laws of the state, may favour the exercise of this prudence at the social level. It is a political ethics which aims to set aside all that might oppose the reign of a well-proportioned happiness. It dismisses a certain number of human phenomena as monstrous aberrations from human nature,[2] notably many sexual desires, as well as the morbidity of transgression, the ferocious superego, the essential guilt which undermines humanity independently of any real transgression.

DOI: 10.4324/9781003055662-17

"Ethics" centred on perfection

Now, psychoanalysis does not follow this general Aristotelian tendency. It does not aim to carefully re-organise happiness and, most of all, it does not put either sexuality or basic guilt to one side. On the contrary, it makes them its central concern. Is this in order to guide the sexual aberrations towards sexual perfection, to erase basic guilt, and to be guided towards perfection in general?

Sexuality and the superego would have to be led in the right direction. The ferocious superego could then make way for a good superego, a beneficent Ideal which simultaneously takes into account reality, the sexual drives, and the Id, under the control of an Ego which provides them with structure. A certain psychoanalytic moral philosophy focused on three types of perfection: the ideal of *genital love* as the final aim of a correct form of sexuality in which the subject would be perfectly fulfilled, the ideal of *authenticity* as a perfect alignment of what the subject says and does with what they fundamentally are, and the ideal of *autonomy* as the independence of the subject from everything that might disturb his perfection. Have we not tried to grasp the moral law at the heart of the unconscious and jouissance at the heart of nascent sexuality in an attempt to allow it to blossom in its full structure, of which *genital love* would be the image? Does not both the Kantian moral law as well as jouissance aim for *authenticity*, the alignment of the subject with his kernel of jouissance? Do the *autonomy* of the moral law and of jouissance not imply putting to one side, not letting oneself be disturbed by the inclinations of the pleasure principle?

Perhaps. But when "genital love", "authenticity", and "autonomy" are proposed as perfection or as *ideals*, they become aims determining the ethics or the morals of psychoanalysis. Now, as we have seen, acting according to aims, as noble as they might be, is always to act *in fine* according to pleasure and happiness. The aim as aim is in fact presented as a reality external to moral action and to the process of morality. The true critique of the ideals of psychoanalysis (genital love, authenticity, autonomy) has to do with the essence of the ideal presented as something which would exist in reality independently of us and not as a part of the subjective architectonic as Freud had already presented it in his introduction to narcissism.[3]

Critique of realism

To understand the major difference between, on the one hand, these false ethics centred on pleasure ("happiness") or on ideals of perfection ("genital love", "authenticity", "autonomy") and, on the other hand, psychoanalytic ethics, strictly speaking, Lacan suggests taking stock of what took place in the intervening years between Aristotle and Freud. We would think of Kant straightaway. Lacan, however, introduces Jeremy Bentham's theory of fictions. Our thought does not solely operate based on given empirical things. To understand and act with our thought, we create for ourselves fictive entities, which it would be impossible to find as such in reality. "Happiness", "genital love", "authenticity", and "autonomy" are, in fact, such fictions, which are in no way realistic. For Aristotle, happiness and pleasure were presupposed to be ready-made in nature – they were waiting for us in reality. With Bentham's theory, we must take stock of the fact that these are only fictions, which may certainly be useful and effective, even though we can never encounter them as such in reality. Before Bentham, Kant had already denounced transcendental realism, as well as the impossibility of founding a true moral philosophy based on realism.[4] We are never in touch with a reality in itself (pleasure, genital love, authenticity, autonomy), but rather with fictions (Bentham) or with phenomena which appear to be "pleasure", "genital love", etc. We are therefore always in an unpayable debt in relation to what would be reality. This is the knot of guilt, the superego and jouissance.

Notes

1 "Freedom" is understood here in the ordinary and everyday sense of the liberation of drive tendencies which obtain pleasure, contrary to Kantian freedom, which should be understood as productive of the moral law (and of jouissance).
2 Let us note that the first of Freud's *Three Essays on Sexuality* (1905) is devoted to the sexual aberrations. It is on these that the whole of the theory of sexuality rests, much more than on a normalised sexuality.
3 Sigmund Freud, *On Narcissism: An Introduction* in *The Standard Edition of the Complete Psychological Works of Sigmund Freud*, Volume 14, London, Hogarth Press, 1957. See Fierens, *The Soul of Narcissism*, Oxon and New York, Routledge, 2019.
4 Cf. Fierens and Pierobon, *Les pièges du réalisme, Kant et Lacan*, op. cit.

Chapter 9

The hole in reality, the real and the thing

Reality, free of all fictions and of what they are accompanied by in their phenomenal appearances, escapes us completely – it is a great void. The Thing (*das Ding*) itself is fundamentally and definitively unsayable. Lacan's genius consists of going and fishing out *das Ding* in Freud, where it is not found in the sense as he understands it and in giving *das Ding*, the exact sense of something fundamentally and definitively unsayable.

In the *Project for a Scientific Psychology* (1895), Freud examines the question of knowing how an infant is able to recover the breast even though it regularly presents itself under different aspects (position in space and other sensorial differences). In the breast or in the person who takes care of the child (*Nebenmensch*), Freud therefore distinguishes that which always presents itself in the same way and that which presents itself in a variable manner. The constant and invariant characteristics of the breast constitute, according to Freud, *das Ding*. They have no need to enter into a process of understanding. The Thing is not judged (*unverstanden*) because it has no need to be judged in order to be understood. It is fundamentally constant and therefore immediately recognisable. The variable characteristics of the breast or of the mother, on the other hand, call for judgement and correct understanding on the part of the infant in order to be able to recognise the source of satisfaction despite variations in its presentation.[1]

Ingeniously, Lacan misunderstands Freud at the same time as he introduces something that will succeed in giving a full sense to the ethics of psychoanalysis. Lacan turns Freud's *das Ding* completely on its head, making it no longer that which is always identical to itself and which poses no problem, but that which *resists* all understanding. *Das Ding* is set apart as a foreign, unattainable, and real term around which the entire movement of representation (*Vorstellung*) and the symbolic revolves.[2] *Das Ding*, as Lacan understood it in order to make his Real from it, is not the Freudian thing which does not pose any problem, it is rather the Kantian thing in itself, *Das Ding an Sich*, the thing independent of all possibility of experience, independent of all processes of representation and understanding.

The Lacanian invention and discovery of *Das Ding* overturn all ethics centred on happiness, including the ethics that would be centred on the highest good as the ultimate pleasure. This is at the same time the discovery of the last reason for

DOI: 10.4324/9781003055662-18

the prohibition of incest. It is to maintain the place of the place of the Thing as unknowable and incomprehensible that it must be said that the Mother is untouchable, forbidden.

> The step taken by Freud at the level of the pleasure principle is to show us that there is no Sovereign Good – that the Sovereign Good, which is *das Ding*, which is the mother, is also the object of incest, is a forbidden good, and that there is no other good. Such is the foundation of the moral law as turned on its head by Freud.[3]

In this quotation, the moral law centred on happiness is turned upside down. The aforementioned "good" in general does not mean the good deduced from the moral principle (as in Kant). It is both "the pleasant" and "the highest good". It is the supremely good object perfectly fulfilling the demand for happiness, which is *forbidden*. The turning on its head carried out by Freud, according to Lacan, is one in which the ultimate aim of the ethics of the pleasant and of the pleasure principle are turned on their heads, by a *prohibition*.

Without this overthrow of the ethics of happiness (Aristotle), without this overthrow which opens up a place for a new "moral law", it is impossible to make progress in the question of psychoanalytic ethics. The overturning of the ethics centred on happiness prepared the way for a very different ethics: the *Critique of Practical Reason* must be read, as it is the central reference of the seminar.[4] Taking up again the opposition between the *Gute* and the *Wohl*, Lacan immediately situates the *Critique of Pure Reason* alongside *Beyond the Pleasure Principle*. *Das Gute* and *das Ding* cannot be thought within the field of the pleasure principle and of the deterministic causality which governs it. They thus open a field or a question beyond the pleasure principle while also shedding light on the workings of the unconscious. *Das Gute* introduces "at the level of the unconscious something that ought to oblige us to ask once again the Kantian question of the *causa noumenon*",[5] in other words of causality on the side of the noumenon, that is, the causality of freedom.[6] "*Das Ding* presents itself at the level of unconscious experience as that which already makes the law."

This law may appear to be "a capricious and arbitrary law, the law of the oracle, the law of signs in which the subject receives no guarantee from anywhere". It appears as such (a capricious and arbitrary law), not because the subject can decide everything, but based on the fact that it is determined at the level of the *unconscious*, which eludes all explanation ("the subject receives no guarantee from anywhere"). Despite this appearance, it is no less a properly moral law (rather than a physical law), which precedes any distinction between Good and Evil. "This is why the *Gute*, at the level of the unconscious, is also at bottom the bad object that Kleinian theory is concerned with. Although it must be said that at this level *das Ding* is not distinguished as bad."[7] With this lack of distinction, we can see that *das Ding* does not appear at all as the "concept of an object of practical reason", like the good or the bad (chapter II of the analytic of practical reason in Kant).

The Lacanian Thing must be situated beyond good and evil, in other words, with the "principle of practical reason" (chapter I of the same analytic). As soon as we speak of *das Ding* in terms of good or evil, what we say appears to be a *false start*, because it short-circuits the unsayable of *das Ding* from which good and bad derive. Speaking in terms of good or evil is a false premise (*prôton pseudos*) which invalidates moral reasoning and unconscious reasoning in its entirety.[8]

Notes

1 "As a consequence, the perceptual complexes are divided into a constant, non-understood *(unverstanden),* part-the thing-and a changing, understandable (*verständlich*), one – the attribute or movement of the thing." (Freud, "Project for a Scientific Psychology" in S. Freud (1950 [1895]). *The Standard Edition of the Complete Psychological Works of Sigmund Freud, Volume I (1886–1899): Pre-Psycho-Analytic Publications and Unpublished Drafts*, p. 382. The non-understood (as it is constant and does not, therefore, pose a problem) must not be confused with the incomprehensible, what cannot be understood.
2 Lacan, *The Ethics of Psychoanalysis 1959–1960: The Seminar of Jacques Lacan Book VII*, edited by Jacques-Alain Miller, translated with notes by Dennis Porter, London, Routledge, 1992, pp. 57–58.
3 Ibid., p. 70.
4 "It is impossible for us to make any progress in this seminar relative to the questions posed by the ethics of psychoanalysis if you do not have this book as a reference point." (Ibid., p. 72).
5 Ibid., p. 73.
6 Lacan carefully avoids the term "freedom" here, because of a possible confusion with the ideology of the liberation of instincts. Kantian freedom has nothing to do with this kind of liberation.
7 [Ibid. Translation modified].
8 The *prôton pseudos* in psychoanalysis classically refers to the case of Emma referred to in Freud's *Entwurf*. This woman had a phobia about going into shops on her own. She connected the story to something which happened to her when she was twelve: some shop assistants had laughed at her. Behind this screen memory was hidden the real trauma: at eight years of age a grocer had groped her genitals. (Freud, "Project for a Scientific Psychology", op. cit., pp. 353–354). In this story, the first error (*prôton pseudos*) consists precisely in being placed at the level of good or evil, whereas it must rather first be related to the absolutely unassimilable Thing that is the arising of sexuality in this trauma experienced at the age of eight.

Chapter 10

The universality of the moral law

As we have seen, Kant's analytic of practical reason begins by excluding all practical principles which presuppose an *object* as determinant of the will.[1] The object is in itself subject to the passions determined by the pleasure principle; the object is in itself "pathological" in the Kantian sense. If the principle of the moral law cannot be in any case an object or *matter*, it can only exist in *form*.[2]

How can this form be understood?

The reduction of this form to a pure abstract formalism is the most frequently accepted one. In this way, Adorno and Horkheimer, in their critique of the Enlightenment (1944) see totalitarianism and fascism as consequences of Kantian formalism by means of the link constituted by Sadean formalism.[3] "According to Adorno, reason placed, from Kant on, within a regime of pure functionality, becomes the support of the most terrifying form of reason."[4]

However, as much from Kant's point of view as from Freud's, "form" does not in any way boil down to an abstract formalism. From the Kantian point of view, the impossibility of determining the moral law by its matter introduces the universality of the moral law not as a pure formalism, but as an *autonomous creation* of the free law-giving subject (the first formula of the moral imperative does not occur without the autonomy of the moral law). From the Freudian point of view, the operation of the unconscious outside of thinking, calculation, and judgement ("it does not think, calculate or judge in any way at all") does not mean that it is content to be purely formal, but that it *gives* things another form. Once more, this involves a *creation*.

Nevertheless, at the moment of analysing the first formula of the categorical imperative expressed according to universality ("So act that the maxim of your will could always hold at the same time as a principle in a giving of universal law"), Lacan does not take into account the creation of form, neither law-giving autonomy (Kant), nor the invention of a new form by the unconscious (Freud).

It is in starting out from form as reduced to a purely formalist and abstract universality, that Lacan can propose an "update", "a renewal or updating of the Kantian imperative" according to advances in mathematics, more precisely in computing. Just as if he had been thinking of having to revise Kant's transcendental aesthetics according to the non-Euclidean geometries which had appeared after Kant, he here proposes a formula which uses the language of computing: "Never act except in such a way that your action may be programmed."[5] Programming corresponds to an abstract universal form, but it completely lacks the principle of *giving things a new form* independently of matter. But "act in such a way that your action may be programmed" can in no way replace the true Kantian imperative. We have seen how, in the *Groundwork*, the universality of the categorical imperative becomes clearer in relying on the universality of the laws of nature and on the *creation* of laws. Here, due to the forgetting of the *creation* or the *donation* of universal form, Lacan (falsely) interprets the Kantian imperative "as the law of a nature in which we are called on to live". Now the Kantian imperative implies, on the contrary, a *will* which would give form. It is the will which must establish this universal law of nature, it is the will which is lawgiving.[6]

In putting to one side the form-*giving* implied by the autonomy of the moral law, we are happy to think about universality by proposing a catalogue of different ways it might look: the universality of programming, the universality of a utopian republic, like the one proposed by Sade in the philosophical text, "Frenchmen, one more effort if you wish to be republicans", inserted in *Philosophy in the Bedroom*.

Among all of these formalist and abstract universalities, the universality of Sade's republic has the advantage of taking the opposite course to what might have been put forward in the others. It is through this opposite course that Sade "opens wide the flood gates that in imagination he proposes as the horizon of our desire; everyone is invited to pursue to the limit the demands of his lust, and to realize them".[7] With this conception of lust pushed to the limit, Lacan proposes as Sade's maxim for our action "the right to enjoy any other person whatsoever as the instrument of our pleasure". Two differences between the Kantian maxim and the Sadean one can be noted straightaway: the first is a duty (an imperative) and is *independent* of pleasure, the second is a *right* (which can be exercised or not) and is completely *dependent* on pleasure. With these differences, these are the central questions of duty and pleasure which must be posed again from scratch.

Kantian duty had been presented under the aspect of universality and autonomy. All Lacan retains of it is its abstract formal universality. He takes out its creative or synthetic moment (autonomy which *gives* form). He had found in Sade early a universality which wishes to be and affirms itself as concrete and pinned to it an act which opens up desire and, alongside it, its creative and synthetic power.

However, Lacan spots that these universalities – Kant's as well as Sade's – give rise to *pain*. From this point of view, "Kant is of the same opinion as Sade".[8] It shall be noted, however, that Lacan abstracts pain from the sole feeling provoked by pure reason in Kant, that is, the respect which implies pain (the pain connected to the moral law is only a correlate of respect). On the other hand, in Sade, the limit of pleasure (on the torturer's side) accompanied by the limit of pain (on the victim's side) remains understood in the sense of "forcing an access to the Thing". Such is the importance of pain in Sade: it would supposedly give sensible access to the Thing (the "Freudian" thing which in fact corresponds to the Kantian thing in itself). It is the Thing which polarises the ethics of psychoanalysis for Lacan.

Notes

1 Kant, *Critique of Practical Reason*, op. cit., p. 19.
2 Ibid., p. 24.
3 Horkheimer and Adorno, *Dialectic of Enlightenment: Philosophical Fragments*, Stanford, Stanford University Press, 2002, pp. 68–69.
4 Marty, *Pourquoi le XXé siècle a-t-il pris Sade au sérieux?* [Why did the 20th century take Sade seriously?], Paris, Seuil, 2011, p. 45. In a similar way to the demonisation of Kantian formalism, Marty reports that, in Jean-Luc Godard's film *La Chinoise* (1967), "beside the cover of Michel Foucault's *Les Mots et les choses*, an inscription:

> "Immanuel Kant, the <photo of Eichmann> of Western philosophy", can be seen on a panel dedicated to the enemies of the people."

(Ibid., p. 44)

5 Lacan, *The Ethics of Psychoanalysis*, op. cit., p. 77.
6 "*So act as if the maxim of your action were to become by your will a* universal law of nature." (*Groundwork of the Metaphysics of Morals*, op. cit., p. 34).
7 Lacan, *The Ethics of Psychoanalysis*, op. cit., p. 79.
8 Ibid., p. 80.

Chapter 11

The human being's essential relationship to the Thing

The Ten Commandments, commandments of speech, were promulgated "by something that announces itself in the following form: 'I am what I am'".[1] They stem from the Real, the unsayable, and are on the side of the Thing. At the end of the lesson of 23 December 1959, Lacan lingers over the last two commandments, "Thou shalt not bear false witness against thy neighbour" and "Thou shalt not covet".

"Thou shalt not lie [or bear false witness against thy neighbour." The unconscious supposes the Real, *the Thing*, the unsayable, and the contribution of the unsayable means that what is said will always be more or less deceptive. That which is said always has to do with a *prôton pseudos*, an unavoidable primary misunderstanding. "Thou shalt not lie" does not command that we avoid this primary misunderstanding or primary "lie". This would be completely impossible. The commandment demands, on the contrary, a positive act; that is, to start out from the Thing to produce a word which creates, giving a new form to things, unique to the unconscious. The "thou shalt not lie" "has as its function to withdraw the subject of enunciation from that which is enunciated",[2] that is, to extract the subject of enunciation and to make it speak from the Thing, which is called "not lying". With this commandment, the speaking subject is already engaged in the enunciation of the moral law and therefore in the operation of the unconscious.

"Thou shalt not covet" deals with all those objects which have a relationship with *das Ding*, that is one's neighbour's house, his wife, his servant, his donkey, etc.

> None of these objects exists without having the closest relationship with [. . .] *das Ding* insofar as it is the very correlative of the law of speech in its most primitive point of origin [. . .]. The covetousness that is in question is not addressed to anything that I might desire but to a thing that is my neighbour's Thing. It is to the extent that the commandment in question preserves the distance from the Thing as founded by speech itself that it assumes its value.[3]

The Law is not at all, however, the same thing as the Thing. The Law is known – it is the *Faktum* Kant speaks about – but the Thing is unknowable as such.

DOI: 10.4324/9781003055662-20

What is the relationship between the known law and the Thing, which is unknowable as such?

> [. . .] I can only know of the Thing by means of the Law. In effect, I would not have had the idea to covet it if the Law hadn't said: "Thou shalt not covet it." Lacan refers here to St. Paul's Letter to the Romans.[4] The covetousness at play in the Sadean ethics and the coveted object as placeholder of the Thing (which cannot, properly speaking, be known) appear, therefore, only as *consequences* of the law. In this line of reasoning, backed up by the quote from Saint Paul, Lacan does no other than to take up Kant's reasoning about the moral law and freedom: if freedom and the moral law refer reciprocally to each other, it must be said that the consciousness or knowledge of the moral law is the necessary condition for knowledge of freedom.[5] Without the moral law, I would never have encountered freedom.
>
> In Freud, the moral law appears in the form of the Superego, the essential Superego which does not operate according to the sins which have been committed. The moral conscience thus, says Lacan, "shows itself to be the more demanding the more refined it becomes, crueller and crueller even as we offend it less and less, more and more fastidious as we force it, by abstaining from acts, to go and seek us out at the most intimate levels of our impulses or desires."[6] It is from the awareness of the moral law, the moral conscience, the Superego, that we may know freedom (Kant), the coveted object (Saint Paul), the Thing and the Real (Lacan).
>
> But what is the relationship between the Thing and the object? How might we reconcile the concrete phenomenal object and the unsayable noumenal Thing? How can the concrete object be retained while opening up to the Thing? The destiny or vicissitude of the drives known as *sublimation* retains an unaltered object cathexis, but it changes the aim (*Ziel*) of the drive. The drive passes from a specifically sexually aim to a non-sexual aim. We should ask whether a "non-sexual aim" is still an "aim", strictly speaking, that is, an external purpose. Because the change of aim at play in sublimation abandons the ordinary sexual (and external) aim to reveal the presence of the Thing, *das Ding*, in the encounter with the object. Sublimation "raises an object [. . .] to the dignity of the Thing."[7]

The "revelation of the Thing beyond the object" implies the surpassing of the opposition of Good and Evil, which can indeed be seen in the art object and in courtly love (*Minne*). To grasp what is at stake in the Thing and the Real (which completely eludes the symbolic), we cannot content ourselves with the ideal and the good, even if this good appears as the ordinary aim of everyday practice. To balance out the Good (which cannot reveal the Thing to us), Lacan here convokes Evil. "The symbolic here is united with the diabolic",[8] says Lacan, and he cites Luther, "You are that waste matter which falls into the world from the devil's anus".[9] It is not enough, therefore, to characterise psychical causality, which takes freedom into account, as a noumenal causality, "*causa noumenon*".[10] Because this noumenal causality in Kant, according to Lacan's conception of it, too much calls to mind the Good (rather than freedom). This noumenal causality, seen as too benevolent, must therefore be counterbalanced by a causality of suffering, of Evil, as a "*causa pathomenon*".[11] The presentation of *das Ding* thus oscillates between Good (a presentation drawn from Kant) and Evil (a presentation drawn from Luther, and then from Sade, as we shall see).

The Thing is not the Law, and sublimation is not ethics. With sublimation, we "have deviated a little from the fundamental problem, that is, the ethical problem".[12] "In order to refocus our discussion onto the level of ethics, one could hardly do better than to refer to [. . .] the Kantian perspective."[13] Sublimation and the level or plane of ethics are both viewed by Lacan from the angle of *weighing up*, on the one hand, the everyday world of appearances, which belongs to the symbolic and, on the other hand, the Thing (sublimation) and the Law (ethics) which belong to the Real. A weighing-up of incommensurable things, because the Real should always end up carrying more weight than the symbolic (cf. Pascal's wager). According to Lacan, the Kantian formula for duty "is another way of making one's weight felt". It must be shown, again according to Lacan, "how reason may make its weight felt". From this point of view, Lacan's weighing-up comes well within the scope of Kant's doctrine of the method of practical reason.[14] The doctrine of method in fact involves showing how the *presentation* of pure virtue can "have *more power* over the human mind [. . .] than all the deceptive allurement of enjoyment and, in general, everything that may be counted as happiness, or even all threats of pain and troubles can produce".[15]

It is to "make us feel the weight of the ethical principle pure and simple" that Lacan invokes the double parable that Kant made use of for a completely different purpose, that is, to support the demonstration according to which consciousness of the moral law comes before faith in freedom.[16] In contrast to the Kantian context, *according to Lacan*, in this double parable Kant wished to "show us the prevalence of duty against all opposition".[17] Intending to "show us the prevalence of duty against all opposition" really is Kantian: it is the intention of the doctrine of method. But the *examples* raised in the double parable do not in any way aim to show us the prevalence of duty, but rather to uphold a *reflection* on the moral law. More precisely, in the case of our double parable, it involves an illustration of the fact that the consciousness of freedom is always dependent on the moral law. Despite this Kantian viewpoint, Lacan understands them directly within the point of view of a weighing-up which would make us feel the weight of the ethical principle.[18]

Let us remember that in the first example or the first parable, there is in fact no ethical principle in Kant; therefore, there is no place to make itself felt. As a consequence, there is no freedom either. The lustful man in front of the bedroom of his desires is not at all confronted with the moral law which ought to master his inclinations. In the Kantian parable, he just measures his passion against its consequences (the scaffold), without the moral law intervening in any way. It is not a question here of either the moral law, or sublimation, or of the Thing or *das Ding*. It is Lacan who introduces here the theme of the possible overvaluing of the object, of its possible elevation to the dignity of the Thing and with this the question of having to make the weight of an ethical principle or of a jouissance felt. Depending on a sublimation and/or a perversion, which is always possible according to Lacan, it is not impossible that the lustful man will coolly accept the possibility of the scaffold "for the pleasure of cutting up the lady concerned in small pieces, for example".[19] So Lacan did nothing other than introduce a third principle (a principle of jouissance, differing from the technical principle and the pleasure principle) into an example which had purposely chosen by Kant as *solely* operating according to the pleasure principle (because there is no other place for the "scaffold").

In the second parable, that of a subject ordered to give false testimony against someone who would lose his life as a result, there really is on this occasion an opposition between two registers: on the one hand, that of appearances and the pleasure principle and, on the other hand, that of reason and the moral law. The moral law – here somewhat reduced to a caricature for the purposes of reflection on the freedom which is always dependent on the moral law – the moral law therefore which would consist in not bearing false witness, is radically opposed to the love of life and to happiness. Kant's story is simple: we know what the Good is (refusing to bear false witness, with one's own downfall as a consequence) and we know what the Bad is (bearing false witness, with the benefit of the tyrant's good graces as a consequence).

In the form of the neighbour, of the *Nebenmensch* as a representative of the Thing, Lacan introduces, however, a new complexity into the example: "Let's talk [. . .] about a case of conscience which is raised if I am summoned to inform on my neighbor or my brother for activities which are prejudicial to the security of the state." Here, Good and Evil fall down, they can no longer serve as simple criteria for guiding the moral law: "And I who stand here right now and bear witness to the idea that there is no law of the good except in evil and through evil, should I bear such witness?"[20] Let us note that Good and Evil, despite the somewhat caricatured nature of the second parable, in which one is radically separated from the other, are never criteria of the moral law in Kant.

Into both parables, Lacan introduces a weighing-up, which is not without a double deviation in relation to Kant's presentation.

Firstly, the parables, which should have served to show how there is no freedom without moral law (the first parable) and how there is always freedom with the moral law (the second parable), are interpreted by Lacan in the sense of a methodology or doctrine of method, that is, for a weighing-up.

Secondly, while Kant's weighing-up of the doctrine of method is played out between the incentives involved in the search for pleasure and the reasons [*les motifs*] involved in the moral law, it is displaced in Lacan towards a weighing-up of the moral law against jouissance, which is not the same thing as pleasure. In Kant, we know what the hoped-for verdict of the weighing-up is: the moral law should weigh heaviest in the balance. In Lacan, this is less sure. And for good reason: the moral law and jouissance should be understood as two sides of the same coin.

Should it not be said that it is the moral law which should weigh the heaviest, not without again invoking reason, that is, the jouissance of the unconscious which had remained hidden until the advent of psychoanalysis?

Notes

1. Lacan, *The Ethics of Psychoanalysis*, op. cit., p. 81.
2. Ibid., p. 82.
3. Ibid., p. 83.
4. "What then should we say? That the law is sin? By no means! Yet, if it had not been for the law, I would not have known sin. I would not have known what it is to covet if the law had not said, 'You shall not covet.'" "The Letter of Paul to the Romans", 7:7, in *The Holy Bible, New Revised Standard Version*, Grand Rapids, MI, Zondervan Publishing House, 1995.
5. Kant, *Critique of Practical Reason*, op. cit., p. 27.
6. Lacan, *The Ethics of Psychoanalysis*, op. cit., p. 89.
7. Ibid., p. 112.
8. Ibid., p. 92.
9. Ibid., p. 93.
10. Ibid., p. 73.
11. Ibid., p. 97.
12. This sentence does not appear in the version of the seminar published by Éditions du Seuil, and it is taken from p. 163 of the edition of seminar VII produced for members of L'association lacanienne internationale. It will be referred to as "ALI". [Footnote modified by translator.]
13. Ibid., pp. 107–108.
14. See Chapter 5 of Part II of the first section of this book.
15. Kant, *Critique of Practical Reason*, op. cit., p. 121.
16. Ibid., p. 28.
17. Sentence not included in Seuil version of seminar (ALI, p. 164).
18. The question of this double parable is taken up much later in the same seminar, still in the sense of demonstrating "the weight of the Law, formulated by him [Kant] as practical reason, as something that imposes itself in purely reasonable terms" (Lacan, *The Ethics of Psychoanalysis*, op. cit., p. 188). It is very curious to remark that on this occasion, Lacan refers again to Saint Paul and to the primacy of the Law over covetousness and gleans from it that the moral law can serve "as a support for the *jouissance* involved; it is so that the sin becomes what Saint Paul calls inordinately sinful" (Ibid., p. 189) and adds that "That's what Kant on this occasion simply ignores", whereas it is Lacan who simply ignores that the double parable is introduced by Kant precisely to show that the moral law must act as a support for freedom or for the question of jouissance.
19. Ibid., p. 109.
20. Ibid. We shall return to the interpretation of this double parable in our reading of "Kant with Sade".

Part II

"Kant with Sade" (1962–1963)
The object *a*

The text "Kant with Sade", published in the review *Critique* (no. 191, April 1963), had been intended as the introduction to the third volume of the complete works of Sade (Cercle du Livre précieux, 1963), which included *Justine, or the Misfortunes of Virtue* and *Philosophy in the Bedroom*. Its publisher, Jean Paulhan, seems to have withdrawn it due to the difficulty of pinpointing its argument. It was to have been a preface; the opening theme was explicitly meant to have introduced Sade. But how and why could he be introduced by relating him to Kant?

As early as 1944, Horkheimer and Adorno[1] had situated Sade alongside Kant: the latter's pure *formalism* would have led to Nazism by way of Sade. For these authors, Sade is "the mediator which explains the appearance of fascism and Nazism within European culture: Sade is the missing link between Kant and Auschwitz".[2] As we shall see, Lacan also undertakes a reading of the *Critique of Practical Reason* on the side of a pure formalism. But this pure formalism attributed to Kant will precisely be *corrected* in the right direction by Lacan's reading of Sade. Before Lacan, a series of great readers of Hegel – Blanchot, Bataille, Klossowski – wanted to use Sade to reject "absolute knowledge" and so as not to "retain anything from Hegel other than negativity (negation) as subversion and the liberation of desire". They wanted to "leave Hegel behind through Sade"[3] Sade – completely de-Nazified – would stand as an alternative to Hegel's totalisation. He would thus correct the universality attributed to Kant, even before it had drifted towards the Hegelian system.

We shall see how Lacan's text basically aims to tease out the ethics of desire centred on the jouissance inherent to the unconscious, by first clarifying the hows and whys of the universality of the categorical imperative, with Sade standing in for it [*Sade y faisant office*]. The function of the fantasy is therefore clarified and, following that, the place of desire. The text finishes with an evaluation of Sade and criticises his limitations, especially in relation to the recognition of the mother's castration, a castration which is fundamental to the structure of desire.

***

(We cannot agree with Marty's evaluation of "Kant with Sade", which reduces it to a lesson given by Lacan to the pervert Sade, in which Lacan is content to deliver his verdict from a "mandarin-like position",[4] whereas *The Ethics* would be the fundamental text for understanding Lacan's position. Certainly, at the end of "Kant with Sade", Lacan does show Sade's limits, but this is only to bring to light the function of the radical nothing, the *nihil negativum*, the "vocal object" for the position of the ethics of the unconscious, not without relaunching the dynamic inherent to Kant's practical reason, as we shall see by following Lacan's text step by step.)

***

Lacan's text does not have a subtitle. Only fourteen-line breaks allow us to distinguish fifteen sections, or fifteen big groups of paragraphs, in the text, which we have grouped together in four chapters: 1) an introduction to Kant and to Sade (four sections), 2) a study of Sade's contribution to psychoanalysis (four sections), 3) the account of a struggle against Kant on the part of Lacan (three sections), and 4) a presentation of the consequences for the practice of psychoanalysis (four sections).

Chapter 12

Introduction to Kant and to Sade

General introduction

The Thing – *das Ding* – is not good, nor is it evil. It cannot be defined by an ethics centred on good or an ethics centred on evil. However, ethics is regularly presented as an ethics of the good. In order to counter this one-sidedness, it seems it would be advisable to oppose to it an ethics of evil before we can develop a true ethics of the Real, an ethics of the Thing. The Sadean utopia of a universality oriented towards evil would stand against the Kantian utopia of a universality which, *in Lacan's eyes*, remains still forever oriented towards good.

Despite an omnipresent theory of nature, Sade's body of work does not at all consist in providing a general survey of the natural tendencies that can be observed in human beings.[5] It is an ethical *oeuvre*. Lacan indeed intends to give the Sadean bedroom a place equal to that of the Academy, the Lyceum, and the Stoa. It is a case with Sade of rectifying the position of ethics, that is to say, to clear away the ethics which had remained overly centred on the good ("as with Kant", Lacan thought) rather than on the Thing.

Philosophy in the Bedroom (1795) thus prepares the way for Freud's work and the question of the Thing, which Lacan had begun to track down based on his reading of the *Entwurf*, the "Project for a Scientific Psychology" (1895). Freud's pleasure principle is certainly in line with the quest for happiness, but it also contains the seeds of its supercession. In fact, the Freudian pleasure/unpleasure principle is distinct from the principle of happiness, because it really is the avoidance of unpleasure which commands it, and the relative good that it seeks is positioned according to an unavoidable evil. Freud could not have discovered *his* principle revolving around *un*pleasure if Kant, then Sade, and finally "the insinuating rise in the nineteenth century of the theme of 'delight in evil'"[6] had not existed one after the other. And well before these references, the mystery of the feminine itself, already highlighted in courtly love, "the eternal feminine does not elevate us".[7]

"Sade represents the first step of a subversion" – is the good overturned here by evil? – and Kant "represents [its] turning point". Even if Lacan thinks that his ethics remains focused on the good, it was he who began to separate ethics from the quest for good in order to centre it elsewhere (the first chapter of the analytic

DOI : 10.4324/9781003055662-22

of practical reason). Lacan's project is to show that *Philosophy in the Bedroom* is in agreement with the *Critique of Practical Reason* in that both of them are based on the principle of universality and that the first "completes" the second in that it adds the ethics of evil on to the ethics of good, while also bringing in a greater clarification of what "universality" ought to be. Lacan's thesis is therefore that *Philosophy in the Bedroom* "yields the truth" of the *Critique of Practical Reason*.

The Lacanian understanding of the postulates of practical reason, that is, the immortality of the soul and the existence of God, confirms his idea that Kant's ethics remains an ethics focused on the Good (the "highest Good"). According to Lacan, Kant confined these postulates to a simple "function of utility". Lacan still thinks in terms of a weighing-up, and these Kantian postulates would serve, according to Lacan, to weigh the balance in the direction of the moral law. Someone hesitating should therefore be persuaded due to the rewards (for the Good) to be expected in the afterlife, and God's will would be the guarantor of this. As we have seen, the dialectic of practical reason is radically opposed to this way of conceiving the postulates, to this weighing-up commanded by the "highest Good" [*le souverain Bien*] understood in fact as the highest good in terms of pleasure or well-being [*le souverain bon*], which reduces the motivation for action to the *pleasure* hoped for in the hereafter, which operates according to a heteronomous principle (the pleasure of the soul and God's will).

However, despite this erroneous interpretation of the dialectic of practical reason, which completely side-lines the cutting edge of the *Critique of Practical Reason*, Lacan believes that these postulates "reduce the work to its subversive core". This is because these two postulates bear witness to the unshakeable persistence of the ethical project (due to its "*categorical*" character). Kantian immortality will be taken up again as the immortality of the victims in the Sadean system: the (certainly utopian) process does not give way in the face of the contingencies of life. The intelligent will to set up the ethical process (represented by the postulate of the existence of God) does not give way either. These explanations (by means of Sade) in the end come back to finding the true meaning of Kant's postulates. The strongest subversion does not involve blowing evil out of proportion. Or doing the same for good. It is on the side of the radicality of practical reason and of the Thing. "This explains the incredible exaltation [felt] upon reading it."

Lacan's introduction to the *Critique of Practical Reason*

As we shall see, Lacan proposes a reading of the *Critique of Pure Reason* completely built around a logical formalism (this was also Adorno and Horkheimer's reading of it) and skewed towards the Good (this was already the viewpoint of all the pre-Kantian ethics). This vulgar and distorted reading of Kant, the easiest and still most common reading of the second critique even today, nevertheless opens up the necessity for thought of going beyond it. In Lacan's text, it is Sade who will play this part: as we shall see further on, Sade will, it might be said, correct the bad reading of Kant.

Morality's false start in the weighing-up of the good

In Lacan's eyes, Kant's ethics does not at first seem like an ethics of the Thing or the Real, it would present itself first as an ethics of good or of the Good. Let us recall that is not this at all: it is an ethics of *principle*, of a principle that is irreducible to any matter at all (including the good). The question of good and evil only arises in the *Critique* secondarily (in the second chapter of the analytic). Rather than the functioning *principle* of morality, Lacan starts out from the *object* aimed at and from the *concept* of the "good" (the Kantian opposition between well-being – *wohl* and the good – *gut*). His argumentation is supported by the equivocation inherent in the term "good", the good of pleasure vs. the good of virtue.[8] "The pleasure principle is the law of feeling good [*bien*], which is *wohl* in German and might be rendered as "well-being" [*bien-être*]". This pleasure comes into play at the level of appearances, which determines objects in general (cf. the *Critique of Pure Reason*). Now, "no phenomenon can lay claim to a constant relationship to pleasure". There is therefore no *law* which can "lay claim to a constant relationship to pleasure". Sooner or later, the search for well-being or for "the good" as pleasure must lead to its reversal. "The quest to feel good would thus be a dead end were it not reborn in the form of *Das Gute*, the good that is the object of the moral law."

The second type of "good" – *das Gute* – is indicated to us by the experience of the categorical imperative, and it puts itself forward as the Good only by opposing itself to all the (pleasurable) goods that objects might bring. The Good and the different goods first appear "according to some theoretical equivalence" [*dans une équivalence de principe*], and the Good seems only to weigh the scales on its side by its own weight alone, and this weight is shown by emptying the plate on the other side of the scales. It involves *excluding* the goods pertaining to the pleasure principle, that is to say, the "pathological" interests (Kant), or the drives or feelings that the subject might experience in relation to these different objects. The Good is not generalised induction or the universal principle of good (as had been the case for the "Sovereign Good of the Greeks"). It does not act through its own weight as a "counterweight". It acts "as an anti-weight – that is, as subtracting weight" on all the effects of pride or contentment related to the pleasure principle.

Lacan very clearly reconsiders the perspective of the weighing-up that he believed he had understood in the double parable (whereas for Kant it involved explaining the relationship between the moral law and freedom) and he observes that Kantian ethics is not at all dependent on an ordinary weighing. Just as logic empties the semantic content of propositions to replace it with weightless letters, so Kant would also empty out all the comparative weighings-up of different goods. With this "anti-weight", with the emptying out of content from the plates of the scales, the thematic of the Good as a gateway into morality presents itself as a simple *absence of an object*: "the subject no longer has any object before him".[9] An absence in which one can already sense the arrival of the question of the object *a*, that is, the very structure of the object highlighted by the disappearance of all particular objects (this structure is equivalent to the gaze, the scopic object, the third form of the object *a* in Lacan, or again to the "empty intuition without object" in Kant).[10]

"No object at all", this is effectively theorem I of the analytic of practical reason: "All practical principles that presuppose an *object* (matter) of the faculty of desire as the determining ground of the will are, without exception, empirical and can furnish no practical laws."[11] The absence of the object on this side of the scales lends weight to the moral law, which is uttered in the "phenomenon" of the "*voice*" (fourth form of the object *a*), which counts as the voice of conscience,[12] not without obvious paradox as the voice presents itself as a phenomenon, while it only counts for the emptying-out of all phenomena. This "voice" *produces* the maxim as a signifier. It is a making on the basis of an absence of phenomena, of a nothing. But how does this production of the voice that the maxim is become a law? It is here that we see that as soon as it is put forward, the "voice" falls back onto the contemplation of everything that might happen, onto the "gaze". At the same time, that which should have presented itself as an active production (universality produced by a synthetic a priori judgement, which is how Kant conceives it) falls back on the logic of the product (a universality given in a purely analytical judgement, which is how Lacan understands Kant).

The universality of the law presented as essentially analytic by Lacan

The production of the voice is reduced here to a pure logical formalisation.

> For the maxim to constitute a law, it is necessary and sufficient that, being put to the test of such [purely practical] reason, the maxim may be considered universal as far as logic is concerned.

"Necessary and sufficient", says Lacan. With this necessary and sufficient condition, everything seems to have been said – all there is to do now is to "analyse" the process, more precisely the products. What does "universal as far as logic is concerned [*universelle en droit de logique*]" mean? We notice the slippage from "duty" in Kant to "right" [*droit*] in Lacan: "*droit*" or right does not mean that the law [*loi*] "forces itself on everyone" (this would be a duty and it must be done), "but rather that it is valid in every case". In other words, the rule *may* be valid in all cases (it is a right and it is sufficient to analyse it). At the same time as duty moves aside to give way to right, the universality appealed in the first formulation of the Kantian categorical imperative is thought of as a purely *logical* universality. And Lacan makes it clear what he understands this as: this test of universality "can only be passed by maxims of the type that allows for analytic deduction". In other words, if the universalisation of the maxim leads to a contradiction, the (particular) maxim cannot become a (universal) moral law.

Everything takes place here at the level of the supreme principle of all analytical judgements: "Nothing can have a predicate that contradicts it".[13] It is not fitting to say that the "maxim" may become a "a moral law" if this universalisation leads to a contradiction. Let us note well that what is deduced from this condition is never the acceptance of such a maxim as a moral law – it is solely a criterion of "*exclusion*". Also, all the examples invoked by Kant are only ever maxims which *cannot* become moral laws because of this contradiction. For it to be *possible* that a maxim become moral law, its universalisation must not be self-contradictory. This is a prohibitory condition that certainly allows us to put many maxims to one side. However, contrary to what Lacan says, *this is not sufficient*, because the moral law is, above all, a synthetic proposition, *it must be made*, and it is even a synthetic a priori proposition: it must be made without being constructed from phenomenal elements.[14]

Before returning to the *synthetic* principle of the moral law (to which Lacan pays no attention in this part of the text), let us insist on its necessary (but not sufficient) condition: for the maxim to have a chance of being taken as moral law, this universalisation must not produce any contradiction (or again, must remain in conformity with the supreme principle of all analytical judgements). Kant illustrates this *a contrario* with the example of the deposit – there is no deposit without a trustworthy depositary. Lacan illustrates the principle of analytic judgements in his own manner: "Long live Poland, for if there were no Poland, there would be no Poles."[15] We see that these two illustrations are very differently presented. In Kant, it is the depositary's loyalty which *makes* [fait] *the* deposit, in other words, the depositary *inspires* trust [fait *confiance*],[16] *makes a commitment*, situates himself or herself already at the level of a *synthetic* judgement. The example of Poland is, on the other hand, purely *analytic*: a Pole is analytically defined as an inhabitant of Poland, without needing to do anything to prove it. Lacan did sense the reduction inherent to this properly analytic side of things and already announces "the need for a more synthetic foundation", but does not take advantage of this at this point in the text. Because he reserves this fundamental task of the synthetic foundation for Sade, as we shall see further on.

The example of the deposit, cited by Lacan, is situated in Kant's text as a *preliminary but not sufficient* condition for the enunciation of the moral law. With this enunciation, the other side of the moral law must again be taken into consideration according to Kant, that is, freedom (cf. the double parable of the moral law and freedom). *Freedom* is precisely the carrying-out of what must be done, the carrying-out of the moral law as synthetic a priori judgement and not simply as an analytic judgement. There is no deduction of the moral law;[17] it can only be deduced that a particular maxim *cannot* be made universal, as making it universal would entail a contradiction; it is therefore unable to become a moral law. For there to be a moral law, there must *additionally* be law-giving freedom.

Lacan does certainly assure us of his "attachment" to "freedom". But this "freedom" to which Lacan says he is attached, is "a freedom without which the people mourn".[18] Lacan also adds that the explanation of this freedom "is analytic" – that is, it is sufficient to analyse the resistance of the Poles, "their remarkable resistance to the eclipses of Poland, and even to the lamentation that ensued" to deduce the freedom that they were demanding. All this obviously has nothing to do with Kantian freedom nor with the foundation of the moral law in a synthetic a priori judgement.

The absence of an object in Kant and the scopic object

According to Lacan, it is all played out for Kant at the purely analytic level of *concepts* (this is certainly not Kant's position, because everything must stem from *principles*). According to Lacan again, this analysis of formal logic would be the reason for or basis of a regret, attributed to Kant, "his regret that no intuition offers up a phenomenal object in the experience of the moral law". This purely formal and analytic universality must be given flesh. The reader will have already understood for a long time that Kant does not at all "regret" this absence of a phenomenal object which could firmly establish the moral law in knowledge. On the contrary, Kant states, "I must [. . .] abolish *knowledge*" and with it intuition of all phenomenal objects, to find a place for morality and lawgiving autonomy.[19]

Whatever the case, Lacan, above all, remembers that "this object slips away throughout the *Critique* [of practical reason]".[20] It slips away in terms of the strictly *logical* side accentuated by Lacan within this *Critique* to the point of reducing universality to a purely analytic question. If the object slips away, all that will remain of it is its empty frame, "the empty intuition without object" or again the simply formal condition of the object. It is not nothing, but it is not something either. Between the something and the nothing, this for Lacan is the object cause of desire, the object *a*. It is from this object that the *Critique of Practical Reason* "derives an eroticism that is no doubt innocent, but perceptible, the well-foundedness of which I shall show through the nature of the said object". This object is presented, here in the *Critique of Practical Reason*, in the guise of "the empty intuition without object", the third form in Kant's table of the division of the concept of nothing, corresponding to Lacan's scopic object. But if the object *a* is surreptitiously introduced here under the form of the *scopic* object (namely, reduced to this form), it is because he presented Kant's ethics as an ethics of Good, of a purified Good (to be contemplated?), to the point of reducing it to a purely formal and analytic logic. This purely formal (analytic) form that the "scopic object" will show is its true function of making a place for another form of nothing, "the empty object without concept", the vocal object, which opens up a (synthetic) *making*. And it is to this effect that Lacan now introduces Sade's *Philosophy in the Bedroom*, in order both to discover the *synthetic* (rather than analytic) value and the *vocal* form of the object *a* (rather than the scopic one attributed to Kant).

Introduction to Sade: *Philosophy in the Bedroom*

THE SADEAN MAXIM AND ITS (SYNTHETIC) ENUNCIATION

With Sade, a rectification of Kant's *Critique of Practical Reason* is involved, more precisely re-commencing the incomplete reading of Kant, a reading which is too easily contented with avoiding the cutting edge of the moral law and that which concerns us in jouissance (an ethics centred on the Good and on universality reduced to a type of formalism). Reading Sade allows us to readdress the question more precisely while articulating it with the tetrahedral schema putting the subject in question again (Lacan's Schema L). Instead of centring everything on Good, it involves developing the architectonic which can alone give access to the Real. Instead of reducing universality to a pure (analytic) form, (synthetic) universality must be fabricated on the basis of the locus of the big Other. This is the intention behind the introduction of Sade into Lacan's line of questioning. Before examining Lacan's text, we shall briefly present the little philosophical treatise inserted into Sade's *Philosophy in the Bedroom*, on which Lacan's argumentation is mainly based.

Sade's text "Yet Another Effort, Frenchmen, If You Would Become Republicans"[21]

King Louis XVI has died, and the first part of Sade's exhorts us to deal "the final blow to the tree of superstition", to every form of allegiance to a God or a Supreme Being. "Atheism is the one doctrine of all those prone to reason." It is on the basis of the radical destruction of these figures of the big Other that the true reform of morality can be begun and to be truly republican.

French mores do not suit a republican government. They must be corrected in relation to the three classical types of duty: duties towards the Supreme Being, duties towards one's peers or one's brothers, and duties towards oneself.

Firstly, as the Supreme Being does not exist, it is sufficient to make fun of the idea. This is how superstition will be destroyed (and not through acts of violence).

Secondly, towards one's brothers, the commandment to "love your neighbour as yourself" goes against all the laws of nature, as there is no universal law valid for all human beings. Sade compares wishing to impose a universal law to a general who would want all his soldiers, tall and short alike, to wear a uniform of the same size. The death penalty is heretofore condemned. It is the height of injustice to strike down by the law (with the death penalty) the one who cannot submit to the supposedly universal law (against killing). Reason, moreover, will never prevent crime.

Sade then inspects the four great classic crimes against one's brothers. 1) *Calumny* is not an evil: because if it speaks the truth, so much the better, and if it is false, it is sufficient to wait for the virtuous person to show themselves as they are. 2) *Theft* is a means for achieving equality between human beings (Sade implicitly believing that is the poor who steal from the rich!). 3) *Impurity* (prostitution, adultery, incest, rape, sodomy, etc.) should be maintained and supported by the republican government. In fact, the immoral state or moral dissolution places the human being within a perpetual movement which is necessary for the insurrection of public life and for its constant renewal. In order to respond to the necessity of lust the government will organise brothels in which women will submit to "men's caprices [as] Nature dictates" (p. 318, translation modified). All men have the right to jouissance over all women, even little girls: "He who has the right to eat the fruit of a tree may assuredly pluck it ripe or green, according to the inspiration of his taste" (p. 323), despite whatever harmful effects this may give rise to. The government will seemingly also organise houses intended for women's libertinage. 4) *Murder* belongs to the laws of nature. Politically, "Is it not by dint of murders that France is free today?" In sociological terms, murder eliminates the poorest people who are a burden to society. Murder is a horror, perhaps, but a necessary one, and never a crime.

Thirdly, towards oneself, suicide is not a crime, but an act of nature.

Lacan's reading of Sade

The form of the "pamphlet within the pamphlet"[22]

With its sexual *mises en scène* "[at] the very limits of what is imaginable", *Philosophy in the Bedroom* offers a ferocious satire of the mores of the republic stemming from the French Revolution. It is already a "pamphlet" against the French Revolution. But its *mise en scène* is interrupted in order to give way to a little philosophical treatise which Lacan calls both a "diatribe" [*factum*] and a "pamphlet within the pamphlet".

By using the word "*factum*"[23,24] Lacan intends to show its equivalence with the *factum* of legal experts, which is opposed to legal right [*droit*] (*qui juris? quid facti?*). This is a factual critique of law, indeed, an attack on the law. But the "factum" is also the term used by Kant (*Faktum*) to designate the *principle* of the *moral law*, which does not present itself as an empirical fact, but which nevertheless forces itself on every rational being. For Lacan, the *factum*, or the pamphlet within the Sadean pamphlet would therefore be relevant to everybody and would impose itself as a "universal" fact. How can it be affirmed that everybody has within themselves the equivalent of Sade's factum or pamphlet within a pamphlet ("*Yet Another Effort, Frenchmen, If You Would Become Republicans*")? This Lacanian affirmation would seem to be as scandalous as Sade's writing itself, that is, a pure mystification. In invoking Sade, does Lacan not do any less than oppose an ethics of Evil (Sade) to the ethics of Good (Kant) in order to arrive, in an illusory fashion, at the ethics of the Real or of the Thing?

Now, Sade's factum does not limit itself to opposing evil to good. By interrupting the narrative of sexual postures and stage directions, it presents itself as a critique of this very narrative – it is a *mise en abyme*. What is the purpose of this doubling? The mechanism of the "pamphlet within the pamphlet" is, according to Lacan, identical to that of the "dream within the dream". In a binary logic, this would be an invalid operation: to dream that the dream is only a dream would mean coming back to reality (and to forgetting the dream), and mocking the mockery that the pamphlet would mean returning to a reality free of mockery, to erasing the satire that the pamphlet is. This is not the case here. Whereas dreaming that it is only a dream seems to erase the importance and the significance of the dream, it only in fact accentuates it, because the doubling (of the dream or of the pamphlet) only proves the impossibility of the erasure (both of the dimension of the dream or of the pamphlet) and the insistence of the real at play in this repetition.[25]

The pamphlet within the pamphlet thus insists on showing how the whole *mise en scene*, and the "action", which is taken "to the very limits of what is imaginable", are to be taken as an unsurpassable *real*. The "deriding of the historical situation", of the republic established by the revolution or, again, the revolution's self-mockery, only point to a real which conditions it and infinitely surpasses it. Sade must therefore be read with that spirit of self-mockery which must focus on Sadean morality and, as a result, on Kantian morality.

The Sadean maxim and its rationality

The real, or the "crux of the [factum]" is expressed in a "maxim" which provides a "rule for jouissance". In speaking of a "*rule*" and a "*maxim*", Lacan lets it be understood that jouissance is approached from a viewpoint which is both subjective (it is a maxim) and technical (it is a rule). It would not be presented as a moral *law* or as *counsel* of prudence in the quest for pleasure (the pleasure principle). This technical maxim nevertheless borrows the Kantian manner: the maxim proposes "a rule for jouissance, which is odd in that it defers to Kant's mode in being laid down as a universal rule." Despite this borrowing from Kant, the maxim does not lead to duty – it is not fundamentally conflictual like Kant's right, and it appropriates a right ("defers to" it [*s'y faire droit*]). Despite its reference to universality, everything seems to oppose it to Kantian ethics.

Lacan himself formulates this maxim which proposes his rule for jouissance and which counts as "the crux of the factum": "I have the right to enjoy your body," anyone can say to me, "and I will exercise this right without any limit to the capriciousness of the exactions I may wish to satiate with your body".[26]

Let us note as an aside that this maxim, formulated by Lacan (and not by Sade), fits in with the Sadean critique of duties towards others where impurity is concerned. The radical suppression of the classical Big Other (the king, God) on which, in Sade's text, the reform of morality depended, is not mentioned in Lacan's text. In contrast, another form of the Big Other had appeared in the person of the one who enunciates the Sadean formula: "I have the right . . . ", which can be found in "anyone". The Other himself has descended from his throne to become (at least potentially) universal, with the slight hint that it is *the unconscious* itself which may be speaking in the enunciation of the Sadean maxim.

"Such is the rule to which everyone's will would be submitted, assuming a society were to forcibly implement the rule." The Lacano-Sadean rule (and, alongside it, the imaginary establishment of fleshpots for each of the sexes) implies a double universality. *Firstly*, that of the Other or of the random person who can say to me *I have the right to enjoy your body*, etc. *Secondly*, that of those limitlessly subjected to the whim of the Other. The rule is, of course, unworkable on both sides, and it appears that "both the maxim (the universality of the Other) and the consent assumed to be given it (the universality of those subjected to it) are at best an instance of black humor".[27] Blanchot had already noted Sade's "bizarre humor" and "glacial joviality".[28] Someone who does not take this humour into account may quite simply condemn the putting into practice of Sadean ethics. Such a judgement pertains to "reasonable" considerations, meaning those which are technical or pragmatic, rather than strictly practical or ethical. The "reasonable [. . .] is no more than resorting in a confused fashion to the pathological (as it was defined by Kant, namely determined by sensibility)", and it must be very carefully distinguished from the rational, which is the faculty of *principles*, and notably of the principle commanding the whole of the *Critique of Practical Reason*.

The "black humour" in the Sadean rule is there to pass from the refined rationality of the principle of ethics to a sensible, comical presentation, while challenging the universality of the enunciation of the maxim, as well as the universality of consent to the maxim. Carrying out such a passage is precisely what is peculiar to humour: "humor betrays the very function of the "superego"(which involves the practical principle) in comedy (that is, in the pragmatic sensible)". Because it is precisely the "superego" which appears under this double universal form. This avatar of the function of the superego, presented by means of the comical nature of the Sadean rule, indicates the difference between the pure rational and the reasonable. The "superego" does not stand for something reasonable imposed by a society or by a social agency ("the renewed obscurantism of our contemporaries' use of it"); it is purely rational, belonging to the universality of the Other present in "anyone" or again, of the unconscious, which would promulgate the Sadean maxim (*I have the right to enjoy your body . . .*), and to its universal applicability.

Precisely because of the function of humour, which is to present the superego within the comical, we are urged to take the Sadean fable completely seriously, not in the comical series of the different Sadean set-pieces (which must not be taken too seriously), but so as to discover the *true sense of the superego*, which belongs to the practical in Kant's sense of the term and which appears in the light of a double universality which is to be criticised. We were introduced into the serious in order to return to the beginning of the series, namely to the universality inherent to the superego, which is always dependent on a *synthetic making*. The Sadean rule henceforth introduces not simply a right, but an *imperative* of jouissance to be fabricated. "The superego is the imperative of jouissance – Enjoy!"[29]

False imaginary universality

It is not necessary that "a society sanction a right to jouissance" (on the side of the comical series of Sadean set-pieces) to assure the imperative of the moral law or the imperative of jouissance. Practice (the imperative) is never caused by pragmatic devices (society's rules). "No *de facto* legality", no regulations can raise a maxim to the level of a universal rule, because a rule is always opposed to another one and a specific legality enshrined in a set of regulations opposes itself to all the others.

It is not a question of finding an imaginary universality and imagining its extension to everybody. "At best one could demonstrate here the mere possibility of generalizability, which is not universalizability; the latter considers things as they are grounded and not as they happen to work out."[30] If how things work out seems to come into play between two individuals, two "subjects", here the victim and the executioner, these only count as two fundamentally and radically different positions, which exclude all reciprocal relations (it is the neurotic who imagines a reciprocity between themselves and the Other). We can understand why Lacan does not take up again the maxim he had cited in Seminar VII, stated by Mme Delbène in *Juliette, or Vice Amply Rewarded*.[31] By implicating reciprocity, it lacks the crux of the imperative, which is situated on the level of a singular (synthetic rather than analytic) making, on the structural level of the principle and not at the level of individuals. Lacan takes advantage of this to "point out the exorbitant nature of the role people grant to the moment of reciprocity in structures, especially subjective ones, that are incompatible with reciprocity".

The question of the subject is posed not on the basis of two individuals, but of four irreducible positions. "[T]he condition of the subject, S (neurosis or psychosis), depends on what unfolds in the Other",[32] and the Other's discourse (here, the enunciation of the Sadean rule) is "drawn to the four corners of the schema: namely, S, his ineffable and stupid existence; a, his objects; a', his ego, that is, his form as reflected in his objects; and A, the locus from which the question of his existence may arise for him". If the subject's structure excludes reciprocity (none of the positions are reducible to any of the others), this does not, however, exclude "my turn next time";[33] in other words, each individual may take up not only the position of the ego – a' – or of its objects – a –, but also that of the ineffable subject S and that of the Other. That which served as a subjected subject may also in turn take up the position of enunciation inherent to the Other.

Every judgement, every condemnation of the "odious social order that would enthrone our maxim" (the Sadean maxim), sidesteps the real question of universality, which was recognised by Kant as the (necessary, but not sufficient) condition for "the unconditional practice of reason", as such a condemnation only envisages an imaginary "universality", in other words one belonging to generalities or examples, which precisely prevent the posing of the question of universality. The judgement condemning the Sadean maxim is founded on the fact that it is not "reasonable", does not suit, is not practicable, or cannot be reciprocated. This condemnation is wholly based on pragmatic, imaginary criteria, on examples. It is not at all based on the true criterion of universality, to which Lacan now returns to give it its real importance.

Universality must be fabricated

The "characteristic of a rule acceptable as universal" must be recognised in the Sadean maxim, "for the simple reason" of "its sole proclamation (its *kerygma*)". In other words, universality is founded here not on analytic logic, not on the phenomenological generality of whomever might be concerned, but on its sole proclamation, on enunciation. Universality here is no longer analytical (as Lacan had presented it, erroneously where Kant was concerned) – it is fabricated from scratch. In Kantian terms, it counts as a *synthetic* judgement. It is synthesised independently of all the particular sensible elements which might be involved in it, counting as a synthetic a priori judgement ("I will exercise this right without any limit to the capriciousness of the exactions I wish to satiate with your body[34]"). In attributing to the Sadean rule the value of a universality founded on its *kerygma*, its proclamation, Lacan in fact finds the real reason for the universality of the moral law in Kant, a reason he had just put to one side in his presentation of *Practical Reason*, that is, its autonomy or the fact that it is promulgated in a free act which *creates* a new temporal series.

Setting off now from this proclamation of the rule or from its autonomy (perfectly stated in Theorem IV of the analytic of practical reason), Lacan rediscovers, as if by magic, two aspects of the Kantian imperative: the negative aspect of the rejection of the pathological as the possible foundation of a true universality (Theorem I and II of the analytic of practical reason) and, on the positive side, the determining principle of the moral law (Theorem III of the analytic of practical reason). These two aspects of the Kantian imperative are presented here as "two imperatives": *firstly*, "the radical rejection of the pathological (that is, of every preoccupation with goods, passion, or even compassion – in other words, the rejection by which Kant cleared the field of moral law)" and *secondly*, "the form of this law, which is also its only substance, insofar as the will becomes bound to the law only by eliminating from its practice every reason that is not based on the maxim itself".

It will have been remarked that "both" imperatives go round in circles: the first clears the way for the second and the second consists in a rejection. The splitting of Kant's moral imperative into these two imperatives by the (technical, it must be said) means of the Sadean rule allows it to be highlighted to what extent "moral life can be stretched, even if it snaps our very life".[35] Beyond the victims in the Sadean comedy, one thinks of the countless lives broken by guilt stretched between the rejection of all sensible (pathological) forms of desire and the form of pure desire, which consists of the rejection of impure desire. The Sadean rule, if it is proclaimed *by the Other*, also imposes the two imperatives in the dimension of the *Other*, and the victim herself may play the role of the Other for the sadistic executioner. From the moment when the Other or the unconscious enunciates the right to jouissance, it is two imperatives which are presented in it. On the one hand, it rejects the "pathological", by which is meant the phenomenal, in its entirety. On the other hand, it opens onto a free and creative will.

The distance between these two imperatives may seem absent in the moral imperative formulated by Kant. This is not the case, because despite the autonomy which seems to come from the same, from the "subject" themselves, the one who promulgates the Kantian imperative really is radically Other, because it only counts if it is necessarily freed of all of the pathological and opened up to a problematic free will. In other words, the sentence which Lacan set aside for Kant – "its commandment requisitions us as Other" – counts, above all, for the Kantian experience. The Kantian subject, who cannot be reduced to an individual, is well and truly divided between the "lower faculty of desire" and the "higher faculty of desire".

The universality of the Kantian moral law can in no way be reduced to a universality "as far as logic is concerned", that is, to analytical judgment and to the exclusion of all contradiction (as was parodied by Lacan in his introduction to the *Critique of Practical Reason*, with his reference to Poland and the Poles). The moral law simultaneously implies analytical judgement (as a prior, but not sufficient, condition) and synthetic judgement (which is sufficient to produce the moral law). In other words, the moral law simultaneously entails purely logical universality (involving the statement) and fabricated universality (involving the enunciation). The moral law is established on the basis of the division of the subject between the pathological (where universality can lodge itself in the form of generality) and the practical (in as much as it involves enunciation). This duality "is nothing but the split in the subject brought about by any and every intervention of the signifier: the split between the enunciating subject [*sujet de l'énonciation*] and the subject of the statement [*sujet de l'énoncé*]. The moral law has no other principle". As soon as there is an intervention from the signifier, there is an enunciation coming from the unconscious, in the dimension of the Other. This enunciation does not happen without the proclamation of the right to jouissance. The unconscious can take hold of the body of the signifier for its limitless jouissance. This is its work, not without a double imperative, finding itself forced to reject all the pathological (all that has to do with the phenomenal) and to permit itself the freedom to give things a new form. The work of the unconscious "does not think, calculate or judge in any way at all; it restricts itself to giving things a new form".

The Other's place

With the staging of different positions, "in coming out of the Other's mouth, Sade's maxim is more honest that Kant's appeal to the voice within, since it unmasks the split in the subject that is usually covered up". Enunciation can no longer be understood as the performance of a subject or of a supposed moral psychological individual. This psychological subject only counts as a provisional fiction (already dismantled by Kant in his critique of the Cartesian cogito). This fiction stems from enunciation. There is no "voice from within": enunciation comes into play on the basis of the Other, the Other in as much as it is not a subject at all, but a locus emptied of all "pathological" determination. The object *a* in its vocal form is precisely the radical impossibility of the phenomenon, the *nihil negativum*. It is therefore well suited for opening up the enunciation coming from that Other place. From there, certainly, faithfulness to the radical rejection of the pathological imposes itself, but, above all, the duty to create a new form.

Enunciation (or autonomy) as a principle of the moral Law is confirmed in the doctrine of "human rights".[36] The right to enjoy (the Sadean maxim) implies a certain constraint on the one solicited by the Other. But this Other is not first of all an external individual who may carry out some kind of violence, but the unconscious itself as principle of jouissance which gives things a new form. The difficulty is not therefore bringing about consent to the Sadean maxim or the Kantian moral Law, but in situating them in their proper place, as *principles*: it is from the unconscious as Other that they are proclaimed, while simultaneously requiring from it the nothing (which rejects all phenomenality) and the freedom to begin a new series.

"Thus, the discourse of the right to jouissance clearly posits the Other qua free – the Other's freedom – as its enunciating subject." This enunciation is found in the "lethal depths [*fonds tuant*] of every imperative". The "pathological" (the sensible, the phenomenal) must be killed, rejected, in order to open up the new form. And every identification based on the unconscious, on the basis of the Other – "*Tu es*" – is dependent on the enunciation of the unconscious, which creates a new form, a new subject. It is not the individual who, in a wholly illusory autonomy, invents a moral Law for themselves – it is the moral Law, the law of jouissance *which has come from the unconscious* and its enunciation, which produces the subject secondarily.

The "discourse of the right to jouissance" always simultaneously implies "the subject of the statement" and "its equivocal content", which the Sadean maxim elicits as a victim. The equivocal nature of the term "jouissance", which we have noted from the beginning of this book (limitless pleasure and beyond the limits of the pleasure principle) is echoed by an equivocation at the level of "subjects", the enjoying subject and the subject who is subjected to enjoyment. The jouissance of the one who enjoys acts as the opposite pole to the suffering of the one who submits. The equivocation is thus played out between enunciation (A and unbarred S) and statement (V and $): it corresponds to the logical equivocation (logic of principle for enunciation vs logic of concept for the statement).[37] Secondly, at the level of enunciation between the Other (A) who enunciates and the one who listens (S): this corresponds to the grammatical equivocation (barred big Other [A̶], unbarred big Other [A]). Thirdly, at the level of the statement, between the character who represents the Will (V) [*Volonté*] of the right to jouissance and the characters who are used for jouissance ($): this corresponds to the homophonic equivocation of jouissance (forbidden/inter-said [*interdit/inter-dit*]). Such is "the cross of Sadean experience":

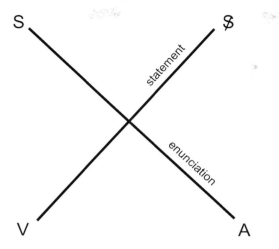

Figure 1

Kant and Sade: pain and the voice as guardians of jouissance

The essential thing that Lacan contributes by the intermediary of Sade is to highlight how enunciation occurs on the basis of the Other, as it is incarnated in the *voice* (in Kantian terms, this highlights synthetic a priori judgement). It is in the experience of *pain* that the voice is inscribed in the place of the Other. It has a function of maintaining the place of jouissance, which radically challenges every form of being.

The function of pain in the Sadean experience: "challenging the circumstances of being"

The cross of the Sadean experience is not unaccompanied by pain. But it is not sufficient to refer to pain to explain the specific nature of the Sadean experience; pain is also part of the Stoical position and of the Kantian moral experience. In the *Critique of Practical Reason*, it would appear as an inevitable thing from the very fact that the principle of the moral law is opposed to the pleasure principle (pain is only the other side of *respect*, the sole feeling provoked by practical reason).

The Stoical will has only an openly declared *contempt* for pain. Lacan cites Epictetus's famous retort to his master who had twisted his leg to make him scream in pain: "You see, you broke it". The Kantian position towards pain *may* appear to be close to the Stoical one here: in Kant, indeed, respect for the moral law necessarily declares a certain contempt (*Verachtung*) for (pathological) pain. Lacan's bringing together of Stoical morals and Kantian morals precisely concerns contempt for pain. If the Other is made present in and through pain (as staged by Sade), then contempt for pain risks being a contempt for the place of the Other, incarnated in the Sadean experience. Now, this place is fundamental, because it is on the basis of this place that being itself can be put in question, as Lacan will show using Sade.

If one imagined a retort similar to that of Epictetus on the part of the victim in the *Sadean experience*, Sadean jouissance would immediately come undone. Because in the Sadean experience, pain always presupposes a "promise of ignominy", a great dishonour, infamy for the victim, and this promise is forestalled by Stoical contempt. In the Sadean experience, pain cannot at all count as a secondary effect of the quest for jouissance. Pain reduced to the misery of an effect would quickly transform jouissance to disgust. By contrast, the pain inherent to Sadean jouissance should crush the victim, radically calling her into question; the Sadean experience is modulated by the pain inherent to jouissance. Jouissance "only proposes to monopolize a will after having already traversed it in order to instate itself at the inmost core of the subject whom it provokes beyond that by offending his sense of modesty".

What is at stake in this attack on the victim's modesty? "Modesty is an amboceptor with respect to the circumstances of being"[38] ("beings" [*étants*] in Heidegger's sense of the term). In other words, it convokes the four places on the Sadean cross. The "circumstances of being" may be understood in several ways at the same time, corresponding to the different equivocations of jouissance. The modesty of one (S and $) allied to the immodesty of the other (V and A) articulates the triple equivocation of jouissance in which the tormentor and his victim are convoked each time in their being. Thus, modesty is capable of uniting and opposing in several ways two aspects of being, the modesty of being as enunciation (A and S) and the immodesty of being as statement (V and $) (logical equivocation), the modesty of the subject's being (S) and the immodesty of the big Other's being (grammatical equivocation), the modesty of the victim of sadism's being ($) and the immodesty of the being of sadistic will (V) (homophonic equivocation). Under all of these forms, it is the immodesty of one which calls into question not only the victim's being but, more radically, calls Being as Being [*l'être en tant qu'être*] into question,[39] or more precisely the being as a being [*étant en tant qu'étant*], "the one's immodesty by itself violating the other's modesty".[40] It is on the basis of the Other and his immodesty that the Subject appears in her modesty. But jouissance in the locus of the Other (the tormentor's) remains precarious because it depends on the echo it attempts to obtain from the Subject. It is thus only excited by itself "like another horrible freedom", the victim's freedom to die, on which it remains completely dependent.

The voice in the big Other's place as guardian of the place of jouissance

According to Lacan, Sade's fundamental contribution (in relation to his reading of Kant) is that he clearly distinguishes the two positions of enunciation, those of the Other and the subject,[41] in the cross of Sadean experience. Enunciation, such as it can be presented in a four-pointed schema, essentially depends on the place of the big Other for the subject. It is a "third term" inscribed in the place of the big

Other, which supports the operation of the Other at the same time as the dimension of enunciation. It is an *object* (the object "that, according to Kant, is lacking in moral experience").

In the place of the object, we shall only have in Kant, if we follow Lacan's reading of him, the pure absence of an object, which in fact corresponds in Kant's vocabulary to the "empty intuition without object" (this empty intuition is equivalent to the gaze or the scopic object *a* in Lacan). In Sade, in contrast, the object in the Other's place is the object *a* in the form of the "voice". With the Sadean experience, Lacan develops enunciation on the basis of the *Other* which would have been unknown to Kant (the Sadean maxim would be more honest than the Kantian law "in coming out of the Other's mouth" and not being an "appeal to the voice within") while introducing the quite specific *object* that is the *vocal* object, while Kant's law would not have an object[42] or, to be more precise, would only have the abstract condition of the object, that is, the scopic object.

(Let us note parenthetically that if the Kantian law is not determined by any object, Kant does not "express regret" in any way for this absence and feels no need to fill it, as Lacan wrongly attributes to him. The three postulates of practical reason [freedom, immortality of the soul and belief in God] and the "unthinkability of the thing in itself" do not intervene at all in Kant as attempts to fill this so-called regrettable absence of the object).

The object (the voice) which comes into the Other's place to support the split in the subject (between A and S) appears to be the incarnation of the big Other. He is at the same time the one that calls into question modesty's "circumstances of being"; through the victim, he is that vocal object, that being which very concretely poses the question of Being. It is he who counts as "the being-in-the-world, the *Dasein*". Heidegger's *Dasein* corresponds very precisely here to Lacan's vocal object *a*. It is present in the Sadean experience as the voice enunciating the maxim or "the tormenting agent". We thus arrive at a radical point which will simultaneously take up again in the Sadean experience the thing in itself as the focus of Kant's question, *Dasein* as the beginning of Heidegger's question and the vocal object *a* as principle of Lacan's invention.

It is the voice which opens the Sadean experience, the emission point or the enunciation of the maxim: "I have the right to enjoy your body." The Kantian thing-in-itself becomes embodied but "retains the opacity of that which is transcendent".[43] This object, which is the voice of the tormentor, "is strangely separated from the subject", from the one subjected to sadism. It is also the voice involved in the verbal hallucinations in psychosis and in the voice of conscience. More fundamentally, the voice is brought to the place of the Other to say that the phenomenal world appears against the background of that which radically defies and contradicts the very conditions of phenomena.[44] And it is on the basis of this voice, as a radical calling into question of Being, that the desire of the lacking Other may appear at the locus of jouissance. "*I* am in the place from which 'the universe is a flaw in the purity of Non-Being' is vociferated. And not without reason for, by protecting itself, this place makes Being itself languish. This place is called Jouissance."[45]

In contrast to what seems to be presented in the Sadean maxim, the Kantian law *cannot* be determined in the transcendental aesthetic, in phenomenality. On principle. But in contrast to what Lacan thinks, Kant does not at all regret this. Phenomenality is not, however, absent from Kantian moral experience: the moral law does appear in sensibility in the form of *respect* (*Achtung*), including the pain for which one must only have contempt (*Verachtung*). "The object", nevertheless, "does not fail to appear in a certain bulge in the phenomenal veil", says Lacan. The Kantian law is not without the fire of desire, without the circumstances of the place and time of moral action, without fantasized unreality and without its effects in reality. This point of the apparition of the Kantian law can therefore be very well described phenomenally.

Despite these phenomenal apparitions of the moral law and despite the long developments that Kant devotes to respect, Lacan claims that he would not have wished to recognise this voice at all. Why does Lacan think this? Why does he want to exclude a priori precisely the *voice* from the Kantian experience? "[T]he voice – even if insane – forces [upon us] the idea of the subject", the idea of a subject completely *subjected to the voice* [*assujetti à la voix*], that is, of a subject who would not be the cause of the moral law, but its consequence (a new subject caused by the unconscious and its freedom). If the voice has taken the place of the Other, this distances us from any morals involving an *individual* in search of the Good. Now, Lacan cannot get rid of the idea that Kant's ethics is played out according to the Good and an individual, a hypostatised "subject". The voice, in contrast, implies a "subject" as the simple locus of enunciation, which is independent of all Good. All of this (the voice in the locus of the Other) may suggest "malignancy on the part of the real God". We see it again here; Lacan does not manage to conceive Kant's ethics according to *principle* alone (and not in dependence on the Good). To save the Good as the so-called centre of his morality and not question God's jouissance, which may just as much wish for evil as for good, Kant would have wished – this is Lacan's conception – to exclude consideration of the point of enunciation of the maxim as a phenomenal object, as voice and to hold on to the purely formal, voluntarist principle of "Law-for-Law's sake",[46] thus taking up "the *ataraxia* of the Stoics" again, of the contempt for pain, in order to transform it into contempt for phenomenality in general. Lacan quite simply reduces Kant to stoicism.

The pure voice expressing the Sadean maxim, which – let us emphasise this – corresponds very closely to Kant's *nihil negativum*, leaves open the question of God's will, which may be good or bad. In the place of Good, it is God's anger (*Zorn*) or Being-in-fury (*Grimmigkeit*)[47] which may come to us; as Jacob Boehme had already suggested.[48] Lacan only convokes the "supremely-evil-being" to counter a "supremely-good-being" supposed to be the determining factor in Kantian morals.[49] This "supremely-evil-being" is not taken from the pamphlet "Frenchmen, One More Effort . . . ", which claims precisely that the Supreme Being does not exist and that it enough to simply mock this type of belief. It comes from *Juliette, or Vice Amply Rewarded* and it is used in Saint-Fond's speech to round off Juliette's libertine education: "Having seen all that was vicious and criminal on earth, the Being Supreme in Wickedness will say unto them, 'Why did you stray into the paths of virtue?'"[50] Why must we stray onto the paths of virtue determined by the highest good? On "Kantian" paths, as Lacan thinks? It must be reiterated, however, contrary to Lacan's reading, Kantian is precisely not determined by the highest good, but by the autonomy in which the subject arises and which leaves no place for God in the creation of the moral law.

Notes

1. *Dialectic of Enlightenment: Philosophical Fragments* (1944), op. cit. Simone de Beauvoir also insisted on the Kant-Sade connection (*Faut-il brûlerSade?* 1955, cited in Marty, *Pourquoi le XXe siècle a-t-il pris Sade au sérieux?* op. cit., p. 77).
2. Marty, *Pourquoi le XXe siècle a-t-il pris Sade au sérieux?*, op. cit., p. 48.
3. Ibid., p. 52.
4. Ibid., p. 233.
5. "The notion that Sade's work anticipated Freud's – if nothing else, as a catalogue of the perversions – is a stupidity" (Lacan, *Écrits*, op. cit. p. 645). This acerbic criticism maliciously takes aim at Blanchot: "Lacan, in *The Ethics of Psychoanalysis*, invites his audience to read Blanchot's text on Sade, but the first sentence of his 'Kant with Sade' was to refute Blanchot by mocking as a 'stupidity' the idea that Sade had anticipated Freud (op. cit., p. 645), a statement which directly targets Blanchot, according to whom Sade 'outstrips Freud' (Blanchot, *Lautréamont and Sade*, translated by Stuart and Michelle Kendall, Stanford, Stanford University Press, 2004, p. 39)" (Marty, *Pourquoi le XXe siècle a-t-il pris Sade au sérieux?*, op. cit., p. 187).
6. Lacan, "Kant with Sade", op. cit., p. 645.
7. Ibid., p. 646.
8. This opposition is dealt with in the second chapter of the analytic of practical reason (see earlier).
9. Lacan, "Kant with Sade", op. cit., p. 647.
10. Kant, *Critique of Pure Reason*, op. cit., p. 232; A290/B346. See Fierens, "Logic of Truth and Logic of Erring in Kant and Lacan", in *The Issue with Kant*, Ljubljana, Filozofski vestnik, 2015.
11. Kant, *Critique of Practical Reason*, op. cit., p. 19.
12. In Kant, the voice of the moral conscience (*Gewissen*) cannot be reduced to a phenomenon, as Lacan claims to do, while simultaneously transforming the voice of conscience [*la voix de la conscience*] into "a voice in conscience", which is understood here as *Bewusstsein* (Lacan, "Kant with Sade", op. cit., p. 647).
13. Kant, *Critique of Pure Reason*, op. cit., p. 149; A149/B189.
14. The categorical imperative (or the moral law) "is an a priori synthetic practical proposition, and since gaining insight into the possibility of propositions of this kind causes so much difficulty in theoretical cognition, it can easily be inferred that in practical cognition there will be no less" (Kant, *Groundwork of the Metaphysics of Morals*, op. cit., p. 33). The theme of the moral law as a synthetic a priori judgement is taken up again in the *Critique of Practical Reason* on the basis of the autonomy of the moral law. Yes, there is great difficulty here.
15. Lacan, "Kant with Sade", op. cit., p. 647.
16. Translator's note: "*Faire confiance*" more commonly means "to trust", which in this example would refer to the one making the deposit, rather than the depositary.
17. "The objective reality of the moral law cannot be proved by any deduction." But the thing that cannot be deduced on the basis of the moral law is that freedom must be part

of it. (Kant, *Critique of Practical Reason*, op. cit., p. 41). In other words, analysing the fact of the moral law leads to freedom which is none other than the synthetic a priori principle of the moral law.
18 Lacan, "Kant with Sade", op. cit., p. 647.
19 Kant, *Critique of Pure Reason*, op. cit., p. 21; BXXIX.
20 Lacan, "Kant with Sade", op. cit., p. 647.
21 Sade, *Justine, Philosophy in the Bedroom, and Other Writings*, compiled and translated by Richard Seaver and Austryn Wainhouse, New York, Grove Press, 1990, p. 296 ff.
22 This form thus comes to replace the bad start in form as analytical universality.
23 Littré's dictionary gives two definitions of *"factum"*: 1. A presentation of the facts of a trial. 2. A memoir, published to attack someone or something, or to defend oneself.
24 [Translator's note: Fink translates "factum" here as "diatribe". "Factum" can be defined in Canadian English as "A written argument or brief filed with the court that is used by a lawyer to argue a motion or case before a judge" or, more simply, "A statement of the facts of a case".]
25 Cf. Freud, S.E. IV, p. 338, and S.E. V, p. 575. Also see Lacan, *The Logic of Fantasy*, lesson of 25th January 1967.
26 Lacan, "Kant with Sade", op. cit., p. 648.
27 Ibid. Text in brackets by the author.
28 Blanchot, *Lautréamont and Sade*, p. 39: "There exists in Sade a purely traditional moralist, and it would be easy to assemble a selection of his maxims which would make those of La Rochefoucauld appear weak and uncertain. We reproach him for writing badly and he does indeed often write in haste and with a prolixity that exhausts our patience. But he is also capable of a bizarre humor, his style reaches a glacial joviality, a sort of cold innocence within his excesses, which we prefer to all of Voltaire's irony and which is found in no other French writer."
29 Lacan, *Encore*, op. cit., p. 3.
30 Lacan, "Kant with Sade", op. cit., p. 649.
31 In *the Ethics*, Lacan cited *Juliette, or Vice Amply Rewarded*, in which Mme Delbène said to Juliette: "Lend me the part of your body that will give me a moment of satisfaction and, if you care to, use for your own pleasure that part of my body which appeals to you." (Lacan, *The Ethics of Psychoanalysis*, op. cit., p. 202).
32 Lacan, "On a Question Prior to Any Possible Treatment of Psychosis", in *Écrits*, op. cit., p. 458.
33 Lacan, "Kant with Sade", op. cit., p. 649.
34 Ibid., p. 648.
35 Ibid., p. 649.
36 Lacan, "Kant with Sade", op. cit., p. 771.
37 Big Other refers to capital A (Autre) in French which translates to English as capital O for Other.
38 Ibid., p. 651.
39 Cf. in The Story of Juliette, Pius VI's speech, as a "coherent anti-creationist" (Marty, *Pourquoi le XXe siècle a-t-il pris Sade au sérieux?*, op. cit., p. 214).
40 Lacan, "Kant with Sade", op. cit., p. 651.
41 "In coming out of the Other's mouth, Sade's maxim [...] unmasks the split in the subject that is usually covered up" (Ibid., p. 650).
42 According to Lacan's reading, Kant would have "expressed his regret" (Ibid., p. 647) at the absence of the object and would have been compelled to find a substitute for the accomplishment of the Law, a substitute he found in the two postulates of the dialectic of practical reason (the immortality of the soul and the existence of God, or again, according to Lacan, "the unthinkability of the thing in itself"). We have seen earlier that this reading does not correspond to the heart of Kant's line of thinking, which does not

seek an object as a substitution, reward, or replacement, but instead seeks not to give way on the principle of pure reason.
43 Ibid., p. 651.
44 The voice is thus the *nihil negativum*, impossible because it contradicts the very conditions of sensible experience, such as "a figure composed of two straight lines" (Kant, *Critique of Pure Reason*, op. cit., p. 232; A290/B346).
45 Lacan, "The Subversion of the Subject and the Dialectic of Desire", op. cit., p. 819.
46 Lacan, "Kant with Sade", op. cit., p. 651.
47 [Translator's note: *Grimmigkeit* can also be more simply translated as "ferocity" or "ferociousness".]
48 Cf. Arjakovsky and France-Lanord, translation notes in Heidegger, *La dévastation et l'attente*, Paris, Gallimard, 2006, p. 81. [English translation: Heidegger, *Country Path Conversations*, translated by Bret W. Davis, Bloomington and Indianapolis, Indiana University Press, 2010].
49 Let us note that Kant himself introduced the concept of "radical evil" in *Religion within the Bounds of Bare Reason*, translated by Werner S. Pluhar (1792), Indianapolis and Cambridge, Hackett Publishing Company, 2009. On this topic, see Éric Weil, "Le mal radical, la religion et la morale [Radical evil, religion and morals]", in *Problèmes kantiens*, Paris, Vrin, 1998, p. 143ff.
50 Marquis de Sade, *Juliette*, translated by Austryn Wainhouse, New York, Grove Press, 1968, p. 399.

Chapter 13

Sade's contribution to psychoanalysis

Desire as the articulation of pleasure and jouissance by the intermediary of the object *a*

The place of the Real is never attained in its pure form, and the pleasure principle always comes to be mixed up with the jouissance principle. The object *a* (and more especially the object *a* in its vocal form) simultaneously allows for the distinction and the articulation of pleasure and jouissance.

The non-existence of the Supreme Being (not unrelated to the barred big Other [Ø] in Lacan) may definitively open up the place of the Real and jouissance. But despite the fact that this non-existence is proclaimed from the start of *Frenchmen, One More Effort* . . . the Supreme Being (good or bad) reappears in the form of the supremely-evil-being or Supreme Being of Wickedness in opposition to the Being of Supreme Good (in *Juliette, or Vice Amply Rewarded*). The Real is thus filled in by these images of the Supreme Being (good or bad), which hold the place of the Thing. Let us chase these images away. "But humph! *Schwärmereien*, black swarms – I chase you away".[1] They come back. "*Schwärmereien*", fanaticisms which Kant had always wanted to put to one side to make way for the principle of practical reason.[2] It is not enough to chase away these "black swarms" in order to finally reach the Thing and the Real in their pure state. The expulsion of impassioned fanatical positions makes way for another form of the imaginary, overlapping the Thing and the Real, that is, the fantasy which imposes itself on us as impossible to eliminate.

The Sadean experience will lead us to analyse the structure of the "Sadean fantasy", in which the structure of the fantasy in general is unveiled. For this, "return[ing] to the function of presence" in the fantasy is involved. It is the object *a*, which is the agent of torment, which holds the function of presence, as *Dasein* (cf. Heidegger). But this object *a* is only one of the two terms of the fantasy which always implicates the fading subject (barred subject) in its dynamic. When the subject is effaced, "the quest [the object] figures" dies out and jouissance is petrified in this object (petrification of the object *a*, of the voice becoming the agent of torment) which becomes a "black fetish". Instead of the non-existence of the big Other, instead of the "black swarms" of the *Schwärmereien* which themselves

DOI:10.4324/9781003055662-23

are substituted for this transcendent big Other (which does not exist) the "black fetish" presents itself quite concretely, that is, the object as a fetish, the latest *concrete* object permitting the sight of the radical lack in the big Other to be avoided, the sight of the mother's castration and the radical calling into question of Being. "This is what becomes of the executioner (or of the object *a*, or the agent of torment) in sadism when, in the most extreme case, his presence is reduced to being no more than the instrument." This is the leading instrument in the sadistic experience, the one which counts as a fetish. We shall we see how it is the instrument which veils the mother's castration. The object *a* thus petrified (agent of torment, executioner, instrument) fixates, crystallises jouissance in the Sadean fantasy.

This crystallisation of jouissance in the object of fantasy also entails "the humility of an act", because the tormentor who serves as the object *a* in the Sadean experience comes into it as "a being of flesh", that is, equally subject to the pleasure principle. Inside the same object *a* (instrument or agent of torment), the principle of jouissance (not first of all counting as a being of flesh but being made present in the "circumstances of being") and the pleasure principle (which essentially involves a being of flesh) will therefore have to be articulated and distinguished. Even if the object *a* is situated in the place of the big Other, the duplication of principles (jouissance vs pleasure) remains within the object *a* (this duplication within the object *a* does not correspond to the duplication of the alterities of the subjects S and A).

The agent of torment is thus split by the duality of principles. It is he who causes desire. Then it is desire, which supports the "subject's two alterities" (S and A), thus amounting to a calling into question of the subject on the basis of the object *a* (and the duplication of principles), in other words, it is what introduces the subject's two alterities, S and A. Desire, here connected to the difference between the pleasure principle and the jouissance principle at the level of its cause (object *a*), "would no doubt be willing to call itself "will to jouissance" at the level of the "subject" (Kant's higher faculty of desire). In this sense, the agent of torment's[3] desire may invoke another will to jouissance "in the Other", that is, his victim. To elicit this will to jouissance in his victim, he must radically divide her from her pathos, that is, from all that still belongs to the pathological and the pleasure principle. But it cannot be forgotten that this division of pleasure and jouissance *starts out* [*part*] from the question of pleasure (such as it is first encountered in the object *a*): it is not possible to directly start out from jouissance or freedom (even in Kant, who starts out from principles, we do not directly start out from jouissance: we know nothing of freedom if we do not first know the moral law, guilt, and the superego).

Now, it is a natural law of pleasure to "make [desire] always fall short of its aim: the homeostasis of the living being, always too quickly re-established at the lowest threshold of tension at which he scrapes by". Desire wants to tear itself away from pleasure and to fly off towards the place of jouissance "from which "the universe is a flaw in the purity of Non-Being" is vociferated",[4] but "the ever early [is the] fall of its wing" (a fall at the level of Kant's lower faculty of desire). This fall of the wing signs "the reproduction of its form", the short cycle of erection-fall specific to pleasure. This wing must, however, here "rise to the function of representing the link between sex and death", that is, to reveal the articulation between sex approached from the viewpoint of pleasure and death opening up the question of jouissance. Let us leave this question of the elevation to jouissance to rest beneath a mythical veil, articulating jouissance and pleasure as if they were two distinct entities.[5]

The pleasure principle, which makes desire fall short of its aim, seems well made to die off as quickly as possible. It is not the same with jouissance, which always calls for more. From this point of view, pleasure and jouissance fundamentally *clash* [*discordent*]. On this basis, it can be imagined that pleasure should quickly succumb, should falter, to definitively make way for jouissance, which arises beyond the pleasure principle and towards the question of the beyond of death. Now, the question of pleasure never disappears. How does it happen that it does not disappear? "At the moment of climax [*jouissance*], it would simply be out of the picture if fantasy did not intervene to sustain it with the very discord to which it succumbs." Pleasure, which would succumb in its discordance, in its discord with jouissance, is in fact recovered *by the fantasy*. "Fantasy provides the pleasure that is characteristic of desire."[6]

In the operation of sustaining desire, the fantasy does indeed enlist the object and the divided subject. But not in the same way. It is object *a*'s duplication (pleasure and jouissance, pleasure is always there) which initiates the fantasy. It is based on the object *a* that it is possible to approach the fantasy and not on the basis of the divided subject. Desire itself cannot be understood on the basis of the subject, based on "that which a signifier represents for another signifier". It cannot therefore "be indicated anywhere in a signifier of any demand whatsoever". It is impossible to hold oneself outside it to articulate it: it "cannot be articulated". But it is already perfectly "articulated", by what causes it, by the object *a*, and it is on this basis that it can be "the henchman of the subject's split",[7] a split which pre-exists every particular subject, who always already finds themselves taken up in the pre-existing opposition between the pleasure principle and the jouissance principle (an opposition primordially brought into play by the object *a*).

"Taking pleasure in fantasy is easy to grasp here": it is contained, implicated in the fantasy under the form of the object *a* (which simultaneously counts as the instrument of pleasure and instrument of jouissance), which means that pleasure is constantly relaunched despite its short cycle: despite its premature faltering, it is continuously recovered.

Pain presents itself as opposed to pleasure: "pain has a longer cycle than pleasure in every respect, since a stimulation provokes pain at the point at which pleasure stops". If, through the object *a* (instrument of pleasure and jouissance), the fantasy relaunches pleasure at the moment at which it flags, the fantasy also takes advantage of this datum of pain to represent "in the sensory aspect of Sadean experience" – the prolonging of desire and its subjective effect which, pushed to its extreme, leads to "the subject pass[ing] out", $.

> Such is the vital datum (pleasure's short cycle, centred on the object *a*, and pain's long cycle, centred on the barred subject) that fantasy takes advantage of in order to fixate – in the sensory aspect of Sadean experience – the desire that appears in its agent (on the basis of the object *a*, the voice or the tormentor).[8]

On the basis of pleasure (object *a*) and pain (the barred subject [$]), we now come to the articulation of the fantasy which implicates the fourfold structure of schema L.

The structure of the fantasy demonstrated in the Sadean experience

The fantasy ($◇a) articulates the dialectic of desire in two directions. In going from *a* to $ (this is the first and principal direction), the object *a* is the desire of $ or again the impossible quest for pleasure on the side of the agent of torment (object *a*) aims for pain and is the desire for the victim's ignominy to the point of her passing out ($). Going from $ to *a*, the victim's extremely mortifying jouissance is supposed to desire the tormentor's pleasure. But the object *a* and $ only take on their consistency in the complex movement – to and fro – of desire. It is in relation to this double-entry desire that the object *a* and the barred subject take on a fixed identity even though tormentor and victim *only* exist within the complex articulation of the fantasy. The fantasy always supposes the complex articulation of the question of the subject, that is, the schema L with its imaginary axis of the statement and its symbolic axis of enunciation, which we recall here:[9]

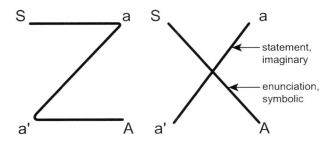

Figure 2

Let us give these two schemata a quarter turn clockwise to obtain the following schemata:

"Kant with Sade" (1962–1963)

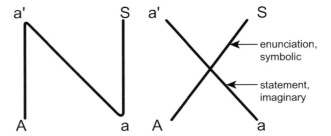

Figure 3

This articulation of the fantasy does not correspond either to the imaginary axis of the statement or to the symbolic axis of enunciation, but to the articulation, on the one hand, of the object *a* in the position of the big Other in enunciation *in as much as it has already been extended* in the statement *towards the will* (the tormentor's will, V) and, on the other hand, from the barred Subject (reduced to its passing out) in the position of nondescript object ("a") in the statement *in as much as it is already extended* in enunciation *towards a subject effect* (the effect of the Sadean experience, S).

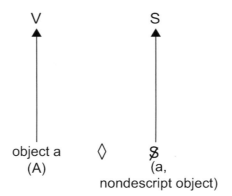

Figure 4

Let us now complete the schema with the purely imaginary line which goes from the tormentor's will (V) to its object, which is the barred subject:

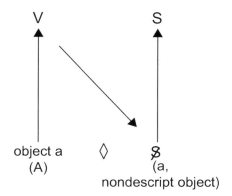

Figure 5

The classic, simplified articulation of the fantasy is situated on the lower line of the schema (without an extension towards V and S). This articulation of the fantasy "only occurs when its apparent agent freezes with the rigidity of an object" (the fixated, "frozen" object *a*).

Under this apparent rigidity, the fantasy only exists because it is, above all, engaged in speech and in the complete schema L. Everything seems to be in the right place in this classic presentation of the fantasy: the object *a* is in the place of the Other (source of enunciation) and the victim counts as the imaginary partner of the torturer's will (statement).

But enunciation – which really is present in the voice – also has the effect of turning all the hardened positions upside-down: the tormentor's words (the enunciation of the Sadean maxim, object *a* with a view to an extension towards V) also implies its other, that is, the victim ($) and its subject effect (S). If the agent of torment insists in his speech at the same time as he freezes it so far as to reduce it to the pure instrument of torment, he *also* places the other, the victim, in a position from which he expects a response. "The structure of speech [. . .] is that the subject receives his message from the other in an inverted form."[10] He addresses a message to her with the aim that his own message will also be sent back to him with the extension that entails the articulation of the four places (whereas in the simplified formula, everything appears in dual form – object *a*/ barred subject).

By what sequence of operations, by what calculus, does the subject make their appearance? How are they produced in the complex structure of the fantasy? We have seen "the condition of the subject, S (neurosis or psychosis), depends on what unfolds in the Other",[11] not without passing through the chicane of the imaginary. Schema L presented the zigzagging route through A, a' (the ego), a (the nondescript objects, not to be confused with the object *a*) and, at last, S. The object *a* (understood as the voice and the agent of torment) is at the beginning of the chain, it is the cause of the chain, that is, the deployment of the articulation of desire by the fantasy as far as the subject effect (S). On its own, the emission point of the maxim "I have the right to enjoy your body . . . " counts in the rigidity of posing the rule as universal. It presents itself as "object a in the place of the cause". But it only finds its *raison d'être* and its existence in the general articulation of desire, which commands the whole business: desire, while it is articulated everywhere ("desire – which is the henchman of the subject's split"), is presented as not being fulfilled anywhere: the fantasy "props up the utopia of desire". The schema should thus be completed by the incidence of desire (d) on the object a which counts as the cause and by bringing back schema 1 of the "Kant with Sade".

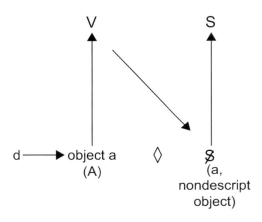

Figure 6

This incidence of desire on the object a fundamentally calls into question the category of *causality* implied in the object a, but not without completely turning it upside down.

Let us explain how it is turned upside down. In the field of appearances or phenomena (in the analytic of *The Critique of Pure Reason*), a particular cause determines a particular effect and every phenomenon is thought of as determined by a cause. The object a, convoked here in the fantasy, is not content to be one cause among others. It presents itself as the universal and categorical cause (the right to be the cause of desire, "I will exercise this right without any limit"). Thus, the emission point of the maxim arrogates an absolute freedom to itself, that is, a causality through freedom, the right to begin, as the creator of one's universe, an infinity of new temporal chains. The universality demanded here is not an analytic universality, it is a synthetic universality, a true creation: on the basis of this object a, the subject is synthetically created following the sequence indicated in schema 1: $a - V - \$ - S$. Such a causality goes beyond, forces "its way into Kant's transcendental deduction" (the causality deduced in the transcendental analytic of pure reason is a purely deterministic causality) to open onto the *Dialectic of Pure Reason*, more precisely the third antinomy, whose thesis states, "Causality according to the laws of nature is not the only causality. [. . .] A causality of freedom is also necessary".[12] The object *a*, in the Sadean fiction which allows itself every freedom of invention, a "horrible freedom"[13]– essentially falls into the framework of this thesis implying freedom. This indeed is why it is presented in the form of the voice, under the form of the *nihil negativum* which contradicts the very conditions of phenomenal experience to open up the field of that which cannot be said or represented, that is, the Real.

In forcing the limits of the *Critique of Pure Reason* in the part of it dedicated to appearances (Transcendental Analytic), the object *a* in the place of cause would establish "a new Critique of Reason" which would no longer be founded on appearances (like Kant's *Critique of Pure Reason*) but on the workings of *practical reason*. Moreover, in order to avoid all practice biased towards Good, the object *a* would establish this critique "on the linchpin of impurity". The impurity of Evil, which comes to be opposed to the Purity of Good, would thus belong, from what Lacan says, to the *Critique of Practical Reason*.

The agent of torment or the voice *seems*, however, to be commanded by V, "the will that dominates the whole business". Everything – notably the place of the fantasy ($\$ \lozenge a$) – would be commanded by the will as in Kant ("good will" in fact commanding the pedagogical exposition of the moral law in the *Groundwork for the Metaphysics of Morals*, but not the structure of pure reason). Now, the letter V, as well as the aforementioned Sadean, will evoke the symbol of union or and/or. Above all, this will, the letter V is the *union* of two parts of the fantasy, on the one hand, the division of the subject, that is, the barred subject (the subject passing out in pain) and, on the other hand, the impossible quest for pleasure and jouissance on the side of the tormentor (object *a*). This same will also implies the extension of the barred subject on the side of a subject which in fact corresponds to the tormentor. If it starts out from the object *a*, the will necessitates passing through the barred subject and its pain to finally arrive at S, the brute subject of pleasure, which remains an enigma.

It is "Kant's will that is encountered in the place of this will". If in Kant the will is encountered as "occupying the place of honour", it is because, as good will, it can be recognised by everybody. But this will, good will, is only a *pedagogical introduction* to the moral law (cf. the first section of the *Groundwork for the Metaphysics of Morals*). In the *Critique of Practical Reason*, everything depends in contrast on the questioning of causality and freedom rather than on good will. In other words, the course of the fantasy can be perfectly well read in Kantian morality. The voice (or the *nihil negativum*), which stands for the calling into question of determinist causality and the opening up of another causality (through freedom), is extended in will to divide the Subject (between pleasure and jouissance) and to make the "pathological" subject appear as an effect of the moral law. The "brute subject of pleasure" or the "pathological" subject does not exist in itself (it is a pure abstraction) – it is always the result of the whole course of the Sadean fantasy, first of all implying the duality of pleasure and jouissance in the initial object a. The will (preceded by the voice, as the point of departure of the whole trajectory, even though the will may *appear* to be first) "can only be said to be a will to jouissance if we explain" that unfolding the chain, allowing the effect of the subject, that is, how the "pathological" subject (S) only occurs after passing through the barred subject, in other words, how the "pathological" subject is to be situated on the basis of the division of the subject. The will situated on this trajectory is firstly dependent on the object a (the voice which enunciates "I have the right to enjoy . . . "), this is why it is called "will to jouissance". In entailing the *whole* course through the barred subject and the "pathological" subject, such a will "is the subject reconstituted through alienation", provided that it is conditioned by the instrument of jouissance, commanded by the object a in the position of cause. It is the subject reconstituted "at the cost of being nothing but the instrument of jouissance".

Kant had seen well how will operates. But he had overlooked the point of departure on the near side of will, that is, the object a. With this exposition of the Sadean fantasy, the will, which also seems to dominate the whole business, is called into question – it is dependent on the object a, more precisely on the voice. Kant is called into question "with Sade", that is, through the introduction of the voice, of the instrument, of the object a of which Kant would have been unaware and of which Sade himself would have held the place in a certain way (see later). But let us say it again: this voice is quite present in its place in Kant in the fourth form of the nothing, the *nihil negativum*. It is the radical absence of the object, the nothing as contradiction of the conditions of sensible experience, which precisely opens up the field of freedom and morality. Kant would have regretted the absence of the object in the experience of morality (p. 647 and p. 651). Lacan triumphs: here now is the object that Kant had thought was lacking. It is indeed delivered by Sade in person who would come in here to yield the truth of the *Critique of Practical Reason* (p. 646). Will "is obvious"; it becomes sensible under the form of the object a which describes desire's question, the sense of "*Che vuoi*", "What do you want?" "What do you want?" is explained not by the will, but by the voice promulgating the impossible maxim that the Sadean maxim is, "I have the right to enjoy your body."

This schema 1 makes the formula of the fantasy explicit (a$\diamond$$, the lower line of the schema) in showing how the fantasy, which at first seemed to consist of two basic terms (the object and the barred subject), ought to be completed by what is presented on the surface (on the upper line of the schema): V and S. Sade systematically develops this structure of the fantasy throughout his work. But it can be used for any fantasy, perverse or otherwise.

Thus far it is mainly the left-hand side of the schema which has been developed, concerning sadistic positions (the will and the tormentor). We can now turn towards what follows, the right-hand side, the victims' side (as barred Subject and pathological subject, undergoing the Sadean experience). Let us first note that in the fantasy, the object is petrified, is rigidified in his insistent posture of the cause of desire (and this rigidity is not without a relationship to the substitution of an *object* for the operation of a *principle*, as we shall see further on). This is why "there is a statics of the fantasy" and all the other terms of schema 1 will undergo the consequences of this and will also be indefinitely presented as monotonous and insistent in their position and their rigidity.

Thus, the barred Subject, purified of all pleasure and of everything pathological, the Subject lacerated by pain on the point of passing out, the Subject who stands for the "point of aphanisis" does cease not dying. The subject's point of aphanisis should reply, should respond to the tormentor. But if he really died, this would also be the aphanisis of desire (no desire without the subject's response); this point also "must in one's imagination be indefinitely pushed back. This explains the hardly believable survival that Sade grants to the victims of the abuse and tribulations he inflicts in his fable." And if one of the victims dies, it is to be replaced in a combinatory in which the function of the victim is always one and the same, to *almost* pass out in pain, to represent the Subject, responding to the tormentor, the Subject in the process of passing out, in the process of being barred. Whereas the barred Subject signifies the punctual moment, the instantaneousness of the death or the passing out of the Subject, it is presented in the fantasy as persisting eternally according to the pressing and rigidifying insistence itself of bringing structure into play through the object *a* in the fantasy. The victims have the function of representing the Will for its own aim, which is to finally produce the brute subject of pleasure, S. Their sole role is to accomplish "the subject's relation to the signifier". The barred subject (the victim) is what is represented by a signifier (S1 or the Will) for another signifier (S2 or the brute subject of pleasure, S). And it is all initiated by the vocal object in the place of the Other.

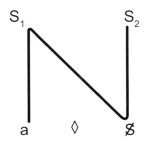

Figure 7

The first cause which fixes this relation to the signifier resides in the object *a*. However, the rigidity of the object *a* is only obtained by the *repetitive* insistence of the voice and the instrument in the real. From this insistence which must always be taken up again, it follows that the object *a*, "the troupe of tormentors [. . .] can have more variety"[14] than the representations of the barred subject in the victims on the point of passing out. It is this continual agency of the object *a*, proper to the fantasy (and in particular to "primal fantasies") which means that the fantasy supports the pleasure principle in the very place where one would think that it should disappear to make way for the jouissance principle. But we shall see, this continual insistence of the fantasy (which supports the pleasure principle in the very place it would disappear) is itself dependent on the Real and jouissance.

"The requirement that the victims' faces always be of incomparable (and, moreover, inalterable) beauty is another matter." This beauty of the subject, of the "pathological subject" (S), precisely hides the horror of the Real and jouissance. It belongs to what underlies the fantasy, above all the decisive, irrevocable engagement in the ethical act which nothing can stop, not even the perspective of certain death (the subject is put through the extreme of the pathological, that is, death). At the moment when Antigone is, so to speak, already dead as she has been condemned by Creon to be buried alive for having wanted to bury her rebellious brother despite the laws of the city, at the moment when Antigone finds herself between the two deaths – the death sentence and the death that will ensue from it – the chorus sings: *Erôs anikaté machan*, "Love unconquered in the fight", because Antigone's love for what she should do will not step back in the face of anything. She will no longer take any pathological pressure into account. Antigone's beauty is none other than the veil of the basic horror of being buried for her ethical act, the "ultimate barrier that forbids access to a fundamental horror".[15]

It is the condemnation here that introduces "the discordance between the two deaths", the death in the condemnation and damnation and then physiological death (everything here is "pathological"). Death in Antigone's condemnation by Creon comes *before* physiological death. But the temporal order of the two deaths can also be inverted. Thus, when the same Creon, champion of condemnation, forbids a tomb to Polynices, he inflicts a "second death" on him *after* his physiological death, which had already taken place.[16] "The between-two-deaths of the shy of [*l'en-deçà*] is essential to show us that it is no other than the one by which the beyond [*l'au-delà*] is sustained." Sade himself wants to have it both ways, the between-two-deaths of the shy of and that of the beyond: condemnation and damnation can come into play before physiological death, but also *afterwards*, in *hell*. In *The Story of Juliette*,

> Saint-Fond forces his victims to sign a pact with the devil which would send them to hell and would indefinitely prolong the suffering that had been inflicted on them in this world ("and yours will be the unspeakable delight of prolonging them beyond the limits of eternity, if eternity there be").[17]

However, an objection immediately presents itself here: the idea of hell had been refuted by Sade on the very basis of the fact that it is dependent on a Supreme Being that does not exist and only stands as "religious tyranny's way of constraining people".[18] How can Sade now reintroduce hell? Despite his radical atheism, Sade does not hesitate to condemn his victims to eternal torment; because it is radical condemnation, the return to absolute nothingness, which opens up the field of the between-two-deaths under one of these two forms or another, however implausible this business might be, because it involves opening up the space of a radically ethical (as in the case of Antigone). With the certainty of the second death, everything is put in place for the radical rejection of every "pathological" consideration in the determination of the ethical act (it is senseless to act towards one goal or another, as everything is consigned to death and condemnation in advance) and physiological death, on the other hand, comes under the heading of nature's ("pathological") routine. In accordance with this second death, which can be understood in the Sadean tortures of the here-below or in the hereafter, Sade's philosophy demands that condemnation attacks Nature itself,[19] so that everything may commence with the voice. "Against the awful routine of nature", it demands that the subject's indefinitely postponed passing out ($) is echoed in the extreme violence which condemns the subject to radical annihilation: "that the very decomposed elements of our body be destroyed so that they can never again be assembled".

Despite all the possible ways of presenting the "second death", death is not a matter of before or after. It is a radical calling into question of time, which allows a new sequence to begin, of which the point of departure is the vocal object, which allows a new form to be created, beyond all presentations. This is what gives an atemporal or eternal character to fantasy precisely on the basis of the object a as voice.

Transcendental value of the pain of existence: the second death and the death drive

The between-two-deaths entails the death drive. The death sentence which introduced it had closed pleasure's account, and nothing more functions according to possible retributions in the sense of the pleasure principle. The emptying-out of every consideration of pleasure leads to the steadfast decision of the ethical act (Antigone) and the purification of the field of jouissance. If we ignore the stakes of the death drive and the jouissance principle, psychoanalytic practice is reduced to a pure "technique", in which language "has effects that are [. . .] simply utilitarian or, at the very most, for purposes of display".[20] This indeed is what happens when the work of the unconscious is reduced to a pure mechanism without taking into account what "giving things a new form" means, without taking account of the fact that this new form does not correspond either to a technique aiming at one goal or another, or to the pleasure principle.

Despite the quite understandable tendency to ignore the death drive and the jouissance principle, there are many arguments, however, in favour of recognising its universal importance in human history. At the level of religious history, "the pain of existence is the original reason for the practices of salvation" that "millions of men [. . .] base on their faith in Buddha". It is also present in Christianity,

Islam, or Hinduism. At the level of psychiatry, this same pain of existence, in its pure state, "model[s] the song" of those suffering from melancholia. At the level of psychoanalysis, this same pain of existence is central to those dreams which not only turn the dreamer upside-down, but also call them to an "inexhaustible rebirth". (We could cite countless dreams here: the dream of Irma's injection, the dream of the dead father, the Wolfman's dream, etc.) At the level of everyday life, the perspective of death is always on the horizon. If we had to imagine "our everyday life as having to be eternal", that is, without death, it would indeed quickly seem like a hell. And "hell's torments" which Sade talks about are nothing other than the signature of the insistence of the death drive.

Despite their importance and their stakes, the death drive and the jouissance principle are almost systematically ignored. This "stupidity" is "sociological" in as much as it depends on the structure of crowds which always gather together around an ego-ideal reduced to the imaginary, which precisely aims to efface the perspective of death. It is futile to hope that this ignorance might be reduced through rational arguments. Associated with the identification with an imaginary ego-ideal figure, this ignorance is constitutive of every human group, as Freud has shown in *Group Psychology and the Analysis of the Ego*.[21] The circles of those whose claim to have "a surer experience of forms of sadism"[22] (and thus claim to have a surer experience of the Real) do not escape this any more than any other group. All this precisely reduces the Real to an imaginary. In the same sense as rejecting the real stakes of the pain of existence and the death drive into a pure imaginary, the Sadean fantasy is reduced to "the relation of reversion that supposedly unites sadism with a certain idea of masochism". Certainly, Freud had indeed noted the reversal of the active drive to the passive one, and one could understand here the reversal of sadism (I torment, active verb) into masochism (I am tormented, passive verb). But this reversal does not happen without the middle reflexive verb (I torment myself). This complex reflexivity is not deployed within an imaginary dual opposition, but within the quadrature of the Sadean *mise en scène* and fantasy, as we have seen. The binary sadism vs. masochism opposition has to do with a pure imaginary and reciprocal relation that could humorously be described as "the exploitation of one man by another", of the sadist by the masochist and the masochist by the sadist,[23] one being no other than the imaginary complement of the other. This conception of an essentially imaginary sadism is equivalent to attributing to it the negation of the dimension of the big Other and the symbolic. "This results in the claim that the sadist "denies the Other's existence."[24] This imaginary relation boils down to the V-$ couple in the schema of the Sadean fantasy.

The second death and the eternal condemnation which introduces it, by evacuating the taking into consideration of the benefits which may result from a certain action, obligate us to put to one side everything which seems to directly have to do with the pleasure/unpleasure principle (that is, everything that may be situated in relation to the statement, V and $) to accentuate the importance of the two other corners of the schema. Thus, in the articulation of the fantasy and in taking the death drive into account, $ only makes sense because it leads to the pathological subject which bears the pain of existence, and alongside this, bears the death drive and the jouissance principle: "the sadist discharges the pain of existence into the Other". The victim must suffer as a subject in her flesh. If the subject is presented as being on the verge of passing out (the barred subject), it is in order to be well present for the sadist as his Other, from who the sadist himself receives his message of jouissance in an inverted form (where it is seen that Sade's characters only take a provisional place in the fourfold schema of the question of the subject).[25] Far from simply disappearing or passing away, the subject who had been presented as barred, must turn into the pure pathological subject, hiding behind her beauty the basic horror of the second death (S). In a similar manner, still within the articulation of the fantasy and in taking the death drive into account, V, the will only has meaning because it is derived from the object a. Provided the fourfold *mise en scène* is understood, the sadist is not firstly a will which would determine its object, he is quite, above all, an atemporal object (as we have seen where the vocal object is concerned, outside the conditions of sensibility, therefore outside of time), "an "eternal object". He holds the place of the object a, the agent of torment. He is the voice which promulgates the Sadean maxim and, in order to obtain the fantasy (and the division of the subject), the object a "freezes with the rigidity of an object",[26] he appears eternal. In Lacan's reading of Sade, the symbolic or symbol-making object (the object a that is the tormentor in the form of the voice) determines the imaginary Will. In the conception of Kantian morality, it may seem that it is (the symbol-making) Good Will which determines the (properly imaginary) Moral Law. But as we have seen, Good Will is only a *pedagogical* manner (first section of the *Groundwork of the Metaphysics of Morals*) of making the Moral Law appear to everyone. The true creation of the Moral Law must come from freedom, which only exists when it is presupposed to escape the conditions of sensible experience, in other words it is the *nihil negativum* (as the nothing in as much as it denies the conditions of sensory experience). In other words, it is still the voice which determines the Moral Law.

We should acknowledge the question of the death drive as well as the jouissance principle which entails the dialectic of the fourfold schema.

From the viewpoint of this architectonic, should we not push Sade a bit further and think that this object a, or the eternal object may well fabricate, may well produce the "common good", the common good of "redemption and the immortal soul", the common good as it would be revised by Sade in accordance with jouissance? The Christian, in his sin of jouissance, would be in the place of the Sadean agent of torment himself, in the place of the object a, and would address himself to his victim (his big Other) who should respond with extreme pain. Christ, as victim, the Other of the Christian, as sadist, may be appealed to respond to the latter's voice. "Let us not proceed too quickly, so as not to go too far either", Lacan already warns us. Because Sade does not push his logic far enough to be able to articulate it to the Christian commandment, *Thou shalt love your neighbour as yourself*, at play in the Christic construction. This question will be taken up again

144 "Kant with Sade" (1962–1963)

at the end of the text: Sade "refuses to be my neighbour" not out of sadism, but rather out of a lack of sadism: he "does not have neighborly enough relations with his own malice [*méchanceté*] to encounter his neighbor in it".[27]

Sade's thought does not lead to Christianity, but to another, new history, which is the logic of his life.

Sade's work and his life

The various Sadean scenes, which count as so many presentations of the fantasy, arise as particular, distinct. Everything seems far from the sought-after universality. As we have seen based on the Sadean maxim, universality is only aimed for as "synthetic", meaning that it is to be constructed and it can only be constructed on the basis of something that is not universal, the object *a* (situated in the place of the Other), more precisely on the basis of the fourth form of the object *a*, the tormentor's *voice*.

Sade's own *voice* is, however, very different from the voice of the tormentor in the Sadean scenes. From the outset, it universalises, involving the universality of human beings and it proclaims from the outset a universal declaration of human rights, it is the "fact that Sade delegates a right to jouissance to everyone in his Republic".[28]

The passage from the tormentor's voice (a voice which appears in the particularity of one staging or another) to Sade's voice (which aims at human universality), in other words, the passage from a particular voice to a universal one, is presented by Lacan by "a 90-degree rotation of the graph"; this is the passage from schema 1 (p. 653) to schema 2 (p. 657):

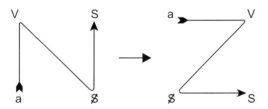

Figure 8

What can be read in this 90-degree rotation?

Let us first insist on the common characteristics of the two schemas, which link both of them to Schema L's zigzag. In each case, the production of S on the basis of *a* is played out by means of the passage through the axis of the statement, by means of the imaginary filter which articulates the sadistic Will (V) to the victim's barred subject ($). Each time, the object *a* is in the position of the big Other and it finishes by producing S (the line A-S, unrepresented in the schemas counts as the axis of enunciation).

What is more, also in each case, it is desire which motivates the schema. The function of desire always operates in the same place and does not undergo the 90-degree rotation (we shall see that this place on the lower line of each of these schemas has a particular rather than a universal value).

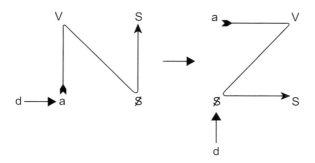

Figure 9

Now let us take a look at the differences. The object *a* and the S produced have different positions in each of the schemas. The 90-degree turn by which the first schema is transformed into the second raises the object *a* to the upper line while demoting the S subject to the lower line. What is the value of these "upper" or "lower" positions?

In the first schema, which stands for a *particular* Sadean scene, it is the "brute subject of pleasure ("pathological" subject)" which is produced at the end of the zigzag and this subject counts as a *universal* (we go from the particular "*a*" to the universal "S"). This indeed is how universality is produced or synthetic. In the second schema, which stands for a *universal* theory presented through Sade's work and life, it is "the brute subject characteristic of the pathological" which is produced and it is incarnated in the *particulars* who play the part of heroes or in the particular reader of Sade's work (we go from the universal to the particular). Here, it is the analysis of Sadean universality which produces particular effects, for example, on the reader.

In both schemas, the upper line is occupied by purportedly universal values. In the first schema, it is "the will that dominates the whole business"[29] and the beautiful subject purified by the second death. In the second schema, it is the object *a* as Sade's voice (which purports to be universal), enunciating the universal rights to jouissance and the will to jouissance (V). In both schemas, the lower line is occupied by particular values. In the first schema, it is the particularity of one tormentor's voice or another and the particularity of one barred subject's pain or another. In the second schema, it is the barred subject and "the brute subject incarnating the heroism characteristic of the pathological".[30] In this rotation, the values of universality and particularity are transmuted for object *a* and the subject produced. But let us note, in both schemas, the imaginary terms do not change: will (V) remains universal and the barred subject remains particular.

It can be read in these two schemas that desire remains what motivates them in each case, only doing so at a particular level, that is, on the lower left-hand of both schemas. In the schema of the fantasy, desire creates the tormentor's voice (object a). In the schema of Sade's work, desire creates $, which stands for the effacement of Sade himself as a subject in this schema.

The articulation of the fantasy, that is, the lozenge uniting a and $, is only articulated in particularity, on the lower line, and this is only possible in the first schema. In other words, if the voice is developed in the second schema as Sade's voice, it is torn away from the very conditions of sensible experience and, at the same time, from the particular pathological conditions of the fantasy in order to stand for the principle of the creation of a universality on the basis of freedom, on the basis of enunciation. But in being thus developed in the sense of freedom, the voice loses its particularity and its direct articulation in the fantasy with $. The writing of the fantasy ($a \diamond \$$) disappears. There are oral fantasies, anal fantasies, scopic fantasies. It is much more difficult to imagine vocal fantasies, because they immediately drift towards enunciation, in which the statics of the fantasy is overcome by the enactment [*mise en acte*] of a dynamics of the drive.

In the second schema, Sade's voice (a), and $ can only be articulated by the enactment of a will to jouissance (V), a will represented by Madame de Montreuil, Sade's mother-in-law, an uncastratable mother who pulls the strings of Sade's destiny: his incarceration in the fortress of Vincennes, then in the Bastille and at Charenton asylum (1778–1790), his imprisonment under the young First Consul Bonaparte in 1801, and his transferral once again to Charenton, where he died in 1814.

As $, Sade disappears, is barred and wishes not to leave any traces behind. In his will and testament, he had asked for a non-religious burial:

> The ditch once covered over, above it acorns shall be strewn, in order that the spot become green again, and the copse grown back thick over it, the traces of my grave may disappear from the face of the earth as I trust the memory of me shall fade out of the minds of all men.

"*Mè phunai*, "not to be born" – Sade's curse is less holy than Oedipus's and does not carry him towards the Gods", but towards nothingness. This radical position of the barred subject stands for Sade's imaginary position faced with the uncastratable Mother's position. The *Mè phunai* curse lasts for eternity to ensure the "unsinkable buoyancy" of his work. At the price of its author's nihilation, Sade's written work lasts forever as a universal voice with a scientific purpose, as a body of work fundamental to all humanity, even if its importance, touching on the Real, is regularly hidden in a library behind works which limit themselves to the symbolic, that is, by rhetorical works (like the writings of St. John Chrysostom) or by works based on thought (like Blaise Pascal's *Pensées*).

It might have been said that Sade's work was annoying.[31] Yes, it is annoying in as much as the Real in it is disturbing. Because its function is to provide a universal place to the fantasy which "is, in effect, quite bothersome, since we do not know where to situate it". We do not know which of the drawers of technique or the pleasure principle to put it in, because it always already implicates the jouissance principle. It also implicates the structure of Schema L in its entirety, which is none other than the structure of discourse: on the basis of the Other, the object a which stands for the truth of discourse, the imaginary agent of the Will addresses itself to its imaginary respondent the barred subject, to produce the pathological Subject, the result of the Sadean experience. Discourse is not mastered by the supposed agent of discourse, it eludes "your powers" (the power of "your honour and member of the Académie Française", and that of Madame de Montreuil as well). It is commanded by the small a, which interpellates your desire, and it is this, inserted in the fantasy, which asks you to "square accounts with your own desires". Schema 2 is finished by the reader which it touches as "the brute subject incarnating the heroism characteristic of the pathological". In Sade's life, it was represented by his loyal subjects, "those who at first tolerated his excesses – his wife, his sister-in-law, and why not his manservant too?" It is the will to jouissance, incarnated in the uncastrated mother (La Présidente de Montreuil) in the position of V, of Vel, which divides the subject into the barred Subject [$] (Sade) and S, the brute subject (those close to him and his readers "who at first tolerated his excesses"), but it not this which commands the Sadean discourse. We shall return later to the all-powerfulness of this mother.

***

To which of the four classic discourses does each of these schemas correspond?

We are in habit of designating (and, therefore, of thinking about) a discourse according to its semblant: the hysterical, magisterial, university, analytic discourses, as they are expressed, respectively, by a hysteric, a master, an academic, and an analyst. These are only semblants, and, in our two schemas, these semblants are represented by the Will. They are thus similar to the Kantian discourses which themselves may also seem to be commanded by the Will, the will to know in the first Critique and "good will" or the will to do the right thing in the second. This is Lacan's reading of them based on the semblant (the *Groundwork of the Metaphysics of Morals* indeed begin with good will, but this is only a pedagogical presentation which must lean on common opinion, that is, on the semblance). But as we have seen, the *truth* of the *Critique of Practical Reason* does start out from the *principle* of the moral law and not a will biased towards the good (good will).

The Sadean schemas can themselves also be specified by the semblance, that is, by the Will. But what is the truth of the two Sadean schemas? Sade "yields the truth of the *Critique*",[32] of the Kantian *Critique*, which would remain a semblance of this truth. The four places in each of the two schemas can be related to the four places in the discourses:

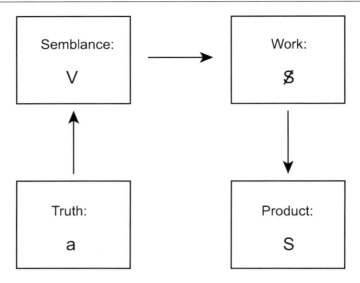

Figure 10

On each occasion the place of truth is held by the object *a*.

It is by the object *a* in the position of truth that they might be differentiated, according to Lacan, from the Kantian discourses which would not leave any place for the big Other or the object *a*. This differentiation presupposes that the Kantian discourses are dealt with the basis of their *semblance*, whereas the Sadean discourses (the two schemas) are approached on the basis of their *truth*. It would be much better to be able to deal with the Kantian discourses as well based on their truth, which implies dealing with the discourse of practical reason on the basis of principles in themselves rather than on the basis of will.

Due to the *Lacanian* approach to discourses, because of truth in Sade and the semblance in Kant, Sade's discourses seem to be truer than those of Kant. That which is found in the place of truth in both Sadean schemas is in each case the object *a*.

Through the object *a* in the position of truth (in the place of the Other), both schemas correspond to the hysterical discourse. In the first schema, the object *a* is present as particular, it is the particularity of one hysteric or another which is in play. In the second schema, the object *a* is present as universal, it is the universality of the scientific discourse (as a scientific researcher or inventor) which is at play, while at the same time remaining within the structure of the hysterical discourse.

If we now characterise the two schemas through the other term ($) of the fantasy ($◇a), in other words, by what is found in the place of work, that is, through the imaginary partner of the semblance or the imaginary partner of the Will to jouissance, then each of the two schemas would correspond to the psychoanalytic discourse precisely inasmuch as it puts the barred subject to work (in the place of the Other); and in this case, there is no need to distinguish universal from particular, because the barred subject is always particular (on the lower line of each of the two schemas).

It seems *truer* to us to interpret the discourse of the fantasy and Sade's discourse according to what is at play in the place of truth, and they both count as a *hysterical* discourse, in which the Will counts as the pure semblance which will put the signifier of the barred Subject or of the subject's passing out to work, to produce the pathological subject, as knowledge. *Both* schemas are articulated in accordance with the structure of the hysterical discourse, the first corresponding to the hysteric's discourse with its particular object *a*, the second to the scientist's (or researcher's) discourse with its purportedly universal object *a*. Both hysterical discourses would respond respectively to the Kantian ones: the first to the magisterial discourse centred on duty (*Critique of Practical Reason*), the second to the academic or university discourse centred on knowledge (*Critique of Pure Reason*). Not without promoting the psychoanalytic discourse.[33]

But how can both these Sadean discourses (schema 1 and schema 2) simultaneously refer back to the structure of the hysterical discourse and to that of the psychoanalytic discourse? And how can they contribute to the *truth* of the psychoanalytic discourse?

If one wishes to consider that the truth of the psychoanalytic discourse is knowledge as knowledge of the structure *of the fantasy* and of what it entails, one notes that the truth of the two schemas implies knowledge of the whole structure (including the opening up of action and freedom), because the object convoked is precisely the *voice* and not the oral object, as in ordinary hysteria, in other words, the form of the object *a* which is difficult to inscribe in fantasy and which compels an exit from the fantasy. This vocal object orders us to square accounts with our desires. It is in this way that the analysis of the Sadean fantasy (first schema) and of Sade himself (second schema) *essentially* contribute to the psychoanalytic discourse.

Despite the major importance of the three short pages on the table of the nothing (at the end of the analytic of the *Critique of Pure Reason*), Kant could have had no idea of what was at stake in the *nihil negativum* or in the vocal object (that is, the hysterical discourse and the psychoanalytic discourse). Repression surely has a rightful place in his architectonic; in his theorisation, it is not at all developed and it is an empty place. In order to introduce repression and give the unconscious its full place, it was necessary to introduce a fundamental opposition, a "counter-cathexis".

The mechanism of cathexis/counter-cathexis is what repression is founded on; it is "primal repression". It is the introduction of repression in the consideration of practical law and jouissance. And it is precisely what comes into play in our following chapter devoted to Lacan's struggle against Kant.

Notes

1 Lacan, "Kant with Sade", op. cit., p. 652.
2 Fanaticism (*Schwärmerei*) "in the most general sense is an overstepping of the bounds of human reason untaken on principles" (Kant, *Critique of Practical Reason*, op. cit., p. 71).

In other words, moral fanaticism or enthusiasm places the main determinant of the moral law outside of the moral law and of respect for it. [Translator's note: Mary Gregor, the translator of the *Critique*, translates *Schwärmerei* as "enthusiasm" in this instance.]
3 Object *a*.
4 Lacan, "Subversion of the Subject and the Dialectic of Desire", op. cit., p. 694.
5 "Let us lay that wing to rest behind its Eleusinian veil." Eleusis was the indiscreet witness to the incantations and manipulations undergone by his son Triptolemus on the part of Demeter to make him immortal, to raise him from the pleasure principle to the jouissance principle, and to thus attain perfect jouissance. Demeter killed Eleusis in anger (cf. Grimal, *Dictionnaire de la mythologie grecque et romaine*, Paris, PUF, 1994, p. 137).
6 Lacan, "Kant with Sade", op. cit., p. 652.
7 Ibid.
8 Ibid., p. 653. Author's remarks in brackets.
9 We take up again here the schema L from p. 458 of the *Écrits* op. cit. (and not the one from p. 40 where *a* and *a'* are inverted: *a* designates the subject's objects and *a'* the ego (Ibid., p. 459). Let us note that the *a* in question both on page 458 and page 40 must not be confused with the object *a*.
10 Lacan, *The Psychoses: The Seminar of Jacques Lacan Book III 1955–1956*, translated by Russell Grigg, London, Routledge, 1993, p. 36.
11 Lacan, "On a Question Prior to Any Possible Treatment of Psychosis", op. cit., p. 458.
12 Kant, *Critique of Pure Reason*, op. cit., p. 329; A444; B472.
13 Lacan, "Kant with Sade", op. cit., p. 651.
14 Ibid., p. 654.
15 Ibid.
16 It was Tiresias who had told Creon after he had banned the burial of Polynices, "A dead man does not need to be killed twice".
17 Marty, *Pourquoi le XXe siècle a-t-il pris Sade au sérieux?*, op. cit., p. 215 note 4.
18 Lacan, "Kant with Sade", op. cit., p. 655.
19 The fact that Sade's philosophy was presented as a philosophy of Nature changes nothing here: it involves destroying all "pathological" considerations (before or after physiological death) to liberate the space of ethics.
20 Ibid., p. 655. [Translation modified.]
21 Freud, *Standard Edition*, Volume XVIII.
22 Lacan, "Kant with Sade", op. cit., p. 656.
23 The "exploitation of one man by another" is "the definition of capitalism, as we know. And socialism, then? It is the opposite". From this humorous viewpoint, capitalism and socialism are both caught up in a purely imaginary relation under the guidance of an imaginarised ego ideal which allows the death drive to be ignored.
24 Ibid.
25 The function of the big Other is not the monopoly of the agent of torment or of the vocal object *a*. It is also appealed to by the victim and this appeal is fundamental to the Sadean experience.
26 Ibid., p. 774.
27 Ibid., p. 666.
28 Ibid., p. 656.
29 Ibid., p. 654.
30 Ibid., p. 657.
31 In 1956, Jean-Jacques Pauvert was accused of offences against morality for the publication of four of Sade's works, *Philosophy in the Bedroom*, *The New Justine*, *Juliette*, and *The 120 Days of Sodom*. His lawyer, Maurice Garçon, called four witnesses in Pauvert's defence: Bataille, Paulhan, Breton, and Cocteau. While he had been condemned in the first instance to a heavy fine and the judge had ordered the destruction of the works confiscated, a later appeal resulted in a suspended sentence. "His honour

the Judge, and *monsieur l'académicien* (Cocteau)" had agreed that Sade's work was "annoying". [Translator's note: *Ennuyeux* could also be translated as "boring".]
32 Ibid., p. 646.
33 We should again recall the predominant place of the equivalent of the object *a* as much in the architectonic of the *Critique of Pure Reason* as that of the *Critique of Practical Reason*. In the former, the possible object of knowledge only ever appears against the background of the impossibility of the object, as the table of the nothing which finishes the Transcendental Analytic shows very briefly, but also very clearly. In the latter, the moral law and freedom appear solely against the background of that which denies the conditions of sensible experience in general, in other words, against the background of the *nihil negativum*, which corresponds to the Lacanian vocal object.

Chapter 14

Lacan's struggle against Kant

How to square accounts with your own desires from the opposition between law and jouissance[1]

Desire for all

The reader is invited to "reverentially approach those exemplary figures who, in the Sadean boudoir, assemble and disassemble in a carnival-act-like rite".[2] At the very interior of the Sadean scenario, there is a "change of positions". The *rupture* of positions, the pause or scansion already represent the putting on hold or a hint of the rejection of the pathological, a rejection by which Kant, according to Lacan, introduced the moral law. "Let us salute here the objects of the law (in this pause and scansion)[3]", inasmuch as they are absent in the moral law and of which "you will know nothing", because the Moral Law would precisely presuppose the absence of the object along with the suspension or *Aufhebung* of knowledge.

To know something of these objects of the law, which are absent from the moral law, it would have to be known how these objects of the law could be "a cause of desire". These objects of the law in their absence stand for the voice as the rupture of the conditions of possibility of sensory experience and the suspension of the entire field of appearances. This *nihil negativum* that is the voice opens up the Sadean maxim's field of enunciation, synthetic universality, as well as the field of Kantian freedom.

In order to find one's way in one's desires, one leans on the fantasy, which also stems from the particular enunciation of the voice, *I have the right to enjoy your body* . . . (schema 1), but also from universal enunciation, "the fact that Sade delegates a right to jouissance to everyone"[4] Sade does us this act of charity. "It is good to be charitable", which is not without also evoking the commandment "Love your neighbour as yourself" (we shall see it's the radical, principled, difference). The question remains of the concrete *application* of this Sadean principle: "*It is good to be charitable/But to whom? That is the question.*"

Who is my neighbour? Does it suffice to recognise in him a figure of the Real?

Sparks of jouissance throwing light on the dialectic of desire

It is jouissance (and not the moral law) which throws light on desire.

Certainly, we would not know the freedom of desire if we did not know the moral law. Desire, however, can only be understood by the jouissance principle inherent to the law.

The examples convoked by Lacan here serve to question the essence of desire (Kant's "higher faculty of desire"), of desire inasmuch as it presupposes "abnegation", the negation of pathological needs. The first example (that of Verdoux) presents desire on the basis of needs, the second (that of Buddha) in the form of pure abnegation.

On the basis of needs, in order to charitably meet the needs of his disabled wife and his son, Monsieur Verdoux, the eponymous main character of a 1947 film by Charlie Chaplin, married rich widows whom he very quickly bumped off after their weddings to divert their riches towards charitable aims. "He thought that his family wanted to live in greater comfort."

On the side of abnegation. It is still "charity" which seems to be at stake. The *Jātaka* tales describe an episode from one of the Shakyamuni Buddha's past lives in which he "offered himself up to be devoured by those who did not know the way", that is, those who did not know the way of emptiness. He offered himself to a hungry tigress, so as she would not devour her own cubs. Both examples involve feeding a mother. The comparison does not end there, however, as with Monsieur Verdoux, no place is left for emptiness, to the *nihil negativum*, which is indeed present with the Buddha. Monsieur Verdoux's case involves an error which "a little lesson from the *Critique*" – the *Critique of Practical Reason* – could have averted. It would have sufficed for him to pose himself the question of the condition of universality in order to notice that the universalisation of his maxim would have meant the disappearance of humanity. Practical Reason could have directly given him a "both more economical and more legal" directive than the ultimate sanction which was set aside for him: the guillotine ("the electric chair", in Lacan's words).

But why present us with such examples, which are hardly relevant it would seem?

The "molecules", the elements of these scenarios (Monsieur Verdoux, his wife, the rich widows, the tigress, her cubs, and all the characters in Sade's scenarios) are gathered together to make up "a spintherian jouissance [*jouissance spintherienne*],[5] which makes sparks fly (from the Greek *spinther*, "spark"). These sparks of jouissance aim to wake us up to the question of jouissance always implicated in desire and inherent to the moral law. A jouissance which, in most cases, most often remains bogged down in the arrangements of the pleasure principle and the reality principle, which seem to be in charge of everything. With all of these sparks, desire can no longer be thought of as all of one piece, it only exists in and through dialectics.

Desire is the other's desire

In the cases of M. Verdoux and the Buddha, the different characters seem to be connected by need or by the extinction of desire. But they are connected solely by the desires which direct the scenarios while also implicating jouissance. In both cases, it is "clear that desire is the Other's desire", M. Verdoux's wife's desire on this side of need or the mysterious desire of the tigress ("it is not clear that a tigress enjoys eating Buddha"). And the voice, which is the voice in the Other's place, is Madame Verdoux's voice, which we do not hear and is the voice of the void, rather than that of the tigress.

"Desire is propped up by a fantasy, at least one foot of which is in the Other, and precisely the one which counts", that is, the object a and, more precisely, the vocal object. "Even and above all if it happens to limp", because the voice only comes to light in a limping fashion, as a *nihil negativum*, a limping within the field of appearances, the conditions of existence of which it denies.

"The object of desire, where we see it in its nakedness" (that is, independently, and as if it were torn from its articulation with the barred subject in the fantasy) "is but the slag of a fantasy in which the subject does not come to after blacking out". However, the object of desire must always be thought according to the complete fantasy. In other words, it does not exist independently of the barred subject. The object seen in its nakedness remains articulated with the barred subject, it "loves" the barred subject. Even when this subject presents itself as the one who "does not come to after passing out", that is, as a dead subject, even then the tormentor – he whose voice stands in the place of the object a – "loves" this dead subject: "It is a case of necrophilia."

Object of desire (Sade) and subject of desire (Kant)

The barred subject and the object a "generally" vacillate in a complementary manner. The barred subject passes out, is barred, disappears; "the subject does not come to after passing out", and the disappearance of the barred subject highlights the object a, the object cause of desire. Conversely, in the Kantian moral law, according to Lacan, it is not the subject who is lacking and vacillates, but the object itself, which completely disappears.[6]

In Kantian moral law, it would be the subject who fills in the still vacant function and place of the voice. It alone would remain present, but "in the form of the voice within". Would the aforementioned voice lose its characteristic nature of *an object* a *which opposes itself to the subject*? What it says is for the most part "nonsensical". For good reason, we would add, because this subjective voice – even from within – necessarily derives from the vocal object a, from the *nihil negativum*, completely detached from the phenomenal and in contradiction with the very conditions of the phenomenal; this is where its "nonsensical" nature arises from.

And if the subject thus appears detached from every object, senseless, it is without a signified which would give it a sense, and it is completely dependent on the signifier. It "what represents a signifier for another signifier". The barred subject (in Kant) is detached from the fantasy (depicted by Sade), "it is released from the fantasy from which it both derives and drifts [*dérive*]".[7] But it is also adrift without the support of the fantasy which fixates desire. It is missing its articulation with the object *a*, which Lacan claims to have discovered in Sade.

The symbol of the bar ($) "returns the commandment from within at which Kant marvels to its rightful place", to the "moral law within me".[8] It would quite simply be dependent on V, on the Will (the commonplace, erroneous reading of the *Critique of Practical Reason*). Now, the subject *as a barred subject* had already been highlighted in the paralogisms of pure reason in the *Critique of Pure Reason*. It is because he or she is essentially barred that we cannot presuppose a pre-existing, substantial subject. We must therefore already presuppose the complete structure of the fantasy *prior* to the subject included in it and this structure necessarily includes the question of the slipping away of the object.

The *slipping away* of the object was presented at the beginning of the *Analytic of the Critique of Practical Reason*[9] (this slipping away is *on principle*[10] and not *de facto*) and Lacan had insisted on it in his exposition of the Kantian moral law.[11] This slipping away leads to desire, as it is the *lack* of an object which causes desire (we can see how this lack is *on principle*). The barred subject's bar introduces an encounter between the Law and desire, "the encounter, which, from Law to desire, goes further than the slipping away of their object, for both the Law and desire".[12]

This encounter is introduced precisely by the voice, *nihil negativum*, the negation of the conditions of possibility of the phenomenal in itself. The "encounter" in question (which is not solely a *tuchè*, a chance encounter, but moreover the very sense of *tuchè* in general, that is, the structural necessity of this "chance" or contingency) cannot be an encounter with what completely eludes us. In this encounter "the ambiguity of the word "freedom" plays a part"; this may in fact be understood either as the possibility of choosing any object at all, any object of pleasure and whim on which one remains dependent, or, in Kant's words, as "altogether independent of the natural law of appearances in their relations to one another".[13] If the equivocation, or ambiguity, between *interdit* (forbidden) and *inter-dit* (*inter-said*, spoken between the lines) articulates jouissance at a certain (homophonic) level, it is because of the ambiguity of the word "freedom".

The ordinary moralist "grab[s] [the word] freedom for himself". He presupposes the freedom to carry out such and such a *phenomenal* action and morals consist in deciding which actions are good, which are pleasant, and which are bad (forbidden). But this conception founded on examples is lacking the principle of the moral law (which, in contrast, plays on the *inter-said*) as we have seen. The freedom introduced through the *nihil negativum*, the freedom to begin a new phenomenal series, to radically change the deterministic course of things cannot be cognised as a given phenomenon within a given sequence, but is postulated on the basis of the factum of the moral law. Moral law and freedom go together: no freedom without the moral law, no moral law without freedom. But the reciprocal articulation of freedom and the moral law is not symmetrical: we have no cognisance of freedom other than through by means of the moral law.[14] And it is, let us recall, in order to illustrate the radical dependence of the postulate of freedom in relation to the moral law that Kant introduced the pair of apologues cited earlier.

Lacan the moralist

As has already been stated, instead of analysing the *structural reason* for these apologues, Lacan, who here takes up the position of the everyday moralist, prefers to linger on the concrete *response* which may be given in both of these examples by one and the same "subject", by one and the same individual (this is neither the barred subject, nor S, the pathological subject), by the "subject, about whom we are first told that a great deal transpires by means of words". According to Lacan, Kant does not give us the "letter" of the response in question, being content to say "one does not have to guess long what he would reply" in the case of the first example (he would resist his passion in order to evade the scaffold!). According to Lacan, everything however is in the "letter" through which our subject should commit or not commit himself. The "subject" convoked by Kant in his two apologues would indeed be none other than the "ideal bourgeois",[15] who stands apart from the "letter" (and from the Real), who reaps the benefits without taking any risks:[16] "in no case would he stoop so low".[17] This so-called Kantian reverence towards the figure of the ideal bourgeois would offset, according to Lacan, the classical reverence towards the figures of the aristocracy, being explained notably by the intention to "counter Fontenelle, the overly gallant centenarian".

Reading Kant's text shows that the main character in both apologues is neither aristocratic, nor bourgeois, nor proletarian, nor does he belong any social stratum at all. He is a fictional character confronted solely with a calculus of pleasure and unpleasure in the first apologue (pleasure principle alone) and with the moral law in the second apologue (pleasure principle and *morality principle*). The reference to "the overly gallant centenarian" is drawn from a completely different context in the Kantian corpus. Far from wishing to counter Fontenelle's aristocracy, Kant relies on an indistinct subject to pinpoint the real object of respect (the third chapter of the A*nalytic of Practical Reason*), which does not involve kowtowing to a great man (whether he be an aristocrat or a bourgeois), but rather bowing before someone more moral than oneself, that is, before true human greatness, independent of social classes.

> Fontenelle says, "*I bow before an eminent man, but my spirit does not bow.*" I can add, before a humble common man in whom I perceive uprightness of character in a higher degree than I am aware of in myself *my spirit bows*, whether I want it or whether I do not and hold my head ever so high, that he may not overlook my superior position.[18]

Let us very temporarily put the second apologue to one side[19] to concentrate, along with Lacan, on the one concerning lustful passion followed by the scaffold. In the fiction invented by Kant, the character is entirely taken up in the calculus of pleasure and unpleasure (the conflict of interests is played out entirely according to the pleasure/reality principle, both where lust and the scaffold are concerned). This character, described by Lacan as the "ideal bourgeois", is radically *outside* of Kantian morality: it is not that he is immoral or amoral, it is that the story does not involve any moral law and it is on these grounds that he does not enjoy any freedom in the Kantian sense.

Whereas this Kantian fiction is situated outside all morals, Lacan substitutes a complete story for it by presupposing "a partisan of passion, who would be blind enough to combine it with questions of honour", that is, to introduce sparks of jouissance into it. The calculation of pleasure and unpleasure alone had completely determined the outcome of the first Kantian apologue. In taking "passion" into account, along with the blindness of a concern for honour, this first apologue is torn from its Kantian fictional context, in which everything was supposed to be calculated according to the reality principle. With this paradigm shift introduced by Lacan, the outcome now seems to be indeterminate. It must be recognised "that no occasion precipitates certain people more surely toward their goal than one that involves defiance of or even contempt for the gallows". Very well. It still remains the case that we are still within the bounds of a purely pathological causality, that is, guided by an unbridled pleasure principle. If it is claimed that we are speaking about "jouissance" here (passion, questions of honour, defiance), it must be recognised that this still and forever has to do with a variant of *pleasure*. None of which contradicts the Kantian spirit of the apologue: everything is played out according to pleasure (it matters little whether that refers to determination or indetermination), there is no morality in this, *therefore there is no freedom*, whether or not, riled up by his passion, he goes to the gallows or, prudently "bourgeois", he does not. While Lacan wishes to introduce a conflict here, a struggle between the bourgeois quest for pleasure and a quest for unbridled pleasure ("jouissance"), *this conflict is not the conflict of the moral law*.

There is no moral question in the first Kantian apologue or in its Lacanian amendment. But Lacan *wishes* to find a new morality in it; he believes he can oppose jouissance to the petty bourgeois morality which has nothing to do with a Kantian morality (the bourgeois' "morality" is only simple good advice). Kant's argument from the fear of the gallows which had kept the first apologue within the bounds of a position *outside morality* is hijacked by Lacan to see in it a "love of life" in which the dignity of living may be found and in order to thus introduce into the first apologue the dimension of morals and jouissance. To this end, Lacan refers to a quote from Juvenal, fished out from a completely different part of Kant's text. *Et non propter vitam vivendi perdere causas*. One must not "prefer life to honour and to lose, for the sake of living, all that makes life worth living".[20] This quote precisely presupposes the framework of morality. One should not lose the moral reasons for living as a cause of one's love of life; one should not lose sight of the question of jouissance because of one's love of life. This quote now *introduces* morality and a possible thematics of jouissance by means of a fictional example which does not, *on principle*, involve it. We have already passed to the *second* apologue which *does* on principle involve it. The quote from Juvenal is in fact included as a commentary on the story of the second apologue:

> If summoned to bear witness in some dubious and uncertain case, though Phalaris (a Sicilian tyrant of the 6th century BCE) himself should dictate that you perjure yourself and bring his bull to move you, count it the greatest of all iniquities to prefer life to honour and to lose, for the sake of living, all that makes life worth living.[21]

Dialectic of the law and desire

But from where does Lacan's doggedness in introducing the conflict inherent to the moral law come from when there is neither a conflict nor any moral law?

"Square accounts with your own desires" implies taking the Kantian distinction between "the lower faculty of desire" and "the higher faculty of desire" into consideration; the former determines the will according to pleasure ("the feeling of pleasure or displeasure"),[22] the second according to the categorical imperative, the moral law and the freedom which is connected to it. "Desire, what is called desire", which echoes the higher faculty of desire alone, "suffices to make life meaningless if it turns someone into a coward".[23] What is a coward? It is the bourgeois who calculates without taking any risks, it is someone who "gives way on their desire" by reducing desire to the quest for pleasure and everyday jouissances (the lower faculty of desire) by forgetting the question of what is beyond the pleasure principle, the moral law and true jouissance (the higher faculty of desire). When the subject is caught within the law, the law in the everyday sense of the word (the law of the bourgeois), when it is really present and regulates all risks, "when law is truly present, desire does not stand up", desire gives way and reduces itself to the quest for pleasure (the lower faculty of desire). "That is because law and repressed desire are one and the same thing." The everyday law (the law of the bourgeois) makes desire disappear without necessarily wiping it out. Therefore the higher faculty of desire is hidden behind the lower faculty of desire.

Desire does not appear otherwise than within this disappearance; it fundamentally emerges as a *repressed desire* – "which is precisely what Freud discovered". In *The Interpretation of Dreams*, Freud had first put forward the thesis *the dream is the fulfilment of a desire or a wish*. He also had to add that the dream, which had however seemed to free itself from the contingencies of the law, is the *disguised* fulfilment of a *repressed or suppressed* wish.[24] Desire can only be upheld by being disguised, suppressed, and repressed in the law. The law, which represses, sustains desire rather than annihilates it: "I would not have known desire if it had not been for the law" (Romans 7:7). "Desire, what is called desire" appears-disappears as always repressed. It is only through this repression of desire that is the Law that you may manage to "square accounts with your own desires". It is only through the moral law and repression that one may encounter "the ambiguity of freedom", such that it always implicates the Kantian freedom of which we know nothing (this really is the context and the reason for both Kantian apologues).

In his *struggle* with Kant over these apologues, Lacan was aiming to highlight desire as repressed, the *struggle* between desire and repression. The struggle waged by Lacan against Kant is identical to the struggle waged by repression against desire.

Lacan now addresses Kant: "We are ahead at half-time, professor".[25] He had taken Kant's first apologue as an example aiming to demonstrate the moral law (we know that it is senseless to demonstrate the *factum* by any kind of example) and he had shown that a particular law is identical to repressed desire. He thought that he had dribbled one around Kant, but the only ball he had played was contempt for the everyday moralist, having first placed himself in the position of the moralist in order to seek out repression in his examples.

For Kant, the higher faculty of desire, even if it eludes us, is situated precisely at the level of the *principle* of the moral Law (to be well distinguished from any old moral law, from a bourgeois moral law for example). It is thanks to this principle of the Law that the law in general may appear as repressed desire.

The tactics used by Lacan to defeat Kant and his supposed attempt to weigh the balance on the side of the moral law

In the previous section, Lacan thought he had defeated the aim of the first Kantian apologue which would have consisted, according to him, in demonstrating the necessity and the universality of the moral law (we have seen how this apologue, in contrast, consists of the basis of an example in which the moral law is completely absent so as to note its complete lack of freedom). Very well. Lacan had highlighted a possible jouissance in opposition to a bourgeois "law", which is only a precautionary calculation. "Squaring accounts with your own desires" does not consist of bringing them under the control of the law (as one might think based on a very simplistic reading of Kant). Squaring accounts with your own desires is rekindling the sparks of jouissance which remind us that desire is always the Other's desire (therefore conflictual and under repression). In his struggle against Kant, Lacan attributes the success of his demonstration to the "infantry", to the desirous pawns without particular qualities, to the common men insofar as they are always already within the complex structure of desire. It is this general structure of desire and of the fantasy which is "the key to the game, as we know". He could, he says, have won the game by bringing in the other pieces in this game of chess with Kant: Sade the knight: the madman [*le fou*] (known in English as "the bishop") from psychiatry: the rook (or "*la tour*", "tower") of human rights: the queen ("*la dame*" or "lady") from courtly love. The most important piece on the board is oddly absent, the king, precisely the one whom it is the aim of the game to checkmate.[26]

Moving all these major pieces around (with the exception of the forgotten king) "would have involved moving too many people for a less certain result". These pieces, which represent widely known *examples*, in fact put us at a distance from the general structure (we are indeed in agreement with Kant: examples cannot be used to determine the will). Each of these pieces could, in its own manner, have countered the "law" of the bourgeois (in fact, the pragmatic principle of caution) to highlight jouissance.

If Sade the knight was convoked to respond to the situation of the first apologue in a more cavalier manner than the ideal bourgeois, the "recompense" for this "partisan of passion, who would be blind enough to combine it with questions of honour" would appear anyway: imprisonment in the Bastille if not the gallows. We would remain within a police-based management of the question.

An appeal could also have made to the Madman's behaviour to counter the ideal bourgeois's risk-free management. The Madman is never totally taken over by his madness, as we have known since Pinel: reason may be encountered within madness. Madness is thus no longer opposed to reason, having become properly "moral", and henceforth, its treatment would also become rational and moral. And, therefore, "bourgeois". Moreover, the Madman remains liable to be locked up. Sade himself had a long stay at the Charenton asylum. "All thinkers agree on this point",[27] that it was not the right place for him. The "right-thinking" man, the one with well-ordered thoughts, the bourgeois, would have sentenced him to hard labour or sent him to the scaffold. By contrast, "those who think well", would have kept him out of any confinement for allowing himself to be deranged by desire. Pinel is solely "a moment in the history of thought",[28] in as much as he attempts to channel excess. No more. "Willy-nilly, he supported the destruction, on the right and the left, by thought of freedoms that the Revolution had just promulgated" in the name of Freedom.[29]

Now, Sade calls on the French, "One more effort, if you wish to be republicans", again to counteract the ideal bourgeois. With the Republic, it is the Tower (or rook) of human rights which would advance. Among these rights must be counted the right to jouissance promulgated by the Sadean maxim itself, "I have the right to enjoy your body". But "everyone now knows" that the truth of human rights, including the right to jouissance, "boil[s] down to the freedom to desire in vain". By convoking the Knight, the Fool, and the Tower, we can indeed "grab [the word] freedom for [ourselves]",[30] but this involves the freedom to die, as the story of Sade confirms, imprisoned in the Bastille, locked up with madmen and coming within a hair's breadth of the guillotine. The gallows is indeed just outside the house of lust. Such a freedom thus also appears to be an empty concept, without sensory nourishment. All it does is renew the conflict between sensory *needs*, forever related to pleasure and the pleasure principle, and *desires*, which indeed seem to remain an empty concept, revolving around the absence of any object. Under the banner of this "freedom", who, out of need or desire, will grab hold of the "*Good*" as a coveted object *par excellence*, the pleaders' oyster (La Fontaine)? In this conflict between need and desire, it is the third arrival, the *judge* of the conflict, "the Law that empties the shell". Again, it must be understood, Lacan imagines that the Kantian Law essentially aims at the Good and that it arises in the middle of the conflict between needs and desires, in order to *judge* them and to run away with the *Good* they covet, leaving behind them nothing but an empty shell.

Is it not Lacan himself who, here, attempts to "empty the shell" of desire?

In this struggle that Lacan attempts to lead "to counter Kant's apologue" and to favour desire at the expense of needs and in opposition to the Law, the Lady of courtly love holds a privileged position because she represents the real of the Thing while introducing a third object to be debated and judged, love, now added alongside need and desire. In *The Ethics of Psychoanalysis*, Lacan mentions the courts of love, "tribunals devoted to the casuistry of love",[31] which entails a whole area of knowledge, "a scholastics of unhappy love". The path of the Lady of courtly love is therefore not at all a return to natural desire. On the contrary, "it requires us to be erudite".[32] "To be erudite by one's position is to bring on the attack of the erudites." Everything is thus situated in the field of knowledge and teaching. But explaining what love should be and making it into a teaching already belongs to comedy. "In this field (the field of love) [the attack of the erudites] is tantamount to the entrance of the clowns."

Kant does not enter the field of love and spares himself from comedy. According to Lacan, he has no sense of comedy. It could indeed be noted that, for him, laughter is no more than what results from a sudden snuffing out of an expectation which had existed on an essentially bodily level.[33] No love involved in that. And this is precisely what "could very easily make us lose our serious demeanour". This is because our serious demeanour is what follows the series of logical consequences of the structure of the fantasy, need, desire, and love.

In order to prevail in his struggle against Kant, Lacan will not bring in his Lady (of courtly love), but rather the general structure of the dialectic of desire, implying the needs and the pleasure principle that go along with it, the Law and love. In the next paragraph we shall follow how Lacan thinks he has dealt the fatal blow to the second Kantian apologue through this dialectic of desire

Love takes part in a comical mood,[34] insofar as it stages the function of the *phallus*, as is well illustrated by Aristophanes's speech in Plato's *Symposium*, a speech in which love appears in the form of wanting to attach oneself to one's complementary half by means of the genital apparatus, the phallus.[35] No love, therefore no phallus in Kant. No love in Sade, but how could one be so bold as to say that there is no phallus in Sade, as the male organ is in constant state of erection in his work?

To shed some light on the function of the phallus in the dialectic of desire (and to show how, contrary to appearances, the true phallic function is deficient in Sade), we here present a schema taken from Lacan's graph of desire,[36] a schema of the functions of the phallus, small phi (φ) and big Phi (Φ). It is here that we can pinpoint the precise manner in which the dialectic of desire and

"Kant with Sade" (1962–1963)

the phallus wavers in Sade. It is also at this precise point that the King should take his place, certainly not Louis XVI, who Sade joyfully did without, without realising that a function which is nonetheless essential to jouissance had eluded him: the function of the Name-of-the-Father, which may be evoked by that of the King in the game of chess.

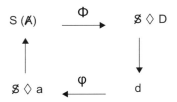

Figure 11

The lower line of φ (quite present in Sade). The imaginary phallus, φ, well serves to fixate desire in the fantasy of the Sadean scenarios, the male organ is constantly erect in order to prop up the passage from desire (d) to the articulation of the fantasy ($◇a). This articulation was developed in schema 1.

The upper line of Φ (absent from Sade). The object *a* inherent to the fantasy is developed as far as the voice – the fourth form of the object *a* – which leaves the fantasy behind (a passage from $◇a to the "signifier of the barred big Other, S(Ⱥ)") and implies the absolute void, the *nihil negativum*, in other words, it in fact entails the definitive impossibility of all proof of the existence of the Supreme Being, of God. It is written here as the signifier of the barred big Other [S(Ⱥ)]. When S(Ⱥ) is left to play out between the absence of all proof (and the absence, even, of every index of the existence of the big Other) and the necessity of making it exist, there is no other way out for the barred subject other than to create, to enter into articulation with its demand, in other words, in the drive which freely creates ("freely" in the Kantian sense) – such is the value of the phallus. It is the operation of capital Phi (Φ) which is completely absent in Sade. With him, the barred subject does not at all enter into his demand, there is none of the drive's invention. The non-existence of the Supreme Being (well affirmed in *Frenchmen, One More Effort* . . . even if it was disowned in *Juliette*) is frozen within the rigidity of the repetitive fantasy (on the lower level of small phi). This obvious presentation of the rigid phallus obliterates the phallus's complete cycle of desire. The complete cycle of desire which fully develops desire is thus absent in Sade: the Phallus () (Φ) is absent, even though the phallus („) steals the scene.

This is why Sade "hasn't the slightest" sense of comedy (which must be supported by the complete cycle of the phallic function). Despite his atheism, the signifier of the barred big Other is not in operation. In Kant, the signifier of the barred big Other indeed has a structural place (cf. the critique and the function of the ideal of pure reason, in the first critique's Transcendental Dialectic); comedy in Kant remains amputated in its presentation, however, as he only develops it within the field of the body and its tensions. The thematic of love is almost absent and comedy is not articulated within the dimension of thought and understanding. The critique of the ideal of pure reason, the radical absence of proof of the existence of God, which would correspond to the signifier of the barred big Other, only leads up to a grave Law (in which the dimension of comedy is lost). This is for want of a sufficiently developed articulation of the conflict, of the struggle inherent to *repression* and the *object a*.

In evaluating pleasure, desire is more judicious than the law[37]

According to Lacan, Kant had introduced his two apologues "to show that the Law weighs in the scales not only pleasure but also pain, happiness and even the burden of abject poverty, not to mention the love of life – in short, everything pathological".[38] It involves weighing up the different pathological goods in order to choose the most appropriate one. In contrast to Kant's aim (to show that freedom does not appear in cognition other than *on the basis of* the moral law), Lacan starts out from these apologues in order to introduce multiple variations onto the plates of the scales of what would be concretely done.

The second apologue presented the case of a tyrant who ordered that false witness be borne against an honest man. The underlying question is that of the possible truth and lies implicated in bearing witness. What is the value of truth in this business of bearing witness?

Let us recall Kant's position in relation to lying. In a little late text entitled, "On a Supposed Right to Lie from Philanthropy" (1797), Kant disproves relativism in relation to the truth. "The πρῶτον ψεῦδος here lies in the proposition '*To tell the truth is a duty, but only to one who has a right to the truth*'".[39] The "*prôton pseudos*", the primal misunderstanding which, in its relativism, radically attacks the categorical imperative and appears to definitively destroy it. The *examples* appealed to in order to support this relativism always consider the truth to be the *adequation* (or accordance) of something said [*un dit*] with a thing.[40] The reductive position of the truth to the aforementioned adequation is the bedrock of the primary misunderstanding (*prôton pseudos*) in the relativist attack against the imperative of truth. In order to grant truth its true place, the truth must in contrast be understood as fidelity to the being of speech, to the speaking-being [*parlêtre*] who is precisely not thought about according to technical or pragmatic situations. We must first question the essence of truth, which forever eludes us and which means that we can do no better than to "hold as true"(*Führwahrhalten*).[41] This question of the truth as "holding as true" (and not as absolute truth) is explicitly dealt with by Kant at the end of the *Critique of Pure Reason*, in the doctrine of method of pure reason.[42]

Kant's reasoning in relation to a proposed right to lie does not consist in promoting "Thou shalt always tell the truth" (this would implicitly presuppose a truth reduced to the perfect adequation of what is said with things), but instead in showing how there cannot be a moral duty to lie (cf. the previously cited example of the deposit).[43] His "examples" are always counter-examples: "Thou shalt lie to achieve your aims" cannot be universalised; therefore, it is not a moral law. Kant's reasoning, completely in the negative, is therefore not the positive promulgation of a "duty to tell the truth as an adequation of what is said with the thing".

Bearing witness as bearing witness entails the truth as a correspondence of what is said with the thing. Now, this truth of adequation or bearing witness are instrumentalised for completely different intentions: Phalaris's servant or slave might wish to get rid of the honest man against whom he bears false witness, he might wish to avoid being thrown into the maw of the burning bull, or he might wish simply to keep the tyrant happy. True or false witnesses do not determine any moral Law here for the simple reason that they are only technical means of achieving a certain end (technical principles). And this end answers to the pleasure principle, the pleasure of seeing one's enemy fall, the pleasure of escaping death, the pleasure of pleasing the tyrant (pragmatic principles).

It is in the framework of a generalised putting into question of truth that Lacan carries the apologue on truth to a higher level. Not without irony. He first transposes the aforementioned slave to Sparta as a "helot", in the course of questioning his tyrant in the Stoic manner in relation to bearing witness to "truth" as a means of satisfying the tyrant's wishes: should he also "bear true witness were this the means by which the tyrant could satisfy his desire"?[44] Should he also tell the tyrant the truths which would make him happy? Then Lacan generalises the apologue to all tyranny. Should one bear true witness for the benefit of all the great tyrants in history (Hitler, Innocent III, Stalin)? Should he denounce a Jew to please Hitler (and thus send him to the extermination camps)? Should denounce an atheist to please Innocent III (and thus send him to the stake)? Should he denounce someone who has broken with the party line to please Stalin (and send him or her to the Gulag)?

In all of these cases, the one from whom a true witness is expected is without any doubt *technically* competent as to the truth of adequation, he has "a better grasp on the import of the accusation [Jewish, atheist or dissident] than a consistory that simply wants to establish a file". He is the bearer of the technical truth of what a Jew is, of what the challenge of atheism consists of, of what the revision of the party line is. But the Jew, the atheist, and the dissident are never completely innocent, nor completely spotless; *truth does not boil down to adequation*. It is the tyrant who reduces truth to a yes/no matter (technical principle) in order to make it into the instrument of his desire (pleasure principle). "A tyrant is someone who appropriates the power to enslave the Other's desire": he perverts the jouissance principle (which is hidden but, however, quite present in the slave, the Jew, the atheist, the dissident) in order to reduce everything to the technique which assures his own pleasure.

"We could make the maxim that one must counter a tyrant's desire into a duty, if a tyrant is someone who appropriates the power to enslave the Other's desire."

Refusing the tyrant's desire, insofar as it boils down here to using witness as a technique for his pleasure, would mean liberating the Other's desire which is deployed in a quaternary logic highlighted in the Sadean fantasy, as we have seen. It is according to this quaternary logic that desire may "weigh in the scales" and take the measure of the different "goods", in short, "everything pathological" that might be judged. In this weighing-up, Lacan privileges desire, in relation to the Kantian law: "desire can have not only the same success but can obtain it more legitimately".

The law/desire opposition is present throughout the match in which Lacan seeks to oppose Kant. According to Lacan, it is Lacanian desire which wins every time, because for him the ("Kantian") law is identical to desire diminished by repression, *repressed* desire. But this manner of opposing law and desire by the intermediary of repression only stands up at the level of the handling of examples, in which a particular law is actually opposed to desire. The Law – the Law as principle, inasmuch as it goes beyond all examples, the Law of which Kant speaks – can be fundamentally *united* with desire and not opposed to it as Lacan himself shall recognise a little bit later.[45] This union is precisely the stakes of Kant's "higher faculty of desire".[46] In contrast to what the expression of the "law as repressed desire" may lead one to understand, desire is not a primary reality that the law would come to secondarily repress, it is never in a pure state or unrepressed. We do not start out from a supposed primordial desire and then bring it under the yoke of a particular law. We must read in Lacan's schema L that the Law is always already presupposed in the place of the Other, not without relying on the support of the signifier of the barred big Other $[S(\cancel{A})]$[47] in order to articulate desire and its quaternary exposition.

Lacan says that he had agreed to follow the *Critique of Practical Reason* (in which he had taken note of the "absence of the object") with the goal of knowing "where it was heading". Now that he thinks he has won out over his adversary Kant, now that he thinks he has proven – by means of the variations he has introduced into the two apologues – that the structure of desire responds better and "more legitimately" to the desired aim of "weigh[ing] in the scales [. . .] everything pathological", he thinks that it might be time to go back over the concessions he has made to Kant, notably to review "the disgrace that rather quickly befell all objects that were proposed as goods because they were incapable of achieving a harmony of wills: simply because they introduce competition".

Lacan speaks of *goods* where Kant speaks of *objects*: the quest for the same good vs. the same object cannot constitute a common will; because everybody wishes for their own pleasure. This impossibility is illustrated by "the pledge of King Francis I to the Emperor Charles V: 'What my brother Charles would have (Milan), that I also would have'".[48] The coveted object (Milan) is incapable of "achieving a harmony of wills: simply because [it] introduce[s] competition".

If Lacan here introduces the good at the place of the object, it is with a view to *weighing* the goods according to a higher *Good* (the moral Law thus remains understood to be dependent on the Good). It is to organise his weighing of the different goods that Lacan introduces a very particular "object" – quite more of a nothing (*nihil negativum*) than an object: "the object of desire" which comes into the place of the Kantian principle.

This is because ordinary objects (Milan, for example) *are not* "objects of desire", no more than principles. While Kant had excluded *all* objects (in the ordinary sense of the term) in the determination of the moral will by the moral principle, Lacan introduces a new, original sense of the term "object", a *new* "object", "the object cause of desire" ("the object *a*"), which is the central determinant in the question of the moral will. "The object of desire" is in no way an object in the everyday sense of the term – it corresponds to the question of the possibility or impossibility of the object in general; it is the *calling into question* of the object. This question is, moreover, perfectly articulated by Kant at the end of the Transcendental Analytic in the first critique (even if only very briefly so): it is the concept "of an object in general – problematically understood, and without its being decided whether it is something or nothing".[49] In order to pose the question of knowing whether it is something or nothing, we shall follow Kant's table of nothing, which corresponds to the different forms of the object *a*.

Armed with this questioning inherent to the object *a*, it can be better understood how desire is "the Other's desire since it is originally desire for what the Other desires".[50] Desire always consists not in desiring *what* the Other desires (Milan, for example), but in desiring that the Other desires, for example for the sexual partner to be taken up in a process of desire.[51] In order for the Other to desire, one may hold for him the position of the "object *a*", an object of satisfaction which is refused (the oral object, for example in hysteria), a contradictory object (the anal object, for example in obsessional neurosis), an object as an empty field open to all possibilities (the scopic object) or an object as the radical absence of all phenomenal objects (the vocal object). With the putting in place of the object *a*, the "harmony of desires" is "conceivable" inasmuch as the complete dialectic of the object *a* (or of Kant's table of nothing) can be followed. But not without danger, because the generalised questioning inherent to the object *a* does not allow one to trust an unmoving material object. Desire refers back to desire which refers back to desire in an infinite quest in which each element solely exists and consists within the entirety of the movements of desire. This chain "resembles the procession of Breughel's blind men, each one, no doubt, has his hand in the hand of the one in front of him, but no one knows where they are all going".[52] The procession of desires, which entails the procession of the different forms of the object *a* (oral, anal, scopic, vocal) eludes any kind of divine gaze which would have put things in order [S($\bcancel{A}$)]. "In retracing their steps, they all clearly experience a universal rule"; but even so they do not know any more about it. In any case, desire and the law are articulated in the expectant absence of knowledge: I must "abolish"(*aufheben*) knowledge to make way for the Law which also magnifies desire.[53]

Desire which is repressed by the law, Law which magnifies desire: "Would the solution in keeping with practical reason be that they go around in circles?"

The *gaze*, the third form of the object *a*, which is equivalent to Kant's "empty intuition without object"[54] (that is space-time, pure form of the intuition) or again to the topology of the loci of the fantasy, is indeed there, even if appears to be "lacking" as with Breughel's blind men led along in the procession of desires. It is indeed there, because this object *a* materialises the cause of desire by linking the two seats of the subject: the centre of the psychological subject who imagines himself or herself to be (*cogito ergo sum*) and the absence of the subject, the barred subject (there where I think, I am not). Around these two seats of the centre and the absence of the subject, the gaze covers the ellipse of all the subject's possibilities [*possibles*]. The gaze, "empty intuition without object" is *pending* the inscription of the object. It thus permits the materialisation of the cause of desire and the expectation of the object (in the most common sense) which will end up being inscribed there.

In contrast to the gaze, the voice, fourth form of the object *a*, appears as the "empty object without concept" because the concept destroys itself by containing within itself the radical contradiction of the possibilities of experience in space-time. The voice is the radical nothing, the radical *impossible*, the *nihil negativum*.

Lacan introduced something into the first apologue that had not originally been there, that is, the jouissance principle, which represents a moral principle (one must risk oneself in jouissance, contrary to the bourgeois spirit). In the second apologue, Lacan reduced the moral principle that could be found there in order to understand it as a technical principle at the service of a pragmatic principle. The moral Law (with a capital L, corresponding to Kant's moral principle) is thus debased to the level of a moral law (with a small l, to a rule in the Kantian sense) which can be opposed to the representatives of desire. The question of desire can thus appear in the opposition of a desire and a law, that is, in repression: the law is repressed desire. The advantage of this presentation is huge: it allows us to show how the moral Law, which is no other than the question of desire, necessarily entails the opposition of the law and desire. In other words, a repression. The practice of the moral Law implies the practice of analysis.

Notes

1 Kant's first apologue.
2 Lacan, "Kant with Sade", op. cit., p. 658.
3 Ibid. Text in brackets added by the author.
4 Ibid., p. 656.
5 [Translator's note: The original (Lacan 1966, p. 780) reads *jouissance spinthrienne*, which Fink translates as "obscene jouissance", providing a note which reads, "*Spinthrienne* (obscene) is an adjective used to qualify medals and engraved stones that depict obscene scenes (Lacan 2006, p. 833).]
6 Ibid., p. 659.
7 Ibid. Translation modified.
8 "Two things fill the mind with ever new and increasing admiration and reverence, the more often and more steadily one reflects on them: *the starry heavens above me and the moral law within me*" (Kant, *Critique of Practical Reason*, op. cit., p. 129).
9 "All practical principles that presuppose an *object* (matter) of the faculty of desire as the determining ground of the will are, without exception, empirical and can furnish no practical laws" (Kant, *Critique of Practical Reason*, op. cit., p. 19).
10 Translator's note: "*de principe*" could also be translated as "automatic".

168 "Kant with Sade" (1962–1963)

11 "Let us consider the paradox that it is at the very moment at which the subject no longer has any object before him that he encounters a law that has no other phenomenon than something that is already signifying; the latter is obtained from a voice in conscience, which, articulating in the form of a maxim in conscience, proposes the order of a purely practical reason or will there" (Lacan, "Kant with Sade", op. cit., p. 647).
12 Ibid., p. 659.
13 Kant, *Critique of Practical Reason*, op. cit., p. 26.
14 Ibid., p. 27.
15 Ibid., p. 660.
16 The figure of the "ideal bourgeois" is probably taken from Kojève's, "Faust ou l'intellectuel bourgeois" (unpublished text from 1936). See Auffret, *Alexandre Kojève, la philosophie, l'État, la fin de l'Histoire*, Paris, Grasset, 1990: "In contrast to the aristocratic spirit, the bourgeois is hypocritical, pretending to take risks; when he calculates them, it is because there are no risks involved but an interest, and when he does not calculate them, it is because there is nothing to lose" (p. 144). According to Lacan, Kant would base his system on a transcendence which would fundamentally have to do with a bourgeois spirit, refusing to get his hands wet. Kant would have brought his system into being on the basis of "the bourgeois who can only imagine transcendence, aesthetic as well as dialectical" (Lacan, "L'Étourdit", op. cit., p. 11). This is a radical confusion of transcendence (protected from risk) and transcendality (concretely implicated in everything seen, thought and done). The first – as a reference to an unattainable Thing in itself – is severely criticised by Kant. The second – as the necessary condition of all phenomenal experience – is at the basis of his *Critique*. More weightily, the introduction of the figure of the bourgeois as a criticism of Kant or Kantianism may also refer implicitly and underhandedly to Horkheimer and Adorno and their *Dialectic of Enlightenment* cited before. Adorno believed he could establish a lineage between Sade and Hitler, by way of the bourgeois, the heir to Kant. "The relationship established by Adorno between Sade and fascism passes precisely through an extremely close and vehement analysis of the formalistic bourgeois rationalism inherited from the Enlightenment, in which the metaphysical infrastructure of all forms of totalitarianism was drawn up" (Marty, *Pourquoi le XXᵉ siècle a-t-il pris Sade au sérieux?*, op. cit., p. 43). The reference to Adorno cannot directly be applied here, as Lacan does not place Sade on the side of the bourgeoisie. Sade would rather be seen as a remedy against them. Lacan thus situates himself on the side of Blanchot and Mascolo, their critique of humanist intellectualism and bourgeois alienation (which could, moreover, be directly related to Kant only with difficulty, as has just been said). "The sole axiom which authorises a radical demystification of bourgeois alienation, is the Sadean thesis *par excellence*, which posits that Evil is more real than Good, that negation is truer than acquiescence, which posits that, because the Good is wholly alienated, Evil is thus wholly inalienable. An axiom which amounts to saying that the sole reality is Evil" (Marty, Ibid., p. 122). The mirage in which Sadean Evil "realises" the inverted image of Good attributed to Kant.
17 Ibid.
18 Kant, *Critique of Practical Reason*, op. cit., p. 64. This citation is drawn from the chapter which deals with respect.
19 "We will excuse the hoodlum, then, from having to testify under oath" (Lacan, "Kant with Sade", op. cit., p. 660).
20 Juvenal, *Satire*, 8.79–84, cited in Kant, Ibid., p. 126.
21 Ibid., p. 126, note *o*. Author's note in brackets.
22 Ibid., p. 23.
23 Lacan, Ibid., p. 660.
24 Freud, S.E., Volume IV, op. cit., p. 160.
25 Lacan, "Kant with Sade", p. 660.
26 It is Kant who holds this place here and, as we have seen, Lacan should have brought this central piece into play in a more serious manner, that is, by bearing in mind that

his opponent's king is not motionless, that Kant, far from being frozen in an analytic conception, is more centred around the synthetic and on enunciation rather than the statement of the moral law and that the absence of an object is an opening up of the field of freedom.
27 Ibid., p. 661.
28 Translator's note: "*un moment de la pensée*". Fink has "an important moment in the history of thought".
29 Foucault had just published his *Madness and Civilization: A History of Insanity in the Age of Reason* (1961), which simultaneously criticises psychiatric confinement and the granting of freedom to the mad, a freedom which, according to Foucault, is solely "the other side of a fall into objectivity" (Marty, op. cit., p. 138).
30 Ibid., p. 659. Translation modified.
31 Lacan, *The Ethics of Psychoanalysis*, op. cit., p. 146.
32 Lacan, "Kant with Sade", op. cit., p. 661.
33 "Whatever is to arouse lively, convulsive laughter must contain something absurd (hence something that the understanding cannot like for its own sake). Laughter is an affect that arises if a tense expectation is transformed into nothing. This same transformation certainly does not gladden the understanding, but indirectly it still gladdens us in a very lively way for a moment. So, the cause of this must consist both in the influence that the presentation has on the body and in the body's reciprocal effect on the mind – but not because the presentation is objectively an object of our gratification (for how could an expectation that turned out to be false gratify us?), but solely because it is a mere play of presentations which produces in the body an equilibrium of the vital forces" (Kant, *Critique of Judgment*, translated by Werner S. Pluhar, Indianapolis, Hackett, 1987, p. 203).
34 "[T]he demand of lovemaking, to *faire l'amour* – if you will *faire l'àmourir*, to do it to death, it's even *à mourir de rire*, to die laughing – I'm not accentuating the side of love that partakes of what I call a comical mood just for the sake of it" (Lacan, *Anxiety: The Seminar of Jacques Lacan Book X*, translated by A.R. Price, Cambridge, Polity Press, 2014, p. 263).
35 "This confirms what I told you was essential to the mainspring of comedy, which is always, in the end, a reference to the phallus. And it is no accident that Aristophanes is the one who talks about it. He is the only one who can do so. But Plato does not realize that in having him speak of it, he has delivered to us – to those of us here – the linchpin that shifts the entire discourse that is to follow into another register" (Lacan, *Transference: The Seminar of Jacques Lacan Book VIII*, translated by Bruce Fink, Cambridge, Polity Press, 2015, p. 94).
36 Lacan, "Subversion of the Subject and the Dialectic of Desire", op. cit., p. 692ff.
37 A response to Kant's second apologue.
38 Lacan, "Kant with Sade", op. cit., p. 662.
39 Kant, "On a Supposed Right to Lie from Philanthropy", in *Practical Philosophy*, translated and edited by Mary Gregor, Cambridge, Cambridge University Press, 1996, p. 611. It is piquant to see that Kant here uses the exact term "*prôton pseudos*".
40 It cannot be upheld that truth for Kant was reduced to this adequation. In this regard, see his questioning of truth beginning with the first pages of the transcendental logic in the *Critique of Pure Reason* (op. cit., p. 73ff; A56/B82). An attempt to answer the question "What is truth?" entails all three of the critiques together.
41 [Translator's note: Previously mentioned in the context of an "assent" to the postulates of pure practical reason.]
42 The third section of the canon of pure reason: "Opinion, knowledge, and belief".
43 Lacan, "Kant with Sade", op. cit., p. 647.
44 Ibid., p. 661.
45 "The true function" is fundamentally "to unite (and not to oppose) a desire to the Law" (Lacan, "The Subversion of the Subject and the Dialectic of Desire", op. cit., p. 698).
46 Kant, *Critique of Practical Reason*, op. cit., p. 20.

47 We shall note that its function is well-represented in Kant, on the one hand, in the radical critique of all the proofs of the existence of God (the ideal of pure reason in the *Critique of Pure Reason*) and, on the other hand, in the necessity for the subject of himself or herself positing the law in his or her autonomy (theorem IV in the Analytic of the *Critique of Practical Reason*).
48 Kant, *Critique of Practical Reason*, op. cit., p. 25.
49 Kant, *Critique of Pure Reason*, op. cit., p. 231; A290/B347. It is following on from this conception of an object of which it cannot be decided whether it is something or nothing that Kant introduces his table of nothing. Lacan himself related his object *a* to this Kantian table of nothing in his seminar *Identification* (unpublished, lessons of 28 February and 28 March 1962). See Fierens, "Logique de la vérité et logique de l'errance chez Kant et chez Lacan", op. cit., pp. 71–73.
50 Lacan, "Kant with Sade", op. cit., p. 662.
51 "Man's desire is the Other's desire [*le désir de l'homme est le désir de l'Autre*] in which the *de* provides what grammarians call a "subjective determination" – namely, that it is qua Other that man desires (this is what provides the true scope of human passion)" (Lacan, "The Subversion of the Subject and the Dialectic of Desire", op. cit., p. 690).
52 Lacan, "Kant with Sade", op. cit., p. 662.
53 Cf. Kant: "I must, therefore, abolish (*aufheben*) *knowledge* (*Wissen*), to make room for *f*aith (*Glauben*)" (Kant, *Critique of Pure Reason*, op. cit., p. 21; BXXX. It is faith which enters into the Law and the Law of desire (the higher faculty of desire).
54 Or "*ens imaginarium*"(Kant, Ibid., pp. 232–233; A292/B348).

Chapter 15

The practice of psychoanalysis

Psychoanalysis recognises the subject's truth in desire

The subject's truth depends on what unfurls in the Other. In the schema of the Sadean fantasy (schema 1, p. 653), what takes place in the place of the Other, the voice, depends on desire. This is a truth which is in no way reducible to the adequation of something said with a thing – it is a truth within the singular exercise of speech: "I, truth, speak". This act of enunciation proper to the truth is hidden, it speaks from "the unconscious". Its pathways of desire may be misrecognised. This misrecognition "demonstrates what it represses", demonstrates desire as articulated with repression, that is, with the law. The misrecognition of the pathways of desire again demonstrates desire alongside repression, that is, the moral Law.

Impasses on the pathways of desire critical commentaries on Kant's morals

Unpleasure and pleasure are always at play in repressed desire or in the law (but Kant was unaware that the law is repressed desire)

Unpleasure always comes to interfere in the paths of desires insofar as the latter always entail repression. Unpleasure is omnipresent. On the one hand, it appears as the pretext which justifies repression strictly speaking; it is because the satisfaction of desire may give rise to unpleasure that desire is repressed under the law. On the other hand, the return of the repressed, in the symptom, for example, only attains the satisfaction of desire in the form of unpleasure. The "pathway of desire" and of its repression therefore always entail unpleasure. The recognition of the Law always passes through unpleasure.

Pleasure always passes through the misrecognition of the Law and the repression which it entails, as much in the repression of desire as in the return of repressed desire. Pleasure has an aversion to recognising the Law: desire is repressed beneath the law. This aversion to recognising the Law echoes repressed desire at the level

DOI: 10.4324/9781003055662-25

of the return of the repressed. Because the return of the repressed entails the desire to satisfy the conditions of the law, that is, the defence against desire.

The quest for happiness is antinomical to the pathway of desire (in lacking an awareness of the repression inherent to desire, Kant would risk being once more taken up in the quest for happiness)

The pathway of desire necessarily entails the law, that is, desire as repressed (articulated in Lacan's four-pointed schema). Desire necessarily implies a *rupture* presented in the four-pointed articulation of the subject. "If happiness means that the subject finds uninterrupted pleasure [*agrément sans rupture*] in his life, as the *Critique of Practical Reason* defines it quite classically, it is clear that happiness is denied to whomever does not renounce the pathway of desire."[1] In happiness, everything is fine, there are no points of rupture. Happiness, thus defined by Kant and by many others who do not take the place of repression (defined according to "consciousness") into account, is absolutely incompatible with the pathway of desire, which implies repression. In the line of pleasure and the misrecognition of the Law inherent to desire, the Epicurean wished to find happiness. On the other side of the same position, the Stoics wished to renounce the pathways of desire through virtue. In each case, it is "at the cost of man's truth, which is quite clear from the disapproval of those who upheld the common ideal", in which the pathways of desire must be respected. The ataraxia of the Epicureans and the Stoics deposes their wisdom, because it evacuates or minimises the place of desire: the Epicureans degrade desire to the level of happiness and the Stoics degrade desire in order to give way to virtue. As Kant does not grasp that the law is repressed desire, he "fail[s] to realize that they degraded desire". The degradation of desire, among both the Epicureans and the Stoics, which is played out in accordance with happiness, as "uninterrupted pleasure" has nothing to do with the repression of desire, which in contrast entails rupture, radical opposition (conflict is quite present in Kant). The degradation of desire does not lead to repressed desire or the law. The law is not "commensurably exalted". On the contrary, "whether we know it or not" (Kant did not know that the law was repressed desire), when the pathway of desire is dismissed, the moral Law – which Kant claims to demonstrate – is "cast down", because the articulation of desire and repression is lacking. In other words, Kant's own moral law is *necessarily* misunderstood due to the lack of an articulation with desire by means of repression (even if the conflict inherent to "duty" had already indicated its place). Lacan could not do otherwise than to start out from a misunderstanding of the Kantian moral Law.

The freedom to desire introduced by the revolution led to its self-destruction

Sade here serves as a representative of the pathway of desire in order to overturn the morals of happiness. In contrast to Saint-Just's proposition, which claimed that "happiness is a new idea in Europe", happiness had been absolutely central in all the pre-Kantian moral systems and the novelty lay on the side of the *pathway of desire*, more precisely on the side of the freedom to desire. "It is the freedom to desire that is a new factor." It is not the term "desire" which is a new factor insofar as it could have inspired the revolution, because "people have always fought and died for a desire", and every revolution is always articulated to a desire. It is the articulation of *desire* with *freedom* which is a new factor. The French Revolution wanted "its struggle to be for the freedom of desire".

It might be though that this new factor of freedom had been introduced by Kant in the third antinomy of the *Critique of Pure Reason* (1781) and that it is at the heart of the moral Law in the *Critique of Practical Reason* (1788). But the "freedom" belonging to the revolution was not at all understood in Kant's sense of the word.[2] The revolution introduces freedom into the law as a fundamental right of the human being and citizen (1789). Freedom is thus like the wife of the law (with a small l). But the revolution also wants the law itself "to be free, so free that it must be a widow." The revolution, backed up by the guillotine (the Widow), kills the husband of the law, that is, freedom. "The Widow *par excellence* [. . .] sends your head to the basket if it so much as balks regarding the matter at hand."[3] Such a will to freedom kills freedom. This lets it be understood that it cannot serve as a universal maxim, because it contradicts itself.

Saint-Just, the exalted young revolutionary, would have been better off remaining inhabited by the voice of desire articulated in his fantasies, notably the fantasies in *Organt* (a racy poem he had written at the age of nineteen while in prison).[4] The poem is a satire on society which also includes a pornographic side to it. If he had pursued this phantasmatic side (on the side of Sade and schema 1), "Thermidor might have been a triumph for" the young genius of revolutionary politics (instead of being guillotined in July 1794 – Thermidor – among Robespierre's main supporters).

To recognise the subject's truth in desire cannot be reduced to a pure search for happiness. Nor is it a case of exalting a false idea of freedom, the "freedom to desire", which leads to its destruction. It must be noted that Lacan dispatches the question of freedom "to the basket" a little too quickly, because the "freedom to desire" promoted by the revolution is not the Kantian freedom of the higher faculty of desire, which remains a pure principle, knowable only by means of the moral law (this is the meaning of the two apologues) and which opens up the possibility of creating a new form forever to be reinvented (on the basis of the Other). He could have articulated this more explicitly with the voice.

The enunciation of the right to jouissance (Sade) goes beyond the egoism of happiness (attributed to Kant, the "bourgeois")

The path of desire is the subject's truth, and it entails jouissance. "Were the right to jouissance recognized, it would consign the domination of the pleasure principle to an obsolete era" (the domination of the pleasure principle, which can be read in the happiness of the hedonists and again in the freedom proclaimed by the revolution). Jouissance is dependent on its enunciation in order to be recognised, and it is through this enunciation in the locus of the Other that "Sade imperceptibly displaces for each of us the ancient axis of ethics, which is but the egoism of happiness".

In Theorem II of the analytic, Kant had already dismissed the egoism of happiness as an axis of ethics which lead directly to the higher faculty of desire.[5] Nevertheless, according to Lacan, this egoism of happiness as the axis of ethics was not extinguished in Kant. He believes he has found decisive proof of this "in the exigencies that make him [Kant] argue both for some retribution in the hereafter and progress in this world".[6] Let us recall that the aforementioned retribution in the hereafter [*au-delà*] intervenes only as a solution for the antinomy of practical reason, of the incompatibility of happiness and virtue: it is necessary to admit that the search for happiness (the pleasure principle) does not disappear, never expires; we must therefore suppose a possible conciliation between virtue and happiness "beyond" [*au-delà*] the life of appearances that we know here. The immortality of the soul is nothing other than the unlimited pursuit of the principle of jouissance – equivalent to the moral principle – which must forever do battle with the pleasure principle. And the existence of God is none other than the existence of a supreme being who would make the conciliation of the two principles possible.[7] As for this world, the so-called "progress" expected by Kant only counts as the sensible inscription of an act which has consequences in the reality of the phenomenal world.

On the side of the hereafter (the "highest good") as on the side of this world ("progress"), Lacan stigmatises the supposedly Kantian Law as determined by the Good towards which it would tend. Let us again remind ourselves that for Kant it is the Law which causes the Good to appear and not the Good which orients the Law. In order to counter this polarization towards the (supposedly Kantian) Good, Lacan takes the opposite course by introducing, with Sade, Evil and "delight in evil" [*le bonheur dans le mal*][8] and thus hopes to reach an ethics of the Real. Thus, "the status of desire would change, demanding a re-examination of it".[9] But the change and the re-examination that it implies has more to do with the Thing, with the Real introduced by Kant himself,[10] than to the opposing force of "delight in evil". And the opposition of Good vs. Evil only serves to introduce the struggle and the counter-cathexis peculiar to repression, which is certainly absent in the work of Kant (despite the highlighting of the *conflict* peculiar to duty, from the *Groundwork* on).

An evaluation of the work of Sade on the basis of desire

Jouissance is introduced through the fantasy

"How far does Sade lead us in the experience of this jouissance?" What is the series of *consequences* which flows from the jouissance principle? How far does Sade lead us in the experience of and the search for the *cause* of this jouissance?

On the one hand, the Sadean scenarios (to be compared with the symbolic) demonstrate the cascade of the effects of jouissance, "these water buffets of desire built so that jouissance makes the Villa d'Este Gardens sparkle with a baroque voluptuousness". On the other hand, this water of desire may spurt up into the heavens (to be compared with the real) and this heavenly source would bring us closer to "the question 'What is it that is flowing here?'"

The water of desire may appear in Sade under the alternating domination of hate and love (as in Empedocles of Agrigentum). In the tormentor's voice, in the object a in the position of the big Other, love and hate are indivisible (from which we see appearing in the exposition of the vocal form of the object a, the structure of opposition and contradiction peculiar to the anal form of the object a, but also peculiar to repression). It is an atom, a something bordering on a nothing or a nothing bordering on a something (cf. Democritus's μηδέν)[11] in which love and hate are inextricably intertwined and the "love/hate atom" undergoes spontaneous random deviations (comparable to Epicurus's *clinamen*), of "unpredictable quanta".

The cascade of jouissance and the animation of the love/hate atom imply "the vicinity of the Thing". They remain dependent on the Thing and remain in the vicinity of their unsayable place of origin on the near side of the opposition between Good and Evil. The Real of the Thing appears as the neighbour (*Nebenmensch*), "the nearest one", more particularly by means of the vocal object a, which, being the negation of the conditions of all sensible experience, calls Being itself back into question.

It is through the voice that the question of Being, which is the very nature of the human being (*Dasein*), emerges. "Man emerges through a scream", the scream which "[vociferates that] "the universe is a flaw in the purity of Non-Being".[12] This is the place of the human being and it is the place of jouissance, deployed in this cascade of effects (to be compared to the symbolic and the imaginary) on the basis of the Real of the Thing.

But that which is felt of this experience of the symbolic and imaginary cascade of jouissance, based on the Thing as its real cause, goes beyond the limits of the fantasy. The fantasy supports desire by freezing it in place, "it is in fact constituted on the basis of these limits", linked to the representation of the scenario.

Desire beyond the fantasy: a putting into question of the approach to the Real through Evil

"We know that Sade went beyond these limits in real life."[13] Lacan presents this process of going beyond the limits in the passage from schema 1 (p. 653) to schema 2 (p. 657). He wanted to disappear after his death, buried in a ditch without a headstone. Without the Real of his own disappearance already in play before his death ($), without the pervasiveness of the Real in his life, Sade could not have given us "this blueprint of his fantasy", presented in "the human pyramids he describes, which are fabulous insofar as they demonstrate the cascading nature of jouissance". Lacan here intends to call into question what Sade's work conveys of the Real, "of this real experience", short of and beyond the fantasy.

In systematically taking the opposite side to the Good, Sade situates wickedness within transcendence, beyond the imaginable and the sensible, on the side of God. Far better than the Good, wickedness on the side of transcendence would have the function of introducing us to the Real. Wickedness *should* introduce us to the fundamental hole in the symbolic, in Kantian terms to the *Aufhebung* of knowledge, in Freudian terms to the mother's castration, in Lacanian terms to S(A̶). But in Sade, this wickedness "does not teach us much that is new" about the "changes of heart" in "a girl's feelings about her mother" at the level of the fantasy, and about that of Sade himself in relation to the mother's castration.

Sade's work as a sermon

Sade's work, which "wishes to be bad", in other words, Sade's work which wishes to introduce the Real *through evil*, should not have "allow[ed] itself to be a bad piece of work [*une méchante oeuvre*]", that is, a work which goes wrong [*méchoit*], a piece of work which fails to truly be an *oeuvre* worthy of the name.[14] It is moralising in the pejorative sense of the term: it claims to tell us what would be good for humanity. "It's a little too preachy." Sade's work wishes to educate young girls, and it is as a treatise on education that it is fundamentally "anal-sadistic". The "anal-sadistic" side brings to light the atmosphere which "obsessively permeated this subject (the education of young girls) for the two preceding centuries". The sermon proclaimed by Sade remains a sermon which by which "the victim is bored to death" and "the teacher is full of himself". The content of the discourse is worth no more than its form: the historical information, physiology, and sex education within it boil down to a number of commonplaces.

The lack of humour and the absence of dialectical reversal in Sade

The intention to educate is usually impotent. This is the source of "the obstacle to every valid account of the effects of education", because it always involves a confession of its failure: its results do not correspond to the intention to educate. This is verified where the treatises from the two preceding centuries are concerned but is equally so for Sade's own. The educative intention always aims to say what must be done. In other words, the law involved in it is heteronomous and action must correspond to the educator's statement of the law. Luckily, this educative intention is fundamentally impotent and the fantasy strives to bring something completely different into play, namely desire and its sudden autonomous appearance in enunciation. The scandal of the Sadean fantasy could have been led further and have shown that "the usual impotence of educational intentions" is precisely the impotence "against which fantasy here fights".

But Sade was not able to recognise the radical impotence of education or "sadistic impotence". If he could have done so, he would have better exploited the fantasy and would have better uncovered the structure of desire which precisely entails this impotence. This deficiency in recognising "the praiseworthy effects of sadistic impotence" is confirmed by the fact that the victim remains the victim without ever consenting to her tormentor's intentions. This reversal could, however, have crowned the fantasy in its development, as an articulation not only of the object *a* (the tormentor) with the barred subject (the victim) but also, in the opposite direction, of the barred subject and the object *a*. But in the Sadean fantasy, the victim remains the victim and the tormentor remains the tormentor.

If the Sadean victim had been able to consent to the tormentor's intentions, it would have shown from another point of view that desire is the other side of the law. Through her consent, the victim would have more clearly shown that this law depends on the desire which conditions it. She would have subscribed to desire more than to the law. This is because the law is only the repression of this desire and consent, as a return of the repressed, would have shown desire in the form of an active desire in she who up to that point had only been a victim.

In contrast, in the Sadean fantasy: the tormentor remains in his place of tormentor and the victim in her place of victim, in a law by which the roles are well-distributed – "one is always on the same side, the good or the bad". It is the dichotomy, of good and evil, of tormentor and victim, which dominates the whole business. Sade's morality is founded on this dichotomy. Justine is the good one and Juliette the bad one (*Juliette, or Vice Amply Rewarded*). If "Justine, or the Misfortunes of Virtue" passes over to the side of vice, it is once more the triumph of the dichotomy which comes into play from the separation of good and evil. The paradox of vice which represents virtue "merely comes down to the derision characteristic of edifying books, the kind *Justine* aims at too much not to have adopted it".[15]

Due to being entirely caught up in this binary logic of good and bad sides, Sade's work completely lacks any reversal. We perceive that the introduction of the Good–Evil opposition, of the law–jouissance conflict, of the Kant–Lacan struggle should lead the reader to an operation in which all principles are reversed within the structure. This is the only honest way to read Kant with Lacan. In contrast, in Sade, there is no reversal and no humour, except perhaps at the end of *Dialogue Between a Priest and a Dying Man* (1782, a very early piece of writing by Sade), in which a priest who has come to convert a dying libertine fails to prove the existence of God to him and lets himself be converted and perverted by the libertine into a voluptuous conformity with "nature".[16] This lack of reversal and, consequently, of humour is certainly veiled by "the invasion of pedantry" in the learned writings devoted to Sade since the Second World War.[17]

Despite its enunciation based on the tormentor's voice, universality in Sade still remains essentially analytical

When Sade "recommends calumny", it is a direct (analytical) result of his attack against the universality of laws.[18] We have seen earlier how Lacan, wrongly, accused Kant of remaining essentially stuck to the *analytical* universality of laws or to universality within the statement [*énoncé*] (which only concerns the first formula of the categorical imperative). According to Lacan, it was Sade who highlighted the *synthetic* universality of the Law or universality dependent on enunciation, notably in the proclamation of the right to jouissance. Here, Lacan returns to the question, turning *against* Sade and now reproaches him for being stuck to the *analytical* universality of statements.

Where can the true critique of purely formal *analytical* universality be found? One might prefer Sade to "add the spice of someone like Renan" in his *Vie de Jésus* (1863). "Let us be thankful", the latter writes, "that Jesus encountered no law against insulting a whole class of citizens",[19] that there was no particular law protecting the particular class of Pharisees, the great defenders of laws as universal statements (analytical universality). This is how Jesus was able to attack universality and how he pinned to the Jew, the son of the Pharisees, representatives of analytical, formal, universality of the law "the Nessus-tunic of ridicule". Remarks mocking analytical universality "have become burned into the flesh of the hypocrite and of the falsely devout". Here at last is a critique of analytical universality which hits home: it touches the heart of the universality constructed by Saint Paul, originally a Pharisee and apostle to the Gentiles, extending the universal scope of the Pharisees' form of universality to the whole of humanity. Here is a much more pertinent critique of universality than Sade's apology for calumny – "that an honest man will always triumph over it"[20] – in which we find, if we really wish to read it, "the ideal bourgeois", as Kant had been stigmatised by Lacan. It is Sade who finally finds himself in the position of the bourgeois.

How to touch the Real beyond Sade?

The flatness of Sade's line of argument attacking the universality of laws "does not encumber the sombre beauty that radiates from this monument of challenges" that Sade's work is. This "sombre beauty" hides the horror of the experience of the Thing, of the Real of desire "that we are seeking beyond the make-believe quality of the fantasy [*fabulation*]".[21] This Real of the Thing is at stake in the tragical experience beyond the emotions of fear and pity provoked and dealt with in Greek tragedy. Sade's work does not linger on fear and pity: it provokes bewilderment in the face of the darkest side of humanity. "Bewilderment and shadows", bewilderment does not lead us here to the spark which lights up the witty remark according to Freud ("bewilderment and light"). In Sade, the absolute lack of a sense of comedy,[22] as well as a sense of wit or witticism,[23] is explained by the tragic nature of a Real which goes far beyond the classical tragedy analysed by Aristotle in terms of fear and pity. The tragic introduced by Sade is one in which everything is put to work to destroy desire itself and the uniquely human vital process.[24] Now, this destruction is again what allows for the desire for rebirth. Lacan here refers to Claudel's Coûfontaine trilogy (*L'otage, Le pain dur* and *Le Père humilié*), which he had just analysed in his seminar on *Transference*.[25] The tragedy in Sade's works as well as in the Coûfontaine trilogy – more tragic than Greek tragedy – is not founded on song and the chorus (on Melpomene, the muse of song) nor on the history of the facts (on Clio, the muse of history).

What is it founded on if both the emotional (the choir) and factual (history) foundations crumble?

The answer, which is not given in Lacan's text, can only imply the introduction of the moral law by Kant, which is not in fact founded either on emotions, which always relate to pleasure (song), nor on the facts of what is the case (history), but certainly on the principle of what *must* be both shy of and beyond all emotion (fear or pity) and shy of and beyond what is actually practised by human beings (anthropology). Here therefore is Kant who must be rehabilitated, provided nonetheless that he has gone through the struggle, the opposition of desire and the law, through repression, provided also that he has gone beyond the field of the gaze (in which the fantasy risks becoming bogged down) and to have opened the door to the voice and the freedom to give a new form to things (cf. the unconscious).

The place of the Real in psychoanalysis

Stepping back from the Real

The step back from the Christian commandment "you shall love your neighbour as yourself."

In his book, *Sade, My Neighbour*, published in 1947,[26] Pierre Klossowski situates Sade's narratives and their fabulous *mises en scène* at the level of ordinary consciousness while connecting them to a Manichean way of thinking which opposes Evil to Good and the supremely evil-being to the highest good. As we have seen, Lacan's analysis does seem to be in line with Klossowski's book: the sadistic scenes expose the ordinary structure of everyone's fantasy while bringing them into relation with Evil, radical destruction, the second death. Lacan had himself posed the question of knowing whether or not Sade's work was "redemption and immortal soul – the status of the Christian".[27] Could we not simply give a Christian theological explanation of Sade?

Lacan is in agreement with Klossowski, "the Sadean fantasy is better situated among the stays of Christian ethics than elsewhere",[28] that is, in the presuppositions of Christian ethics rather than outside it. However, Sade's work fundamentally remains *shy of* Christianity. Because the static opposition of Good and Evil and the complete absence of any reversal between the torturer and the victim does not leave any pathways to a true introduction of the Real (Sade completely lacks a sense of humour, good and bad always remain on the same side). In contrast to Sade, Renan's Jesus contributes a radical calling into question of analytical universality, as well as a radical overturning which together permit the introduction of the Real.

Lacan now pinpoints Sade's step back from Christian ethics, according to the commandment, "You shall love your neighbour as yourself". The neighbour, the *Nebenmensch*, is a figure of the Real, of the Thing.

Klossowski's title presents the thesis, *Sade, My Neighbour*. Lacan is willing to recognise him as his neighbour and, as such, a figure of the Real (it is precisely in order to recognise the Real that he invokes Sadean evil in opposition to the supposedly Kantian Good). But the reverse is not true: "Sade himself refuses to be my neighbour". Sade explicitly rejected "this absurd morality [that] tells us to love our neighbour as ourselves".[29] Freud also rejected this Christian commandment.[30] Whether it has to do with the neighbour on the side of evil or the neighbour on the side of good, on one side or on the other, the fundamental reason for this refusal is the horror of the Real hidden in the *Nebenmensch*. "Sade does not have neighbourly enough relations with his own malice",[31] not to say that either his characters or he himself do not imagine enough horrors, but rather that they remain at quite a distance from the very *principle* of this malice, so much so that any perspective of reversal remains unthinkable. They remain at a distance from the Real of the Thing. This is because the latter does not let itself be reduced to an imaginary opposition between good and bad, but always entails dialectical reversals and the creative act of enunciation found in Renan's Jesus.

Before further examining the reason for Sade's step back from the Real of the Thing, let us again take up the question: What is Kant's position in relation to the Christian commandment "Love your neighbour as yourself"? Lacan says nothing about it, even though Kant had made his position explicit at length in the third chapter of the analytic of the *Critique of Practical Reason*, devoted to respect. Kant *fundamentally* accepts the Christian commandment; the moral law "agrees [. . .] very well"[32] with this commandment, which demands the respect (*Achtung*) reserved for the moral law. Kant's sole reservation regarding the Christian commandment has to do with the formulation which mixes up the field of the moral Law (the categorical imperative) with the field of the pathological inclinations (love).[33] This mix-up in fact risks losing track of the question of the Real.

Death drive and death penalty

The test which allows it to be seen if an author can accept the Real (or, in Freudian terms, "the death drive") or equally, the "commandment" to love one's neighbour, is, according to Lacan, his or her position towards the death penalty, which is "one of the correlates of Charity". Charity[34] is here synonymous with absolute respect for the other and with what he or she does, in other words, respect for the Real of the neighbour. Under the pretext of a respect for nature, Sade repudiates the death penalty. Here is what he says, "Must murder be repressed by murder? Surely not. Let us never impose any other penalty upon the murderer than the one he may risk from the vengeance of the friends or family of him he has killed".[35]

Two years after this rejection of the death penalty by Sade in *Philosophy in the Bedroom*, Kant takes the opposite position in the *Metaphysics of Morals* (1797): "If, however, he has committed murder he must *die*. Here there is no substitute that will satisfy justice".[36] It is not a case here of returning to the debate on the death penalty, but of evaluating the position of *reason*, of *reasoning*, the manner of reason in relation to death and the death penalty. Sade's position is justified from the perspective of a letting *nature* (which acts as a kind of imaginary) be. Kant's position is justified in the perspective of a duty on the part of reason to take the Real of the death drive and its consequences in the criminals concerned into account. The death penalty is pronounced "in proportion to [the criminal's] *inner wickedness*".[37] Supposing that criminals were given the choice of death or life imprisonment: "the man of honour would choose death, and the scoundrel convict labour". The reason for the death penalty is neither vengeance nor prevention. It solely has the aim of bringing the penalty or the consequences of the crime into proportion with the criminal's reason, to his honour.

It is in this sense that Lacan proposes the test of the "death penalty" to know whether or not the death drive is taken seriously (to be understood in the sense of the series or sequence leading from the crime to the punishment):[38] one who categorically rejects the death penalty does not take the Christian commandment seriously. In Sade, the Real and the death drive are precisely not taken seriously, "Sade does not have neighbourly enough relations with his own malice." And the same goes for Freud when he condemns the commandment to love one's neighbour as oneself, which implicates us right within the Real of the death drive. Just like Sade, Freud steps back from the commandment of Charity, the "Charity" (with a capital C) of loving one's neighbour as oneself, of loving the Real of the death drive in the other as in oneself. It must indeed be recognised that Kant's reasoning precisely takes the Real of the crime and its consequences into account. He provides ample space for taking death into consideration without concession.

The stopping point in Sade

Sade stopped "at the point where desire and the law become bound up with each other".[39] "Who would cast the first stone", if he discovers desire on the basis of the law, if, like Saint Paul, he may know covetousness on the basis of the Torah[40] and if, as in Kant, he may deduce freedom on the basis of the law.

This operation may appear to be same each time, but it is exaggerated in Sade, who systematically takes the opposite course to the law, the law which is equivalent to repressed desire, with the idea that he may thus uncover a desire purified of its hindrances.

This cannot suffice, because desire *is bound up with* the law; in other words, it is not without its repression. And this binding or knotting of desire with repression precisely implicates the Real. "It is not simply that his flesh is weak, as it is for each of us; it is that the spirit is too willing not to be deluded."[41] In Sade, jouissance unwinds from the side of the flesh and it is easily reduced to a pleasure pushed to the extreme, all while losing its specific character of a *principle*, as in the most commonplace usage of the term "jouissance". But also in Sade, the spirit is too willing in so easily opposing evil to the good. It is deluded and loses sight of the question of the Real (and of the articulation of desire and the law – in other words, the articulation of desire in the dialectic of repression). "His apology for crime merely impels him to an oblique acceptance of the Law" and not to the recognition of the Real.

Nature (the substantivized big Other) comes to stop up the question of the Real

Also at the place of the Real of the non-existence of the big Other [S(A̸)], Sade re-establishes the reverse side of the highest good or Sovereign Good, Evil, the supremely evil-being. "The Supreme Being is restored in Evil Action [*le Maléfice*]."

Sade thinks "that by replacing repentance with reiteration he can be done with the law within". With its reverse side of guilt, with repentance, the moral Law at the heart of the human being appears as the second of the great things which, according to Kant, "fill the mind with ever new and increasing admiration and reverence, the more often and more steadily one reflects on them".[42] Sade, however, thinks he can have done with the second admirable thing, the moral law. He thinks it possible just to hold on to the *natural law*, the first admirable thing which commands the "starry sky" of the galaxies of which we are nothing but a lowly dust.

He thinks he can reduce everything to the natural principle alone and hold on only to "the promise that nature, woman that she is, will magically give us ever more". "We would be foolish to have faith in this typical dream of potency", in which "nature" is no more than an avatar of the non-castrated, all powerful Mother.

In the sense of Nature as the sole Supreme Being in Sade, we might have thought along with Klossowski that Sade's work was situated in "the prolongations of Spinoza's 'atheist' doctrine of 'Deus sive Natura'".[43]

On the basis of a nature infinitely more respectable than the *human* being, all human laws may and even ought to be transgressed. Whence the radical dependence of the human being in relation to God-Nature in Spinoza's *Ethics*. Whence the human being's relation to original Nature, in which he or she is only one of the instruments of Nature, in Sade.

This parallel, however, ignores the fundamentally different place of Nature in each. In Spinoza, it depends on God's intelligence. In Sade, it depends on sensibility, magnified in the imagination of the all-powerful original Mother.

The non-castrated Mother in Sade

"What Sade is missing here", is the Mother's castration or, again, the signifier of the barred big Other. *Philosophy in the Bedroom* comes to a close with the necessity of sewing up all the Mother's holes[44] with a curved needle which comes to definitively restore the Mother to her uncastratability. But it is also a needle which pierces the voyeur's eye through the keyhole as in Buñuel's *El*, the voyeuristic eye which would precisely attempt to verify the Mother's non-castration (which is not without calling to mind Buñuel's childhood experiences).[45]

We have gained nothing by replacing Socrates's Diotima (who upholds a radical hole in knowledge and therefore the mother's castration) with Sade's Dolmancé (who upholds a hole-less Nature and a non-castrated Mother). On the contrary. In his sexual behaviour Dolmancé is, moreover, frightened by the ordinary sexual pathway, insofar as it precisely puts forward the question of castration. At the end of Sade's text, the mother – Madame de Mistival, in *Philosophy in the Bedroom* – is sewn up, she will remain forbidden, she will remain intact and outside castration. *Noli tangere matrem*, do not touch the un-castratable Mother Nature.

It all certainly appears from the angle of a certain kind of "castration", apparently incurred in sadistic scenes from the book. But this "castration" remains purely imaginary and therefore without an effect of reversal, without symbolic castration and without consequence on the side of the Real. Everything in fact remains within the Mother's essential non-castration, a non-castration which is again reassured at the end of the narrative when the needle comes to sew up all the holes of the Mother, who had been raped as if it counted for nothing: raped and sewn up [*violée et cousue*].

In sadistic rape, it is desire which would like to declare itself freed from the law, freed from a law from which Sade wishes to take the opposite direction, desire which would be freed from repression. But the letters of the French word meaning "rape – *viol* – and "raped" – *violée* – contain the three letters i-o-l which, when they are inverted, spell l-o-i, *loi*, the French word for "law". Even when he attempts to erase the law at heart of rape, a mysterious letter V remains. Is it the V of *Volonté* – "will"? But this is not without convoking the complete structure, even if it remains veiled [*voilée*]: "V . . . ée et cousue",[46] law and castration remain present, even if they are effaced. The law remains subjacent to the aforementioned rape: "My verdict is confirmed regarding Sade's submission to the Law". But it is a submission which we must call "covered up" or "veiled" [*voilée*] (*v . . . ée*, not without again implicating the law) insofar as it absolutely avoids the Mother's castration or the signifier of the barred big Other.

"There is thus precious little here – in fact, nothing – by way of a treatise that is truly on desire." Because it all reaches not as far as the fact of desire, but rather the representation of desire by the fantasy, without ever elevating desire to the real problematic of jouissance, which involves repression, the signifier of the barred big Other and the action [*l'agir*] of the drive (cf. the upper line of Lacan's graph and of our presentation of the phallic function). What is heralded by this radical failing of the treatise, in which Sade does not truly encounter his neighbour or the Real, "is at most but a tone of reason". For want of having truly accepted the stakes of the Real, which passes through the Mother's castration, through the signifier of the barred big Other, Sade's work is finally only a tonal variation of the reasonable, a degeneration of reason.

Notes

1. Lacan, "Kant with Sade", op. cit., p. 663.
2. Kantian freedom must be articulated with the fourth form of the object *a*, the voice, the *nihil negativum*.
3. Ibid.
4. He had stolen jewels and other precious objects from his family and had been imprisoned at his mother's request.
5. Kant, *Critique of Practical Reason*, op. cit., pp. 19–20.
6. Lacan, "Kant with Sade", op. cit., p. 664.
7. Following Lacan's position, Alenka Zupančič also reduces the dialectic of practical reason to a simple reward for services rendered in morality. We understand that she can thus distinguish two ethics: an ethic of the real, founded on the moral law (cf. the analytic of practical reason) and an ethic founded on a supposed reward, such as would be developed in the dialectic of practical reason and which still follows the former axis of the quest for happiness (Zupančič, *Ethics of the Real*).
8. Lacan, "Kant with Sade", op. cit., p. 645.
9. Ibid., p. 664.
10. From the table of nothing and in the whole dialectic of pure reason (Kant, *Critique of Pure Reason*, op. cit.).
11. "Democritus in effect made us a gift of the ἄτομος, of the radical real, by eliding the 'not', μή, but in its subjunctivity, in other word this modal, whose consideration demand recasts. In consideration of which the – δέν was indeed the clandestine passenger whose clam now shapes our destiny" ("L'Étourdit", op. cit., p. 23; see Fierens, *Lecture de l'Étourdit*, Paris, L'Harmattan, 2002, pp. 294–295).
12. Lacan, "The Subversion of the Subject and the Dialectic of Desire", op. cit., p. 694.
13. Lacan, "Kant with Sade", op. cit., p. 664.
14. Lacan had played off the double sense of the word "bad" in *The Ethics of Psychoanalysis* with regard to Sade's work. In that seminar, low literary standing [*la mauvaise tenue littéraire*] was seen as a quality which could suitably refer back to Evil! "The fact that the book falls from one's hands no doubt proves that it is bad, but literary badness here is perhaps the guarantee of the very badness or *mauvaisité*, as it was still called in the eighteenth century, that is the object of our investigation" (Lacan, *The Ethics of Psychoanalysis*, op. cit., p. 201).
15. Lacan, "Kant with Sade", op. cit., p. 665.
16. At the moment of his death, "the dying man rang, the women entered; and after he had been a little while in their arms the preacher became one whom Nature had corrupted, all because he had not succeeded in explaining what a corrupt nature is" (final note at the end of the dialogue).
17. Adorno, Klossowski, Bataille, Blanchot, etc.
18. "To seek to impose universal laws would be a palpable absurdity: such a proceeding would be as ridiculous as that of the general who would have all his soldiers dressed in a uniform of the same size; it is a terrible injustice to require that men of unlike character all be ruled by the same law: what is good for one is not at all good for another" (Sade, *Philosophy in the Bedroom*, op. cit., p. 310).
19. Renan, *Vie de Jésus*, 17th Edition, Paris, Calmann-Lévy, 1863, p. 339, cited by Lacan, "Kant with Sade", op. cit., p. 665.
20. "Either one or the other: calumny attaches to a truly evil man, or it falls upon a virtuous creature. It will be agreed that, in the first case, it makes little difference if one imputes a little more evil to a man known for having done a great deal of it; perhaps indeed the evil which does not exist will bring to light evil which does, and there you have him, the malefactor, more fully exposed than ever before. [. . .] If, on the contrary, a virtuous man is calumniated, let him not be alarmed; he need but exhibit himself, and all the

calumniator's venom will soon be turned back upon the latter" (Sade, *Philosophy in the Bedroom*, op. cit., p. 312).
21 Lacan, "Kant with Sade", op. cit., p. 666. Translation modified.
22 Ibid., p. 661.
23 Ibid., p. 665.
24 This absolute destruction not simply of a particular individual life but of the life principle is notably evoked by Pius IV's dissertation in the fourth part of *Juliette* (see Marty, op. cit., pp. 213–214.
25 "As it develops through the three stages of the tragedy, the drama is that of knowing how – based on this radical stance – a desire can be reborn and of knowing what desire it is" (Lacan, *Transference: The Seminar of Jacques Lacan Book VIII*, translated by Bruce Fink, Cambridge, Polity Press, 2015, p. 303.
26 This is how Klossowski explained the title of his book: "If some strong spirit had been advised to ask Saint Benedict Labre what he had thought of his contemporary, the Marquis de Sade, the saint would have unhesitatingly replied, 'He's my neighbour'" (Annie Le Brun, *Soudain un bloc d'abime, Sade*, Paris, Gallimard, 2014, p. 33).
27 Lacan, "Kant with Sade", op. cit., p. 656.
28 Ibid., p. 666.
29 Sade, *Philosophy in the Bedroom*, op. cit., p. 309.
30 Freud, *Civilization and Its Discontents* in *Standard Edition of the Psychological Works of Sigmund Freud*, Volume 21, edited and translated by James Strachey, London, Hogarth Press, 1961, p. 108.
31 Lacan, "Kant with Sade", op. cit., p. 666.
32 Kant, *Critique of Practical Reason*, op. cit., p. 68.
33 Kant draws attention to the paradoxical side of the order of the term "*loving*". In the Christian commandment, the distinctions between inclination (to love, to "willingly" carry out) and the categorical imperative (the commandment, to love the moral Law and one's freedom), between the pathological and the practical, between the phenomenal and the noumenal are erased. Now, the irreducible opposition inherent to duty between inclination ("willingly") and the moral law (the "commandment") must be maintained. The Real can in no way be reduced to inclination or to what is done willingly.
34 This "Charity", as a fundamental respect on the side of the Real, must not be confused with imaginary charity, which Lacan criticises in *Television*: "A saint's business is not *caritas*. Rather, he acts as trash [*déchet*]: his business being *trashitas* [*il décharite*]" (Jacques Lacan, "Television" in *October*, Volume 40, translated by Denis Hollier, Rosalind Krauss and Annette Michelson, Cambridge, MA, The MIT Press, Spring 1987, p. 19).
35 Sade, *Philosophy in the Bedroom*, op. cit., p. 337.
36 Kant, *Metaphysics of Morals*, translated by Mary Gregor, Cambridge, Cambridge University Press, 1991, p. 142.
37 Ibid.
38 For further development of the topic of the death penalty, see Jacques Derrida, *The Death Penalty*, Volume 1, translated by Peggy Kamuf, Chicago, University of Chicago Press, 2013, and Volume 2, translated by Elizabeth Rottenberg, Chicago, University of Chicago Press, 2017.
39 Lacan, "Kant with Sade", op. cit., p. 667.
40 "What then should we say? That the law [Torah] is sin? By no means! Yet, if it had been for the law, I would have not known sin. I would have not known what it is to covet if the law had not said, "You shall not covet" (Saint Paul, "The Letter of Paul to the Romans", 7:7, in *The Holy Bible, New Revised Standard Edition*, Grand Rapids, Zondervan Publishing House, 1995, p. 1019).
41 Lacan, "Kant with Sade", op. cit., p. 667.
42 Kant, *Critique of Practical Reason*, op. cit., p. 129.

43 Klossowski, *Sade My Neighbor*, translated by Alphonso Lingis, Evanston, Northwestern University Press, 1991, p. 141.
44 "MADAME DE SAINT-ANGE – I believe it is now of the highest importance to provide against the escape of the poison circulating in Madame's veins; consequently, Eugenie must very carefully sew your cunt and ass so that the virulent humor, more concentrated, less subject to evaporation and not at all to leakage, will more promptly cinder your bones. EUGENIE – Excellent idea! Quickly, quickly, fetch me needle and thread! . . . Spread your thighs, Mamma, so I can stitch you together – so that you'll give me no more little brothers and sisters" (Sade, *Philosophy in the Bedroom*, op. cit., p. 363).
45 As a child, "he watched women undress in beach changing huts. Equipped with a piece of glass placed against the keyhole, he could look at them without the risk of having his eye pierced by a needle. That was the method women had used to defend themselves from voyeurs" (Trichet and Marion, "Ce que nous apprend *El* de Buñuel sur l'économie de jouissance dans la paranoia" [What Buñuel's *El* Teaches Us about the Economy of Jouissance in Paranoia], in *Cliniques méditerranéennes*, Toulouse, Érès, 2012/2, no. 86, p. 159).
46 [Translator's note: Fink reads *V . . . ée* as *Vérolée*, which he translates as "syphilized". See Lacan, "Kant with Sade", op. cit., p. 667 and the note on p. 835.]

Section III

Practice of the unconscious

Chapter 16

From one reading the other on Kant and on Lacan

The reading of Kant's morality is most often distorted in more than one way. It is very generally seen as a variant of the morality of a bourgeois individual seeking the Good, without taking any risks, regretting the absence of an object perfectly fitting his or her appetites and having to content himself or herself in the most comfortable way possible with having to be inscribed within the framework of a given law, characterised by its pretension to universality.

There was no need to wait for Eichmann in order to produce this misreading of Kant, on which the "banality of evil" in general can be supported. It could be imagined that it had already been produced where Sade is concerned as early as the publication of the *Critique of Practical Reason*. But whatever the case may be, the divine Marquis had not hesitated to *respond* to this moral system, which takes a step back from really being "republican".

Tasked with writing a preface introducing Sade's work, Lacan wished to show that Sade yielded the truth of Kant's *Critique of Practical Reason*.

As we have seen, Lacan's reading is regularly unbalanced, out of step, and misaligned in relation to the lines of force of the Kantian moral system in the strictest sense: it stigmatizes a quest for the *Good* as primary object of the moral law (in the locus and place of the primordial operation of the moral principle); it supposes a pre-existing *subject individual* (rather than considering the subject as a consequence of the moral factum); it relies on *examples* (rather than playing everything out according to principles); it understands universality as a purely formal *analytic* criterion (rather than understanding it as a synthetic a priori judgement, which must therefore always be created anew); and consequently, it does not delay in encountering in it no more than the "morality" of a bourgeois, the everyday "morality" which consists in inscribing oneself within universality without getting one's feet too wet, by seeking the greatest possible advantage.

A *bad* reading of Kant by Lacan, therefore. Let us not boast of being in possession of the *right one*, however. It is not a case of branching out from the concept of good/bad: but from the operating principle, preliminary to these judgements.

Provided that it is agreed to carefully read Kant as much as Lacan, we thus note the entire movement animating the thinking within Kant, Sade and Lacan.

Lacan certainly starts out from a bad reading of Kant – and it is the classical reading, from which we never entirely escape. But it is on the basis of this unavoidable deficiency that everything needs to begin to shift. This gap must be responded to. And it is Sade who is called to do so. Does Sade do "better" than Kant? Certainly not. He responds and puts back to work what we had too easily and too falsely admitted in approaching the moral system, in approaching the unconscious, in our facile comprehension of jouissance, namely – that there is a subject individual (the *question* of the subject is effaced and the "subject" is taken to be a person), that there is quite simply Good on one side and Evil on the other (the right or wrong, bad or good, reading of a text, for example, but also Good and Evil in what the "patient" should do, good and bad solutions), that examples are guides for our practice (clinical vignettes to explain to us what must be done in clinical practice), formal universalities by which we may straitjacket our patients and our procedures (conceptual or concrete "frameworks" which should format our clinical practice). All this would permit us to organise our bourgeois psychoanalysis (has it not been said that Freudian technique was adapted to the Viennese bourgeoisie at the turn of the 20th century?).

A bad reading certainly. As long as it introduces reversal, the movement of dialectic. Sade, more of a rebel than a marquis and more demonic than divine, does not appear to be anything other at first than the representative of a statics antithetical to the statics of bourgeois morality. But the bourgeois position (the bad reading of Kant) and the Sadean position must be read not as statics, but in the movement of structure. This movement can be approached in "those exemplary figures who, in the Sadean boudoir, assemble and disassemble in a carnival-act-like rite".[1] Lacan teased out the quadripartite, moving structure of the fantasy in general. Not only is the movement of the fantasy inscribed in sensibility; it is also the condition *sine qua non* of the exercise of all sensibility in general. A sensibility, therefore, in which the jouissance at the heart of the exercise of desire emerges. But this cannot suffice. Because sensibility, jouissance, desire are only ever valid with their counterpoint in intelligibility, with refined jouissance, with the difference between the "lower faculty of desire" (which would be on the side of Sade) and the "higher faculty of desire" (highlighted by Kant).

A lack of object in Kant? Never mind, Lacan introduces what will become the object *a*, simultaneously excessively sensible and excessively intelligible, because it is the *question* – something or nothing? – which conditions (intelligible) the appearance of every object (in the sensible and common sense of the term).

On the strength of this "object *a*" at the heart of jouissance, Lacan can return to the struggle against Kant. The law opposes itself to desire. But is it not the other way round instead? The sensible opposes itself to the intelligible. But is it not the other way round instead? These questions probably do not have a univocal meaning, because it is reversal which counts. In this struggle, none of the combatants can declare himself the winner. Because it is the struggle itself which wins the game on its own account. The struggle provides the very structure of repression (of primary repression): cathexis and counter-cathexis, which lean on each other in order to *appear* in a certainly frozen rigidity, but one which remains entirely constructed from live forces peculiar to the unconscious. The Real is not frozen reality, it only exists in the live forces of structure, which bear witness to the creative power of the unconscious.

Even if he could not envisage the fourth form of holding as true that is repression, Kant had been, no doubt, much better equipped to grasp this movement of structure than Sade, for whom everything became too easily fixated in the opposition of Good and Evil, between No and Yes, without any possible reversal.

If Lacan has the measure of this fundamental rigidity (despite the changing of positions in the Sadean scenes), it is not in order to "teach a lesson". *Kant with Sade* does not boil down to a lesson administered to Sade, the pervert, from the "position of a mandarin",[2] as it may appear. Rigidity (the movement which becomes rigid in the fantasy) is indeed inscribed within the dialectical movement of practice, to which Kant opens the door.

What are the consequences of the movement initiated by the *Critique of Pure Reason*, taken up by Lacan with the support of Sade in order to find jouissance in it? How does the unconscious find itself relaunched from it?

Notes

1 Lacan, "Kant with Sade", p. 658.
2 Marty, *Pourquoi le XX siècle a-t-il pris Sade au sérieux?*, op. cit., p. 233.

Chapter 17

The unconscious and the jouissance principle

The unconscious and jouissance

What specifies the unconscious is that it "gives things a new form". It is a tireless factory of new forms. Every psychoanalyst and analysand since Freud may note its efflorescence in the dream. They may also note that this production of forms that is the unconscious does not burden itself with any contingency or any necessity relative to the dreamer's empirical, sensible data: the unconscious does not think, calculate, or judge in any way at all.

On the basis of this observation (the new forms replace the taking into consideration of the sensible data of everyday life), it is possible to conceive the unconscious in two diametrically opposed ways according to the status which will be given to these new forms. They may be supposed as emerging from a purely mechanical, deregulated, lawless machine; the purely random new forms thus have no meaning, even if they are perfectly determined by this transforming machine within a purely empirical world in direct and simple relation with our sensibility. The unconscious, insofar as it produces new forms may respond to a *principle* situated outside the purely empirical world, outside of our sensibility, outside the deterministic laws of nature. The unconscious may be properly creative here not without presupposing the freedom inherent to the unconscious and its creation: it is on the basis of a *non-empirical* principle x, that it makes new forms appear. We can never prove the validity of this second conception, because our knowledge and our science are limited to the empirical world accessible to our sensibility. Neither can we refute it, for the same reason.

Scientism – which claims to explain everything through science (and through sensible data alone) – effectively excludes the second conception of new forms. Scientism is a non-scientific belief, because it is founded on an exclusion which is not at all scientific, an absolute faith in the absolute monopoly of science: everything without exception can be explained according to sensible experience. Directly or indirectly, everything would be science.

Psychoanalysis – which indeed claims to act with the unconscious – *must* accept the second conception. In order to uphold its practice, which consists in acting with the unconscious, in order to transform what had appeared to be well-determined in symptoms, psychoanalysis must believe – this is also a belief – that this is possible, in other words that a new form may be produced that does not consist of variations within the framework of an absolute determinism. It must be possible to start out from the unconscious and to begin a new experience of life.

Nothing permits us to prove or to refute the first (scientistic) conception of the unconscious. Nothing permits us to prove or to refute the second (psychoanalytic) conception of the unconscious. They are solely beliefs or faiths appealed to by a practice. The first by a scientific practice which, wrongly, imagines itself needing to explain *everything* (this is a universalisation of the scientific approach) and to exclude all the other possible practices in order to be able to advance. The second by a practice of speech which has faith in the fundamental transformational power arising from the unconscious and which is certainly *not whole* (because it recognises moreover the relevance of sensible data and, therefore, of science).

The new form produced by the unconscious does not essentially operate by taking the sensible data of experience into account; it does not therefore operate in relation to a (guaranteed or anticipated) gain of pleasure, nor in relation to a certain utility (whether or not it is predicted).[1] This necessary discrepancy (both in relation to pleasure and to utility) corresponds very precisely to what is commonly called "jouissance", always out of step in relation to pleasure (an ex-aggerated, ex-alted pleasure or pain, that is, outside the norms of pleasure), always out of step in relation to any kind of utility (it strictly serves no purpose). This is why we must say that the specificity of the unconscious and of the work of psychoanalysis is to be found *in jouissance*. Again, it must always be specified what jouissance is, as opposed to pleasure. As it cannot be understood either through fixed ideas, or through judgements determining the status of things, nor through calculations aiming at a certain precise goal, it can only be made explicit *as a principle*. How can this principle be made explicit if we cannot rely on everything that is, however, so familiar?

The jouissance principle and the ethical dimension of the unconscious

Theoretical concepts first appear to be statements which constrain the relations between concepts. Practical principles appear to be propositions containing a general determination of the will. On either side, they seem to indicate instructions, the set of instructions for concepts vs the set of instructions for the will: how should we act theoretically or practically? These instructions are generally made explicit by quite concrete operations, which can be inscribed in sensible experience. With an ordinary principle, we can calculate, deduce quite precise judgements on what must be done and not done and produce fixed thoughts on the procedures to be carried out.

It will have been noted, the "jouissance principle", which counts as the fundamental principle of the unconscious, not only does not correspond to the schematism of principles as an algorithm or set of instructions, but is radically opposed to it: the work of the unconscious "does not think, calculate or judge in any way at all; it restricts itself to giving things a new form". Jouissance and the unconscious do not correspond to any set of instructions.

We must tease out a principle, independent of the sensible conditions of experience and irreducible to any algorithm, to any set of instructions at all. Such is the problem of the unconscious.

The formal structure of the problem *of the unconscious* in Freud is identical to the structure of ethics, more precisely that of Kant's *practical reason*. This is why we must say that "the status of the unconscious [. . .] is ethical".[2]

How is the work of the unconscious guided without the help of thoughts, calculations, and judgements on concrete empirical things? How are ethics or practical reason guided without the aid of what can be known on the basis of sensible experience?

Certainly, we can say that the "matter" of the unconscious is "jouissance", whereas that of Kantian practical reason is the "moral law". But we do not know what these matters of "jouissance" and the "moral law" are, impossible as they are to define strictly speaking. The important thing is to clearly understand that "jouissance" and the "moral law" are only found and only let themselves be questioned *through their form*, through the structure and functioning of their *principle*. "Jouissance" and "moral law" may appear as two different matters, but they are essentially only valid through their form, *which is the same*. Whence the fundamental importance of *practical reason* to put the unconscious in place in its essentially ethical dimension. From the perspective of structure and functioning, "jouissance" and the "moral law" are the same thing. In clinical practice (in empirical experience), we shall note, moreover, the ceaseless entanglement of the moral law, guilt, jouissance, and the formations of the unconscious in general. Whence the obligatory passage through a reading of Kant's *practical reason* (the *Groundwork of the Metaphysics of Morals* and the *Critique of Practical Reason*).

A rigorous reading of "jouissance and of the "moral law" is necessarily ascetic, stripped-down, suprasensible, "in the purity of Non-Being". The chapter devoted to "respect" certainly introduces the necessity of passing this blueprint into sensibility, but this passage is only carried out in the form of a feeling, the sole feeling aroused by pure reason. And a rigorous reading of Kant (insofar as the moral law is founded outside of sensibility) remains without any tangible result. Because the subject of the moral law is not a human individual, but a point of pure reason, that is, a functioning point of the principle itself, divested of any sensible elements.

The examples cited only count as preparatory exercises, in order to transport us, by way of reflection, towards the purity of the principle. There are no uniformly effectively moral actions in the past, present, or future.

What remains is form in all its dryness. What can be done in order to present the jouissance peculiar to the unconscious?

Notes

1 Better than anyone, Bataille highlighted the necessity of a radical discrepancy in relation to the notion of utility, for all the essential questions concerning the human being: "Every time the meaning of a discussion depends on the fundamental value of the word *useful* [. . .] it is possible to affirm that the debate is necessarily warped and the fundamental question is eluded" (Georges Bataille, "The Notion of Expenditure", in *The Bataille Reader*, edited by Fred Botting and Scott Wilson, Oxford, Blackwell, 1997, p. 167).
2 Jacques Lacan, *The Four Fundamental Concepts of Psycho-Analysis*, translated by Alan Sheridan, London, Vintage, 1998, p. 33.

Chapter 18

How can the jouissance peculiar to the unconscious be presented?

Lacan had hectored his audience to *read* the *Critique of Practical Reason*, to check "if it does, indeed, have the effect" that he had intended to prove, namely its effect of "jouissance", not without promising his readers "the pleasure that is brought by the feat itself",[1] because the effect of jouissance indeed seems here to be equal to the effect of pleasure. How is this bonus of pleasure possible on the basis of such an ascetic blueprint? It is always the *appeal* to sensibility which never ceases to insist and to return. It is the experience of reading it which proves this. Now this experience always leads at first to a *bad* reading of Kant. The first reading of the practical reason, the classical reading, always presupposes that a well-defined subject, a human individual finds himself or herself faced with a choice regarding a quite concrete action to be carried out. This individual would weigh up, on their own, the for and against according to the Good or the goods which may result from it (Pascal's wager is situated precisely within this weighing-up). It would be only through the abstraction of earthly goods that the value of the highest Good may appear along with the purely formal universality of the law.

Lacan's first reading of practical reason corresponds exactly with this commonplace reading: it is his manner of approaching the supposedly Kantian moral law. Into this reading is mixed up both the purely, mechanically formal side of the moral law and the inscription of the principle *in sensible experience*.

The attentive reader of both Kant and Lacan's texts cannot fail to note how Lacan's obvious "mistakes" in interpreting Kant lead him to reduce the Kantian moral system to a modern Stoical morality, in which virtue and happiness tend to be confused, in which the noumenal and the phenomenal are mixed up. But Lacan's aim does not at all boil down to this mixture or this confusion. The real question posed by the completely virtual and noumenal purity of the Kantian moral law, is of knowing how we may have access to it, concretely, in experience. It is in this question that both Lacan's purpose and the true effect (of "pleasure" or of "jouissance"?) obtained by a reading of the *Critique of Practical Reason* come into play.

How can a noumenal principle (that of the moral law or of jouissance) have such phenomenal consequences? This is the general question of the passage from the plane of the principle to its sensible presentation. How can the principle be schematised? What should be concretely done with it?

DOI : 10.4324/9781003055662-29

Rendering jouissance sensible in the fantasy

How can the jouissance principle be "sensibilised"? How can jouissance be "schematised"?

As we have seen, in Kant, the schematism of practical reason is given in the "typic": moral laws must follow the path of physical laws in their universality. But this schematization remains quite theoretical and abstract. Quite simply taking ourselves for the creator in the process of inventing new laws for a new world seems to lead us straight to a paranoiac position and paranoiac jouissance.

How can we follow the concrete path of the creation peculiar to the *unconscious*, rather than an individual? A first stage consists in noting that reading the moral blueprint is always played out in a skidding off-course ("distortion", Freud's *Entstellung*) towards a "pathological" reading, the commonplace, erroneous reading of the Kantian oeuvre, in which Lacan himself took part. Not without simultaneously upholding the correction of this skidding off-course by introducing Sade.

Because not only does Sade provide an inscription of the moral law within sensibility, he delivers within his *mises en scène* a fantasmatic representation which calls into question all the questionable points in the commonplace, erroneous reading of Kant. The individual, the moral subject who has become a victim in the Sadean experience finds themselves wiped out, barred to the point of becoming a purely sensible effect. The solipsism of the purely moral subject is thwarted by the concrete instrument of torture or by Sade's voice (in the place of the big Other). The problematic centred on goods and the highest Good is obscured by the incarnation of Evil in the Sadean *mises en scène*. The purely formal and analytic universality of the moral law, on which the moral law would depend, gives way to the proclaimed jouissance of a natural law inscribed, above all, in sensibility.

What is the benefit of setting the Sadean cat among the pigeons of Kant's moral law? Kant's law is challenged, not in the abstract, but in the opposite direction, which consists in grasping it as engaged in the flesh, compromised in sensibility. With the sparkling fire of the Sadean scenes responding to the purity of the Kantian law, Lacan introduced the dimension of fantasy: the pure noumenal Kantian moral law is extended and made explicit in the fantasy and its phenomenal dimension.

But it does not involve a simple substitution of moral law with fantasy. Because the fantasy *makes* or *does* something: it consists of a properly ethical dimension (that of the unconscious) made explicit and articulated in its structure with the four terms of the putting of the subject into question (schema 1). Because the monolithic subject as it is presented in the ordinary conception of the subject in general and in the commonplace, vulgar reading of Kantian morality in particular must be called into question (this monolithic subject risks spinning off towards a paranoiac position). As soon as we speak of the subject in the dimension of the unconscious and of the ethics which is connected to it, we must always already distinguish the different positions represented by each of the persons at stake (the torturer and the victim, the object and the subject), but also each one's movement, their becoming and their reappraisal. As we have seen, the fantasy does not boil down to uniting a barred subject to an object a. The lozenge which unites them hides the complex movement of the structure which starts out from an object a in the position of the big Other to produce and imagine for itself a will (V). The latter of which attacks what it has in front of it, namely the subject-individual, in order to bar it ($) and in order to produce a pathological subject effect (S).

The fantasy thus reprises all the terms of common, vulgar morality, which are only mistakes in reading the purity of the moral law and jouissance (the subject-individual, the Good, the exemplary, analytic universality); but it reprises them in order to fundamentally turn them upside-down and reverse them (the barred subject in the place of the subject, the Real in the place of the good, the principle in the place of the exemplary, synthetic universality in the place of the analytic).

It is only in this movement of bad reading and its correction in the play of fantasy that the Kantian moral Law and the jouissance principle can begin to be sensibly said. The "typic" no longer consists in imagining oneself imitating the creator of the laws of the world; it consists in the movement which accepts being mistaken (a bad reading) in the presentation of jouissance in order to let itself be corrected in the dynamics of the fantasy.

The conflict inherent to the jouissance of the unconscious

As we have seen, after highlighting the structure of the fantasy, Lacan came back to Kant, more precisely to his reading (a commonplace reading) of Kant to confront it in a struggle of giants. But who are these giants? Kant and Lacan? No. All the pages devoted to the struggle, presented partly as a game of chess, partly as a game of two halves, in fact ceaselessly deal with the opposition – and the struggle – between "desire" and the "law". These terms remain in inverted commas because they cannot be defined as such. Sadean unbridled desire and the Kantian law, can they be imagined? With Lacan as a referee? No. Because desire cannot be understood as being without the law (despite Sade's ceaseless effort to bring everything back to Nature) and the law convoked here is not Kantian, it is the moral law in the bad reading of Kant, which is opposed to desire. As for Lacan, far from calming down the conflict, he stokes it up and provokes it. His victory is in having stoked up and articulated the opposition of desire and the law – in other words, the dialectic of desire. This articulation is not just any old one: it does not involve first imagining one then the other of the pieces that go to make it up in order to then put them together. "Desire" does not exist independently of the "law". And vice versa. Two sides of the same surface are involved, two faces which are superbly unaware of what is on the other side, which nevertheless constitutes them.

The combat of giants introduced by Lacan in his reading of Kant is the conflict inherent to desire, to the desire which always comprises the two faces of desire and the law. They are the giants of the *conflict* inherent to desire. But these giants in themselves are only paper tigers who draw all of their consistency from struggle, from conflict. In his polemic against the reading of Kant that he had just carried out, Lacan thus puts on the stage not his personal struggle against Kant, but the conflict as conflict. He situates himself there in the very lineage of Freud, who had never ceased to uphold the conflictual foundation of psychical reality (the duality of the sexual drives and the drives of self-preservation, then the duality of the life drives and the death drives), but also within the lineage of Kant in which "duty", constitutive of the moral factum, depends on the conflict between the higher faculty of desire and the lower faculty of desire.

Repression of the law by desire, repression of desire by the law. Law is repressed desire (or the higher faculty of desire) and desire is the repressed law (or the lower faculty of desire). This structure of desire and the law dismisses the hypothesis of an unrepressed desire. Desire and the law are together constituted by the opposition of these two forces, which themselves only exist through the play of their opposition, through repression (more precisely, the mechanism peculiar to primal repression, anti-cathexis).

The structure of repression

Kant could not, of course, have known that Freud would go on to discover repression, the fundamental defence mechanism against knowledge. Basically, Kant recognised *three* essential manners of holding as true: *opinion* (*meinen*), which does not contain a sufficient (either objective or subjective) argument for what it nevertheless holds as true; *faith* or *belief* (*glauben*), which are solely founded on subjective reasons without having objective proofs (the moral law has to do with faith); and *knowledge* [*savoir*] (*wissen*), which is founded on objective reasons, which, according to Kant, are supposed to automatically entail the agreement of any rational being.[2] In this description, a fourth type of holding as true is obviously lacking, which is constructed contrary to nevertheless obvious objective reasons, which, subjectively does not lead to something known [*un savoir*], that of repression "wants to know nothing about" its objective reasons.

Within the moral law so rigorously teased out by Kant, and in his struggle against him, Lacan precisely brings into play the repression of which the former had been unaware. The law does not want to know anything about desire (this underlay in the *Aufhebung* of knowledge, a necessary condition for opening up the field of practical reason according to Kant); but desire also wants to know nothing about the law (this was proclaimed by Sade, as the condition of his entire body of work).

This particular topology [*topologique particulière*], peculiar to the repression unknown to Kant, corresponds nonetheless to a structure that he knew perfectly well. It is the opposition of a sensible force to a sensible counterforce of the same intensity, privative negation (*nihil privativum*).[3] What is given on one side is taken away on the other. A surface is heated on one side and cooled on the other. Or a vehicle is pushed in one direction by a force and in the other direction by a counter-force. The result of this type of double operation, making and unmaking, is nothing, nothing moves. It is a way to manufacture nothing (well-known to the obsessional, who loves and hates in equal measure, who ignites and extinguishes the gas to make sure of . . . nothing). In order to make such an operation of privation possible, force and counterforce naturally must meet at the same locus, at the same meeting point and on the same plane of sensibility.

However, it is not possible that the (pure, true) Kantian moral Law, whose locus is supposed to be *purely* noumenal, is opposed by this system of privation to the technical and pragmatic (pleasure) principles, whose locus is presupposed to be phenomenal. It is therefore not the Kantian moral Law which is opposed to Desire, but the commonplace moral law (an imaginary degradation of the Law, plunged back into the sensible), which is opposed to commonplace desire (an imaginary degradation of desire situated in the sensible). Lacan displaces the problem of the pure principle of the Kantian moral Law by introducing Sade: sensible moral things (drawn from a bad reading of Kant) find themselves countered by sensible amoral things of the same intensity: Juliette is opposed to Justine, the moral subject is opposed to his or her immorality, Evil is opposed to Good, etc. The counterforces appealed to by Sade are supposed to be strictly equal and in the opposite direction to the commonplace moral law. This is a factory of the privative nothing: it is the complete cleaning up of the commonplace moral law.

Does this Sadean operation of privation (peculiar to repression), leading to a privative nothing, suffice to explain the operation of the unconscious and the jouissance principle?

Reversal

Despite what is played out objectively on one side of the coin (desire or the law), the subject adheres to the opposing side (the law or desire). And what is more – and this is the crucial point – one side continues onto the other. As we have seen by starting out from the moral law (the commonplace, erroneous reading of Kant); by extending the logic of formal universality (the first formula of the Kantian imperative), we discover that it drifts towards the Lacano-Sadean imperative of the desire for jouissance ("I have the right to enjoy your body . . . "), in which duty continues into a right. The inverse movement should be made: starting out from the desire for Sadean jouissance taken to its extreme and its very power of destruction over the whole phenomenological world, we would discover the necessity of the moral law. We shall recognise the circuit on a two-sided surface which turns out to be one and the same side, it is the Moebius strip.

The interest of this Moebian structure of desire and the law highlighted by Lacan, as well as of the moral imperative and guilt, and also of jouissance in all its forms, is a *practical* one for the psychoanalyst, practical in terms of methodology in the treatment: in understanding this reversal, we already foresee the principle of jouissance and of the unconscious in all its radicalism (giving things a new form).

Where the analyst hears desire, he knows that it can and must be reversed into law. Where he hears the law, he knows that it can and must be reversed into desire. This reversal counts as an introduction to the jouissance in which the unconscious is said concretely. The readiness to reverse force into counterforce (the two of them opposing each other in primal repression) may be presented under a thousand facets among which we will retain the love–hate opposition. However, the desire–law opposition in jouissance, brought to light by Lacan, seems more fundamental; because it unveils the very reason for repression, namely the essentially practical question (in the Kantian sense of the term): what must I do? Do in accordance with visible, empirical, sensible, phenomenal things (technical and pragmatic principle)? Or do according to a possible creation? Do according to thoughts, calculations, and judgements? Or do according to a new form? The dilemma of practice is rooted in the unconscious. With these questions, the unconscious is given as fundamentally ethical. It is in the reversal from one side to the other, in other words in the circuit of the Moebius strip of desire and the law, that psychoanalysis is directed in its practice. The psychoanalyst does well to not only have meditated on Kant's practical reason (the principle of the *Critique of Practical Reason*), but also on the conflict inherent to repression at the heart of this practical reason (the conflict inherent to the vocal object *a*, in *Kant with Sade*), because it is through the principle and the vocal object *a* that the jouissance of the unconscious can be rightly thought about.

The binary opposition in Sadean argumentation (Good/Evil, etc.) may well serve as an introduction to the structure of repression. In its statics, it is completely insufficient and may well also serve as an obstacle to the dynamics of repression. With Sade, who completely lacks a sense of comedy, there is no place for any reversal: "one is always on the same side, the good or the bad".[4] It is quite different with Freud. Lacan does not fail to insist on the fact that the principal principle in Freud is "*his* pleasure principle [i.e. Freud's]". Certainly, pleasure is opposed to unpleasure, seemingly like two distinct sides of a bilateral surface; everything would seem at first sight to be able to correspond to the binary opposition of Sadean argumentation.[5] This is not at all the case, however, because the treatment of unpleasure – in the history of the symptom as much as in its treatment by psychoanalysis – does not consist in simply countering this unpleasure with an opposed pleasure of equal intensity. The operation of the unconscious entails, on the contrary, giving things a new form, and we already find a first appearance of this in the reversal peculiar to the Moebian surface. In this practice of transformation, unpleasure finds itself displaced towards another form of unpleasure; towards a neighbouring unpleasure. Displacement (which could also translate *Entstellung*)[6] thus leads to finding oneself on what had appeared as the "other" side, finding oneself in the pleasure which is fundamentally continuous with unpleasure. In Sade, there is no place for reversal, in Freud, there is no place for anything other than reversal (on the basis of the unconscious which gives things a new form). *Freud's* pleasure principle is always first of all an *unpleasure* principle. Pleasure or unpleasure? The question is not so much that of a bottle which is half-empty or half-full. It is a Klein bottle, whose "inside" is continuous with its "outside", in other words what appears to be unpleasure is reversed into what appears to be pleasure and vice versa. It is an overturning of continuous values which is in operation (while in Sade, the status of values is frozen once and for all in an eternal rigidity). The primal repression which consists in the opposition of a force and a counter-force (anti-cathexis) is also always articulated in its becoming with its displacement, with its drift, within repression strictly speaking and in the return of the repressed.

Notes

1 Lacan, "Kant with Sade", op. cit., p. 648.
2 Kant, *Critique of Pure Reason*, op. cit., pp. 526–527; A820/B848-A821/B849.
3 Ibid., pp. 232–233; A290–291/B347–348.
4 Lacan, "Kant with Sade", op. cit., p. 665.
5 Lacan stressed from the outset: "The notion that Sade's work anticipated Freud [. . .] is a stupidity" (Lacan, "Kant with Sade", op. cit., p. 645).
6 [Translator's note: Most commonly translated into English as "distortion", see Laplanche and Pontalis, *The Language of Psychoanalysis*, translated by Donald Nicholson-Smith, London, Karnac, 1988, p. 124.]

Chapter 19

It must be made

The practice of the unconscious

There is no Moebius strip given in the psyche's experience. *It must be made.* This means that repression must be made and not passively observed. We too easily insist here on the manufacture of a strip with paper and glue (or any other material) and such an empirical Moebius strip is easily made to the point of making it into an art object. But a strip thus materialised in reality does not have much to do with the question of the psyche and the unconscious, unless as a metaphorisation of the practical *it must be made/done* [*il faut le faire*] (having to do with the ethics of the unconscious and, therefore, the jouissance principle) by a purely artisanal *it must be made* (having to do with purely technical principles). With this metaphor, the trace of the principle of the moral law and the jouissance at stake in the unconscious does indeed risk being lost in topological technicality.

The fantasy is not sufficient to present the jouissance principle

It is the fantasy which supports desire and the ethics of the unconscious. By making the most of his reading of Sade in order to highlight the structure of the fantasy, Lacan did not simply fixate desire within the fantasy ($\$\lozenge a$); he also highlighted the relaunching operation inherent to the fantasy, such as it is developed in the quadrature of schema 1, borrowed from schema L, the schema which calls the subject into question. With this schema 1, we not only have the fixation of desire in the fantasy but also the movement of the fantasy which already represents the ethics of the unconscious. What is more, we can twist the schema of the fantasy in such a way as by forming a Moebius strip,[1] it simultaneously represents repression's continual reversal.

Everything is thus represented and Sade himself seems to be faithfully folded and unfolded in accordance with the paths unveiled by Lacan: the big Other is there, the object *a* is in its place, the subject is called into question. Everything is animated by pre-existing desire. The point of animation is represented in the schema by the *vocal* form of the object *a*, situated in the place of the big Other (the tormentor's voice in schema 1 and Sade's voice in schema 2 command the whole business). In short, everything seems to be represented in the fantasy.

DOI :10.4324/9781003055662-30

We have indeed, with the topology of the fantasy, a complete *representation* of the articulation of desire; but we do not at all have a effective *presentation* of it (including its *making*). Everything is *re*-presented and remains in the imagination of sensible experience. Practice is imagined (obviously so in technique), but its operating principle is completely erased in this blueprint in imagination. And Sade remains absolutely impermeable to any reversal and his characters remain frozen in their roles.

Why? The answer is probably to be found at the origin of the movement of fantasy, that is, in the voice and in the manner in which it is grasped. The voice (the tormentor's as well as Sade's) is always presented there as an *empirical* reality, and it is indefinitely repeated equal to itself. Lacan had pointed out the specific place of the *voice* (the fourth form of the object *a*) in the place of the Other for upholding the operation of desire. But the voice reduced to sensible experience cannot suffice. The experience of the voice, singing exercises and other *sensible* chords (including the tormentor's voice) do not directly correspond to the specific function of the fourth form of the object *a*, which is precisely to contradict the very conditions of all sensible experience. In other words, the voice is (*sensibly*) *represented* as the opposite of what it should *present*: the radical hole in the field of the sensible.

The voice is not a status quo

The ethics of the unconscious – which gives things a new form – relies on the dismissal and the radical effacement of all sensible experience, on which thoughts, calculations and judgements rely. The operation and the ethics of the unconscious are propped up in a totally different manner, namely on the fourth form of the object *a*, the aforementioned "voice" understood as *nihil negativum*.

The question is therefore now one of knowing how to *present* this fourth form, this "voice", in such a way that it does not appear as a phenomenon (an auditory one), but as a nothing and, what is more, a nothing outside all given sensible experience. This involves conceiving, manufacturing, putting in place a nothing which would not be taken back into the series of phenomena, visible or audible things or anything that makes up our sensibility. We have already constructed a nothing, the privative nothing, *nihil privatum*, which is obtained by opposing two forces of the same intensity going in opposite directions (hot/cold, love/hate, etc.) It is the statics of primal repression ("fixation") and the constitution of the bilateral surface as a locus of the opposition of cathexes (forces) and anti-cathexes (counterforces).

Throughout our interrogation of the fundamental principle of the unconscious, we have encountered a series of oppositions which respond to the structure of the privative nothing: evil opposed to good, unpleasure opposed to pleasure, law opposed to desire. On both sides, sensible, empirical, testable [*expérimentable*] things are involved, even if they can be generalised: evil is everywhere, good is everywhere, unpleasure is everywhere, pleasure is everywhere, the law is everywhere, desire is everywhere. This indeed is why these six terms can count as general principles of *sensibility* applicable to all human action in general.

Can these three oppositions referred to in Lacan's text serve to introduce the question of the voice, fourth form of the object *a*? The general principle of evil in Sade is opposed to the general principle of good attributed to Kant, in order to introduce the tormentor's voice, occupying the place of the big Other in schema 1. The unpleasure principle is opposed to the pleasure principle in Freud in order to introduce the death drive and the voice which resounds in the between-two-deaths. The principle of the common moral law is opposed to desire in the struggle Lacan leads against Kant, in order to introduce the function of the voice in the dialectic of desire.

But in opposing something cold to something hot or a thrust to another thrust of the same intensity, a privative nothing is obtained, that is, a *status quo* and not the radical nothing at all. In opposing sensible evil (which is general) to sensible good (which is general), it may be thought that a radical or general nothing is obtained, in which all of the sensible (on the side of good) is cancelled by all of the sensible (on the side of bad). But this manner of constructing a nothing by opposition did not manufacture the *nihil negativum*, because "good" and "evil" are only invoked as *sensible principles* for perceiving the world (optimistic and pessimistic). "Good" and "evil", despite their neutralising encounter, remain sensible things. It is the same for the opposition of pleasure and unpleasure and for the opposition of desire and the law. Each time, we arrive at a status quo, at a stalemate or a stop at which the structure of repression is shown as opposing a force to a counterforce; each time, this form of the nothing absolutely does not empty out the sensible, it does not contradict the general conditions of sensible experience. Despite the generality of a sensible thing opposed to the generality of another sensible thing under a different principle, it is not the fourth form of the object *a*. It is solely a perfectly sensible privative nothing.

With these oppositions, we do not yet have access to the voice, to that which contradicts the very conditions of all sensible experience and thus opens up a true "making", the making of the unconscious. To characterise the work of the unconscious, it is thus totally insufficient to say that it thinks neither of good nor of bad, that it calculates neither pleasure nor unpleasure, and that it absolutely does not judge either desire or the law. The question remains: in accordance with what principle can it therefore give things a new form? It is a "synthetic" principle insofar as it *must make* something (synthesis has to do with pure *practical* reason).

What the unconscious does not do: the opening up of the three fields of jouissance

Each of the oppositions (good/evil, pleasure/unpleasure, desire/law), pushed to the limit, operate an exclusion (the field of good and evil is paralyzed or excluded, the field of pleasure and unpleasure is paralyzed or excluded, the field of law and desire is paralyzed or excluded). Each time a field remains which was not excluded and can be used for Jouissance.

If the work of the unconscious *does not think about good or evil*, it excludes the Imaginary linked to this good/bad polarity. What is left to it is the possible articulation of the real and the symbolic. Jouissance may then *appear* as *phallic* (where thought fails). This aspect of Jouissance, insofar as it attempts to exclude the imaginary, is "*phallic jouissance*".

If the work of the unconscious does not calculate either *pleasure or unpleasure*, it excludes the Symbolic, which calculates the means of finding pleasure and avoiding unpleasure. What is left to it is the possible articulation of the imaginary and the real. Jouissance may then *appear* as *Other* (in which calculation has no purchase). This aspect of Jouissance, insofar as it attempts to exclude the symbolic, is the "*Other jouissance*" and the "*jouissance of the Other*".

If the work of the unconscious *absolutely does not judge* desire and the (common, vulgar) law, it excludes the Real which judges this desire and law. What is left to it is the articulation of the symbolic and the imaginary. Jouissance may then *appear* as the *jouissance or enjoyment of sense or meaning* (in which judgement has no good reason to be). This aspect of Jouissance, insofar as it attempts to exclude the real, is "*jouis-sens*".

Each of the things excluded (the imaginary of thought, the symbolic of calculation and the real of judgement) operates nonetheless on a specific principle. Judgement responds to a technical principle. Calculation responds to a pragmatic principle. Thought remains, which according to the question of good and evil, responds to a moral principle. This moral principle on which thought depends is only the common moral principle, which adapts itself to what is suited for to think about good and evil in order to think correctly, that is, following the general trend. We have indeed three kinds of acting principles: technical principle, pragmatic principle and principle of common morality. And the jouissance principle is defined as not being reducible to any one of these three, as a fourth principle which does not itself follow any of the sensible pathways, an unheard of principle of creation which "does not think, calculate or judge in any way at all".

It is because it denies the imaginary of thought, that Jouissance (the "jouissance principle") can appear as the negative of the common moral principle, in other words, as phallic jouissance.

It is because it denies the symbolic of calculation, that Jouissance (the "jouissance principle") can appear as the negative of the pleasure principle, in other words, as Other jouissance or jouissance of the Other.

It is because it denies the real of judgement, that Jouissance (the "jouissance principle") can appear as the negative of the technical principle, in other words, as jouissance of sense or *jouis-sens*.

It would be tempting to think that the working principle of the unconscious (the "jouissance principle") should synthesize the whole set and be organised quite simply with the *three* dimensions R S I. The fourth principle would thus be represented by Lacan's object *a* at the centre of the three dimensions.

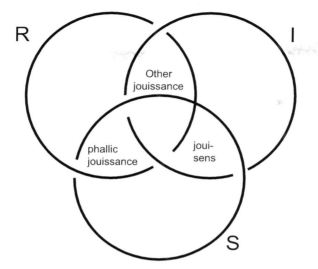

Figure 12

This is precisely what the unconscious does not do: it is not the object *a* which would dominate the structure at its centre, it is not a super-thinker-calculator-and-judge. It "does not think, calculate, or judge in any way at all".

"Synthesis" must be thought "otherwise", that is, without presupposing the Borromean structure as something given. This synthesis corresponds to a pure making on the basis of nothing.

What the unconscious makes: the synthesis of a new form

Different laws are more or less well-known ("Ignorance of the law is not a valid excuse"). *Shy of* these laws (and therefore shy of the sensible data of experience) a fundamental guilt *independent of known laws and the acts committed* imposes itself. This guilt is present in everybody, and the Law, the *Faktum* of which Kant speaks, is only its inverted presentation. It is in accordance with this Law (and the guilt connected to it) that all laws may be called into question. The presence of this Law and this guilt nevertheless imply a point of absolute freedom in relation to the inexorable, deterministic course of the sensible world. We are obliged according to our experience of guilt to suppose that we might be able to do otherwise, "giving [. . .] a new form" to this world, which, moreover, seems to be completely determined.

We speak of "freedom", but we know strictly nothing about it, other than that it is necessarily deduced from the experience of our duty [*devoir faire*], of our guilt: we should have done otherwise and we can do otherwise; a new form can be given to things on the basis of what eludes us, on the basis of what we do not know, on the basis of the unconscious. Instead of "freedom", we can say "the Thing", jouissance, autonomy, even indeed sin and covetousness. All the connotations implied by these names are secondary in relation to the *process* by which these things ("freedom") happen to us. "I can only know of the Thing by means of the Law. In effect, I would not have had the idea to covet it if the Law hadn't said: 'Thou shalt not covet it.'"[2] "What then should we say? That the law [Torah] is sin? By no means! Yet, if it had been for the law, I would have not known sin. I would have not known what it is to covet if the law had not said, 'You shall not covet.'"[3] This is the same reasoning that Kant uses in relation to the moral law and freedom (it is illustrated in the two apologues cited). It is on the basis of the knowledge of the moral law that we may know freedom (Kant), the coveted object (Saint Paul). It is on the basis of the superego, of guilt or of anxiety that we may know the Thing and the Real (Lacan) outside the conditions of experience, with the voice.

We can well define the voice as that which contradicts the conditions of sensible experience; but we can know nothing about it, because all knowledge depends on the conditions of sensible experience. The voice, the fourth form of the object *a*, arising among phenomena, is *nothing other* than a radical hole in the phenomenal world: in sweeping away everything related to the phenomenon, it opens up the field of the freedom to begin a new causal series, to give things a new form. The presence of the moral Law and of guilt (the superego) is thus the necessary entrance to a knowledge of the creative freedom inherent to the unconscious.

The "subject" must never be "freed of guilt". That is only a defence mechanism which bars access to the jouissance principle, to the freedom and creation unique to the unconscious.

Notes

1 Cf. "On a Question Prior to Any Possible Treatment of Psychosis", op. cit., p. 462.
2 Lacan, *The Ethics of Psychoanalysis*, op. cit., p. 83.
3 Saint Paul, "The Letter of Paul to the Romans", 7:7, in *The Holy Bible, New Revised Standard Edition*, Grand Rapids, Zondervan Publishing House, 1995, p. 1019).

Conclusion

The jouissance principle and the object *a*

The jouissance *principle*, which is none other than the functioning proper to the unconscious, would elude us completely if it were not for the unique – but nonetheless common to every human being – experience of the *Faktum* of the moral law and, most of all, of its other side, *guilt* (including anxiety as unconscious guilt).

Can this *principle*, which commands the operation both of the unconscious and of psychoanalytic practice strictly speaking, be rendered sensible? It is not sufficient to observe and examine the moral Law, guilt, and anxiety and to provide a clinical description of them. In so doing, we certainly take facts, the results of the unconscious, into account, but its "*faire*" – "making" – and its particular ethics remain completely unknown; we thus remain in the position of someone who notices an apple which has fallen at the foot of his tree, without grasping the *principle* of how it got there (the principle of universal gravitation). Ignorance of the principle does not prevent the apple falling to the ground.

It is not the same in the field of psychoanalysis, founded on the ethics of the unconscious. Ignorance of the jouissance principle leads practice onto the side of the quest for pleasure, nothing more.

The psychoanalyst's place becomes clearer precisely in relation to the workings of the unconscious, that is, in relation to the jouissance principle. How can it be embodied? How can the principle as such be rendered sensible?

Lacan's reading seems to embody the jouissance *principle* (moral law and guilt) in the representation of the *fantasy*, which originates in the object *a*. We would have the drift from the *principle* (on Kant's side), towards the *fantasy* (unearthed on Sade's side), and finishes up with the object *a* (on Lacan's side). In short, Lacan's object *a* would be a good replacement for *Kant's principle* (that is, in sensible experience).

This substitution (of the principle giving way to object *a*) only finds its meaning on the condition of interrogating the object *a*, which is itself a question. How can the object *a* that the analyst must embody at the place of the semblance in the psychoanalytic discourse be understood in order to allow the jouissance principle peculiar to the unconscious – and to the psychoanalytic discourse – to operate?

Is it something or is it nothing? This question, which is the essence of the object *a*, may take four forms, corresponding to four forms of the said "object" (or of the nothing). At the same time, it corresponds to four types of principle.

The object may be that which is capable of providing full satisfaction (the breast or paradise, guarantors of an infinite pleasure). *The calculation of pleasure and unpleasure is indeed carried out according to this oral object.* Is it something or is it nothing? Something in relation to the fiction of a satisfaction. Nothing in relation to its realisation. The operating *principle* of this object *a* is essentially *pragmatic*: it has to do with evaluating the chances of pleasure and satisfaction, and giving or giving oneself *advice* (or "counsels") as a consequence.

The object may be that which is constructed by the apposition of opposites (gift-and-waste-product, faeces, desire-and-law, love-and-hate). The judgement of desire and the law is made according to this *anal* object. Is it something or nothing? Something as much in relation to desire as in relation to the law. Nothing in relation to repression and the paralysis of one by the other. The operating *principle* of this form of the object *a* is essentially *moral*: it involves learning what one must "do", learning how to keep clean [*apprentissage de la propreté*], as well as how to take hold of things [*l'appropriation*]. It involves taking on and giving oneself *laws* as a consequence.

The object may be the general framework, the spatiotemporal conditions of all sensible experience (the scopic field, the cartography of the different psychical functions presented, for example, in the fantasy and by means of the Sadean scenarios). The thought of good and evil is played out according to this *scopic* object, a field rather than an object strictly speaking. Is it something or nothing? Something in relation to all the sensible experiences which come under its heading. Nothing in relation to the fact that it is itself no more than a perfectly empty field. The operating principle of this object *a* is essentially *technical*: it makes it possible to find oneself in the field of experience in order to discern the appropriate *rules* for attaining a given goal.

Each principle and each form of the object *a* becomes clearer through what they deprive themselves of and what is left to them in order to operate.

The pragmatic (pleasure/unpleasure) principle and the *oral* object do not burden themselves with the symbolic: what is left to them are the workings of the real and the imaginary. Jouissance arises as *the jouissance of the Other*. It is the Other which will give me the object without having to ask for it in the symbolic.

The moral principle (desire/law) and the *anal object* do not burden themselves with the real (and reality): what is left to them are the workings of the symbolic and the imaginary, in other words, the quest for meaning. Jouissance arises as *jouis-sens*. It is sense or meaning which will give me the object without having to take the reality of the Real in account.

The technical principle (good[*bon*][1]/bad) and the *scopic object* do not burden themselves with the imaginary, with the particular quality of the sensible objects which would come to be inscribed in the scopic field: what is left to them are the workings of the real and the symbolic. Jouissance arises as *phallic jouissance*. It is the phallic as a relaunching function, which would give me the object without having to rely on any image (*hypotheses non fingo*).

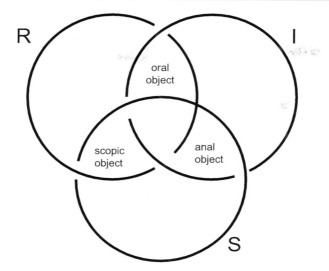

Figure 13

But none of these three principles and none of these forms of the object *a* are sufficient to describe the moral Law, the *new form* given by the unconscious, basic guilt (which remains even though everyday morality is observed with the greatest care).

Despite all the importance of the staging of the fantasy in its relationship to the scopic object, it is not what provides the truth of the Kantian moral law. Neither is it the anal object of common morality, nor the oral object of pleasure. If Lacan claims that Sade yields the truth of Kant, it is indeed because he wishes to hear in him already the *voice*, bearing the *nihil negativum*, opening up the creation of freedom, and not the purely scopic representation of the fantasy. In order to uphold the function of the *nihil negativum*, one could certainly begin from the opposition of desire and the law, an opposition of two sensible things, which nonetheless only amount to a commonplace morality, a bad reading of Kant. If therefore, in his struggle with Kant, Lacan indeed highlights the structure of repression inherent to desire, this repression does not yet open up the voice or the *nihil negativum*.

To grasp the true importance of the "voice" (insofar as it contradicts the conditions of sensible experience and which is therefore not representable), it must look like the opening up of a *principle* which does not correspond to *any* of the three other common principles of action. The jouissance principle does not take up any guidelines, other than the freedom to create or to give things a new form, a freedom underlying the fundamental Law and basic guilt, underlying a superego which no longer has anything to do with commonplace morals, a superego which says "Enjoy!" [*Jouis!*], without knowing what that means.

The true principle of morality and of the unconscious is not a principle, unless it is that of eluding every predetermined principle. If we wish to describe it through the fourth form of the object *a*, it is not wise to place it at the centre of the schema, in the central triangle. It is outside the classic Borromean schema, as the radical nothing which forever again orders to create, to give a new form to our way of approaching the clinic, to our way of dealing with the ordinary (technical, pragmatic, everyday moral) principles. A new "principle".

The vocal object does not provide any guidance.

The opening up of the field of freedom. It must be made. That is the sole "synthesis" which counts; it is invented in the autonomy of the point of freedom of the unconscious which gives things a new form.

Note

1 ["Good"[*bon*] in relation to the pleasure principle rather than a moral good [*bien*].]

Bibliography

Arjakovsky, Philippe and France-Lanord, Hadrien, translation notes in Heidegger, *La dévastation et l'attente*, Paris, Gallimard, 2006.
Auffret, Dominique, *Alexandre Kojève, la philosophie, l'État, la fin de l'Histoire*, Paris, Grasset, 1990.
Badiou, Alain, *Le Séminaire, L'Un, Descartes, Platon, Kant 1983–1984*, Paris, Fayard, 2016.
Bataille, George, "The Notion of Expenditure" in *The Bataille Reader*, edited by Fred Botting and Scott Wilson, Oxford, Blackwell, 1997.
Blanchot, Maurice, *Lautréamont and Sade*, translated by Stuart and Michelle Kendall, Stanford, Stanford University Press, 2004.
Derrida, Jacques, *The Death Penalty*, Volume 1, translated by Peggy Kamuf, Chicago, University of Chicago Press, 2013, and Volume 2, translated by Elizabeth Rottenberg, Chicago, University of Chicago Press, 2017.
Descartes, René, *Meditations on First Philosophy*, 3rd Edition, translated by Donald A. Cress, Indianapolis/Cambridge, Hackett Publishing Company, 1993.
Eisler, Rudolf, *Kant-Lexikon*, Paris, Gallimard, NRF, 1994.
Fierens, Christian, *La relance du phallus*, Toulouse, Érès, 2005.
Fierens, Christian, *Lecture de l'Étourdit*, Paris, L'Harmattan, 2002.
Fierens, Christian, *Lecture du sinthome*, Toulouse, Érès, 2018.
Fierens, Christian, "Logic of Truth and Logic of Erring in Kant and Lacan" in *The Issue with Kant*, Ljubljana, Filozofski vestnik, 2015.
Fierens, Christian, *The Soul of Narcissism*, translated by Michael Gerard Plastow, London, Routledge, 2019.
Fierens, Christian and Pierobon, Frank, *Les pièges du réalisme*, Louvain-la-Neuve, EME, 2017.
Freud, Sigmund, *Civilization and Its Discontents* in *The Standard Edition of the Complete Psychological Works of Sigmund Freud*, Volume 21, London, Hogarth Press, 1961.
Freud, Sigmund, *The Ego and the Id* in *The Standard Edition of the Complete Psychological Works of Sigmund Freud*, Volume 19, London, Hogarth Press, 1961.
Freud, Sigmund, *Introductory Lectures on Psychoanalysis* in *The Standard Edition of the Complete Psychological Works of Sigmund Freud*, Volumes 15 and 16, London, Hogarth Press, 1963.
Freud, Sigmund, *On Narcissism: An Introduction* in *The Standard Edition of the Complete Psychological Works of Sigmund Freud*, Volume 14, London, Hogarth Press, 1957.
Freud, Sigmund, *Project for a Scientific Psychology* in *The Standard Edition of the Complete Psychological Works of Sigmund Freud*, Volume 1, London, Hogarth Press, 1966.
Grimal, Pierre, *Dictionnaire de la mythologie grecque et romaine*, Paris, PUF, 1994.

Horkheimer, Max and Adorno, Theodor W., *Dialectic of Enlightenment: Philosophical Fragments*, Stanford, Stanford University Press, 2002.
Kant, Immanuel, *Critique of Judgment*, translated by Werner S. Pluhar, Indianapolis, Hackett, 1987.
Kant, Immanuel, *Critique of Practical Reason*, translated by Mary Gregor, Cambridge, Cambridge University Press, 2015.
Kant, Immanuel, *Critique of Pure Reason*, edited by Vasilis Politis, London, J.M. Dent, 1993.
Kant, Immanuel, *Groundwork of the Metaphysics of Morals*, translated by Mary Gregor, Cambridge, Cambridge University Press, 2012.
Kant, Immanuel, *Grundlegung zur Metaphysik der Sitten* in *Werkausgabe Band VII*, Frankfurt am Main, Suhrkamp Taschenbuch, 1974.
Kant, Immanuel, *Kritik de praktischen Vernunft* in *Werkausgabe Band VII*, Frankfurt am Main, Suhrkamp Taschenbuch, 1974.
Kant, Immanuel, "On a Supposed Right to Lie from Philanthropy" in *Practical Philosophy*, translated and edited by Mary Gregor, Cambridge, Cambridge University Press, 1996.
Kant, Immanuel, *Religion within the Bounds of Bare Reason*, translated by Werner S. Pluhar (1792), Indianapolis/Cambridge, Hackett Publishing Company, 2009.
Klossowski, Pierre, *Sade My Neighbor*, translated by Alphonso Lingis, Evanston, Northwestern University Press, 1991.
Lacan, Jacques, *The Ethics of Psychoanalysis 1959–1960: The Seminar of Jacques Lacan Book VII*, edited by Jacques-Alain Miller, translated with notes by Dennis Porter, London, Routledge, 1992.
Lacan, Jacques, *On Feminine Sexuality: The Limits of Love and Knowledge*, translated with notes by Bruce Fink, New York, W.W. Norton & Company, 1999.
Lacan, Jacques, *The Four Fundamental Concepts of Psycho-Analysis*, translated by Alan Sheridan, London, Vintage, 1998.
Lacan, Jacques, "Kant with Sade" in *Écrits: The First Complete Edition in English*, translated by Bruce Fink, New York, W.W. Norton & Company, 2006.
Lacan, Jacques, "L'Étourdit" in *Autre Écrits*, Paris, Seuil, 2000.
Lacan, Jacques, *L'insu que sait de l'une-bévue s'aile à mourre*, lesson of 11th January 1977, translated by Cormac Gallagher, unpublished. Available at lacaninireland.com.
Lacan, Jacques, "On a Question Prior to Any Possible Treatment of Psychosis" in *Écrits: The First Complete Edition in English*, translated by Bruce Fink, New York, W.W. Norton & Company, 2006.
Lacan, Jacques, *The Psychoses: The Seminar of Jacques Lacan Book III 1955–1956*, translated by Russell Grigg, London, Routledge, 1993.
Lacan, Jacques, "Subversion of the Subject and the Dialectic of Desire" in *Écrits: The First Complete Edition in English*, translated by Bruce Fink, New York, W.W. Norton & Company, 2006.
Lacan, Jacques, "Television" in *October*, Volume 40, translated by Denis Hollier, Rosalind Krauss and Annette Michelson, Cambridge, MA, The MIT Press, Spring 1987.
Lacan, Jacques, *Transference: The Seminar of Jacques Lacan Book VIII*, translated by Bruce Fink, Cambridge, Polity Press, 2015.
Lacôte, Christiane, "Jouissance" in *Dictionnaire de la psychanalyse*, edited by Roland Chemama, Paris, Larousse, 1993.
Le Brun, Annie, *Soudain un bloc d'abime, Sade*, Paris, Gallimard, 2014.
Le Brun, Jacques, *Le pur amour de Platon à Lacan*, Paris, Seuil, 2002.
Marty, Éric, *Pourquoi le XXe siècle a-t-il pris Sade au sérieux?*, Paris, Seuil, 2011.

Plastow, Michael Gerard, "L'émergence de la pulsion de mort chez Sabina Spielrein" in *Essaim*, Toulouse, Érès, 2019/2, no. 14.

Plastow, Michael Gerard, *Sabina Spielrein and the Poetry of Psychoanalysis*, Oxon, Routledge, 2018.

Sade, Donatien Alphonse François de, *Juliette*, translated by Austryn Wainhouse, New York, Grove Press, 1968.

Sade, Donatien Alphonse François de, *Justine, Philosophy in the Bedroom, and Other Writings*, compiled and translated by Richard Seaver and Austryn Wainhouse, New York, Grove Press, 1990.

Spinoza, Baruch de, *Ethics*, translated by Andrew Boyle, edited by G.H.R. Parkinson, London, J.M. Dent, 1993.

Trichet, Yohan and Marion, Élisabeth, "Ce que nous apprend *El* de Buñuel sur l'économie de jouissance dans la paranoia" in *Cliniques méditerranéennes*, Toulouse, Érès, 2012/2, no. 86.

Weil, Éric, "Le mal radical, la religion et la morale" in *Problèmes kantiens*, Paris, Vrin, 1998.

Zupančič, Alenka, *Ethics of the Real: Kant, Lacan*, London, Verso Books, 2000.

Index

Adorno, Theodor W. 99, 101n3, 107, 110, 168
anal object 13, 166, 210–211
Antigone 22n3, 140–141
antinomy of practical reason 73–75, 174
Aristotle 24, 93–95, 97, 178
Aufhebung (hole in knowledge) 19, 21, 21n2, 75, 79, 152, 176, 183, 199

Badiou, Alain 59n2, 71
barred big Other 3–4, 122, 130, 162–163, 165, 182–183
Bataille, George 107, 150n31, 184n17, 195n1
belief 4, 77–79, 125–126, 169n42, 192–193, 199
Blanchot, Maurice 107, 118, 127n5, 128n28, 168n16, 184n17
Borromean knot 5
bourgeois 156–160, 167, 168n16, 173, 178, 189–190
Buddha 141, 153–154

categorical imperative 21, 22n3, 32–33, 35–37, 47, 49, 54, 57–58, 75, 99–100, 107, 111–112, 127n14, 158, 163, 178, 180, 185n33
cathexis (and counter-cathexis) 103, 149, 174, 191, 199, 202
charity 55, 152–153, 180–181, 185n34
Che vuoi 32, 138
Christian commandment ("love your neighbour as yourself") 55, 68–69, 115, 143, 152, 179–181, 185n33
Claudel, Paul 178
comedy 118, 120, 161–163, 169n35, 178, 201
contempt (*Verachtung*) 67–68, 123–124, 126, 157, 159

Dasein 125, 130, 175
death drive 9, 13, 27, 50, 141–143, 150n23, 180–181, 199, 205
death penalty 56, 115, 180–181, 185n38
Democritus 175, 184n11
diabolic 103
dignity 26, 36–37, 103–105, 157
discourse 119, 122, 147–149, 169n35, 176, 209

Emperor Charles V 50, 165
Epictetus 123–124
Epicurean 72–74, 77, 172
Epicurus 74, 175
evil 13, 24, 28n1, 44, 56, 61–65, 70–71, 88, 97–98, 98n8, 103–105, 109–111, 115–116, 126, 129n49, 130, 137, 168n16, 174–177, 179–180, 182, 184n14, 184n20, 189–191, 197, 200–201, 204–206
existence of God 22n2, 72, 76–77, 79, 110, 128n42, 163, 170n47, 174, 177

factum (*Faktum*) 53–54, 57, 102, 116–117, 128n23, 128n24, 155, 159, 189, 199, 207, 209
faith 21n1, 45, 75, 79, 104, 14, 170n53, 182, 192–193, 199, 203
fiction 47, 94–96, 121–122, 137, 156–158, 210
Fontenelle, Bernard Le Bovier de 156
forbidden 3–4, 64, 97, 122, 155, 183

gaze 112, 125, 166–167, 179
genital love 94–95
good will 21, 23–27, 27n1, 28n1, 29–30, 33, 39, 47, 137, 143, 147
grammatical equivocation 62, 122, 124

guilt 10–11, 14n16, 15, 19, 22n4, 24–25, 30, 52, 70–71, 76, 80, 93–95, 120, 131, 182, 194, 200, 207–209, 211

Heidegger, Martin 124–125, 129n48, 130
heteronomy 38, 55, 63
higher faculty of desire 13, 48–49, 58, 61, 69n2, 121, 131, 153, 158–159, 165, 170n53, 173–174, 190, 199
highest good 24, 57, 71–77, 79–80, 80n12, 96–97, 110, 127, 174, 179, 182, 196–197
Hitler, Adolf 164, 168
holding as true 78, 163, 191, 199
homophonic equivocation 62, 122, 124
Horkheimer, Max 99, 101n3, 107, 110, 168
hysterical discourse 148–149

immortality of the soul 72, 75–80, 110, 125, 128n42, 174
impossibility 29, 35, 56, 59n17, 70, 74, 95, 99, 117, 122, 151n33, 162, 165–166
Innocent III 164
interpretation 6–8, 10, 14n4, 27, 72, 80n11, 93, 106n20, 110, 158
inter-said 3–4, 14n2, 122, 155

j'ouis sens 5, 206, 210
Juvenal 157–158, 168n20

kingdom of ends 37
King Francis I 50, 195
Klossowski, Pierre 107, 179–180, 182, 184n17, 185n26, 186n43

La Fontaine, Jean de La 161
logical equivocation 62, 122, 124
lower faculty of desire 48–49, 69n2, 121, 158, 190, 199

Marty, Éric 101n4, 107, 121n1, 121n2, 121n5, 128n39, 150n17, 168n16, 169n29, 185n24, 191n2
Mè phunai 146
methodology 43, 45, 82, 105, 200
Moebius strip 200–201, 203
mother's castration 107, 131, 176, 182–183

narcissism 27, 67, 94, 95n3
Nebenmensch 96, 105, 175, 180
nihil negativum 55, 108, 122, 126, 129n44, 137–138, 143, 149, 151n33, 152–155, 162, 166–167, 184n2, 204–205, 211

opinion 79, 88, 100, 147, 169n42, 199
oral object 13, 143, 149, 166, 210–211
Other jouissance 5, 206–207
overdetermination 24, 27, 29, 45

pain 52, 56, 67–69, 69n2, 82–83, 88, 100, 104, 123–124, 126, 132–133, 137, 139, 141–143, 145, 163, 178, 193
paralogisms of pure reason 12, 21n2, 77, 155
Pascal, Blaise 104, 196
Paul (St-Paul) 103, 106n4, 106n18, 178, 181, 185n40, 208, 208n3
perversion 105, 127n5
phallic function 161–162, 183
phallus 14n14, 161–162, 169n35
Plato 161, 169n35
prôton pseudos 98, 98n8, 102, 163, 169n39
psychoanalytic discourse 148–149, 209

Renan, Ernest 178–180, 184n19
repressed (repression) 8–9, 11, 13, 93, 149, 158–159, 163, 165–167, 171–172, 174–175, 177, 179–183, 191, 199–205, 210–211
respect (*Achtung*) 8, 25–26, 28n16, 34–38, 45, 54, 67–70, 74, 82–83, 87–88, 100, 123–124, 126, 132, 150n2, 156, 168n18, 180, 185n34, 194

Saint-Just 172–173
schema L (Lacan) 115, 133, 135, 144, 147, 150n9, 165, 203
Schwärmereien (fanaticism) 78, 84–85, 130, 149n2, 150n2
scopic object 13, 112, 114, 125, 166, 210–211
second death 140–143, 145, 179
self-love 29, 34n1, 48, 55–56, 67, 85n1, 87
signifier 3, 7, 112, 121, 132, 139, 149, 155, 162–163, 165, 182–183
Socrates 183
soul 19, 21, 39n14, 44, 64n3, 71–72, 75–80, 95n3, 110, 125, 128n42, 143, 174, 179
Spielrein, Sabina 50, 60n27
Spinoza, Baruch 46, 59n5, 80n4, 182
Stalin, Joseph 164
Stoic 72, 74, 77, 164
subject effect 134–136, 198
subject of pleasure 137, 139, 145
sublimation 103–105

superego 3, 15, 20–21, 22n4, 93–95, 103, 118, 131, 208, 211
supreme Being 19, 71, 115, 126, 130, 140, 162, 174, 182

Thing, the (*das Ding*) 2, 53, 64, 79, 88, 96–97, 98n1, 100–105, 109–111, 116, 125, 125n17, 128n42, 130, 161, 164, 174–175, 178, 180, 208
truth 8, 11–13, 28n16, 43, 88, 110, 115, 127n10, 138, 147–149, 160, 163–164, 169n40, 171–173, 189, 211

Verdoux, Monsieur 153–154
vocal object 13, 108, 114, 125, 139, 141, 143, 149, 150n25, 151n33, 154, 166, 175, 201, 212
voice 55–56, 69n7, 70, 112, 121–126, 127n12, 129n44, 130, 133, 135, 137–139, 141, 143–146, 149, 152, 154–155, 162, 167, 168n11, 171, 173, 175, 177, 179, 184n1, 197, 203–205, 208, 211

wish-fulfilment (Wunscherfüllung) 1
Wo Es war soll Ich werden 27, 38